TAXONOMIC CHARTS OF

THEOLOGY
AND
BIBLICAL STUDIES

ZONDERVAN*CHARTS* BOOKS IN THE SERIES

Charts of Christian Theology and Doctrine
(H. Wayne House)

Charts of Cults, Sects, and Religious Movements
(H. Wayne House)

Chronological and Background Charts of Church History
(Robert C. Walton)

Chronological and Background Charts of the New Testament
(H. Wayne House)

Chronological and Background Charts of the Old Testament: Revised and Expanded
(John H. Walton)

Chronological and Thematic Charts of Philosophers and Philosophies
(Milton D. Hunnex)

Taxonomic Charts of Theology and Biblical Studies
(M. James Sawyer)

Timeline Charts of the Western Church
(Susan Lynn Peterson)

TAXONOMIC CHARTS OF THEOLOGY AND BIBLICAL STUDIES

M. JAMES SAWYER

GRAND RAPIDS, MICHIGAN 49530 USA

Taxonomic Charts of Theology and Biblical Studies

Requests for information should be addressed to:

ZONDERVAN™

Grand Rapids, Michigan 49530

Library of Congress Cataloging-in-Publication Data
Sawyer, M. James
Taxonomic charts of theology and biblical studies / M. James Sawyer.
p. cm.
ISBN 0-310-21993-0
1. Theology, Doctrinal—study and teaching Audio-visual aids. 2. Bible—Study and teaching Audio-visual aids. 3. Theology, Doctrinal Charts, diagrams, etc. 4. Bible Charts, diagrams, etc.
I. Title.
BT77.3.S29 1999
230'.02'02—dc21 99-28262
CIP

Interior design by Pamela J. L. Eicher

Printed in the United States of America

99 00 01 02 03 04 05 06 /❖ ML/ 10 9 8 7 6 5 4 3 2 1

CONTENTS

PREFACE

During many years of teaching introductory theology courses to seminarians, I have found that students are consistently intimidated and baffled by the nature, structure, and vocabulary of the discipline. On many occasions students have asked if there weren't some kind of charts they could use to help them get a handle on the scope of the subject. This idea of charts that serve as simple road maps through the maze of issues seems to appeal to the increasingly visually oriented culture we live in.

This volume came out of work done on a larger project for Zondervan. As I worked on structuring a database for that project, Ed van der Maas, then senior acquisitions editor, suggested that these charts would do well on their own. Skeptical that such a work would find an audience, but mindful of the persistent requests of students over the years, I showed some of the charts to friends who are seminary graduates. They all said that they wished they had had a tool like this when they first undertook the study of the theological and biblical disciplines.

I used some of the charts in my theology classes to gauge student interest. I was both surprised and gratified. I found that students appreciate having a visual map of the area of theology they are studying. The taxonomic arrangement helped them to visually grasp the structure of the topic as well as its comprehensiveness and complexity.

The intent of the charts is to communicate structure, not content. Issues and questions are raised and set forth, not answered. The glossary, which includes only terms taken from the charts, gives the beginning theologian, overwhelmed by jargon, some quick, rough-and-ready definitions. The definitions make no claim to being exhaustive.

Any attempt to map the landscape of theological studies must recognize that charts are a form of shorthand that will on occasion force divisions and distinctions where in reality there is a great deal of overlap and interdependence. Furthermore, I recognize that there is no single "right" way to organize theological material and questions, or even one "right" set of questions and issues to be addressed. A quick perusal of several evangelical systematic theologies, such as those by Charles Hodge, William G. T. Shedd, Millard Erickson, and Wayne Grudem, will provide ample evidence of this. Finally, it is impossible to avoid a subjective element in describing a discipline, and at points my own areas of particular interest and expertise will show through.

A work of this type can make no claim to originality. The categories and questions set forth are generally common in the theological disciplines, but there are certain authors whose succinct articulation of categories and questions have been particularly helpful and whose concepts can be clearly seen in various charts. Among these are Oscar Cullmann, *The Christology of the New Testament*, rev. ed. (Louisville: Westminster John Knox, 1980); Millard J.

Erickson, *Christian Theology* (Grand Rapids: Baker Book House, 1996); George Eldon Ladd, *Theology of the New Testament*, rev. ed., ed. Donald A. Hagner (Grand Rapids: Wm. B. Eerdmans, 1993); Alister McGrath, *The Genesis of Doctrine* (Grand Rapids: Wm. B. Eerdmans, 1997) and *Intellectuals Don't Need God and Other Modern Myths* (Grand Rapids: Zondervan, 1993); Tom Oden's *Systematic Theology: The Living God* (1992), *The Word of Life* (1992), *Life in the Spirit* (San Francisco: Harper Collins, 1994); Grant Osborne, *The Hermeneutical Spiral* (Downers Grove, IL: InterVarsity Press, 1992); and Vern Poythress, *Symphonic Theology* (Grand Rapids: Zondervan, 1987).

A final word of explanation is needed on the structure of the charts. Items on the same level structurally are to be assigned the same level of relative importance. Items first on a list are not necessarily more important than subsequent items that appear on the same level. I anticipate that many will question my placing the Apocrypha between the Old and New Testaments in regard to biblical studies. While I personally do not accept the inspiration of the Apocrypha, it is so accepted by the majority of professing Christendom; moreover, the literary nature of the body of texts parallels that of the Old and New Testaments. Hence, for organizational purposes alone, the Apocrypha found a place between them.

My heartfelt thanks and appreciation go out to my colleagues who contributed to this work with their expertise: Dr. Merilyn Hargis, who provided the categories and structure for the charts on archaeology and geography; Dr. Robert O'Connell for his initial suggestions for the structure of the Old Testament charts; Dr. Roy Low for his invaluable assistance in preparing the Old Testament charts; and Dr. Daniel B. Wallace for his generous assistance in working over the New Testament charts and making many suggestions for improving them.

TO THE READER

Charts are not for everyone. Some people find charts exceptionally helpful; others try to use them but find them of little value. It all depends on how your mind processes information.

These charts are not the last word on theological taxonomy. In many cases there are alternative ways of organizing the material.

If you simply memorize these charts, they will have failed their purpose. If, by contrast, you interact with them and find yourself disagreeing with some, they will have achieved their purpose: to help us learn about the doing of theology, not in the memorizing of theology.

The glossary is included for quick reference and review. The definitions reflect to some extent my personal interests and priorities. They are not intended to be used as the description "delivered once for all to the saints," but as an aid to learning theology as an ongoing, personal process.

A number in a box serves as a cross reference to indicate where a chart or charts on that particular topic are located. The number refers to the chart number, not the page number.

For practical reasons, the charts use the word man rather than inclusive terms such as humanity. The term is to be understood in the sense of the German *Mensch* and the Greek *anthropos* as encompassing the totality of humanity.

May these charts assist you in your study of the greatest and most exciting discipline: God and his revelation.

Chart 1

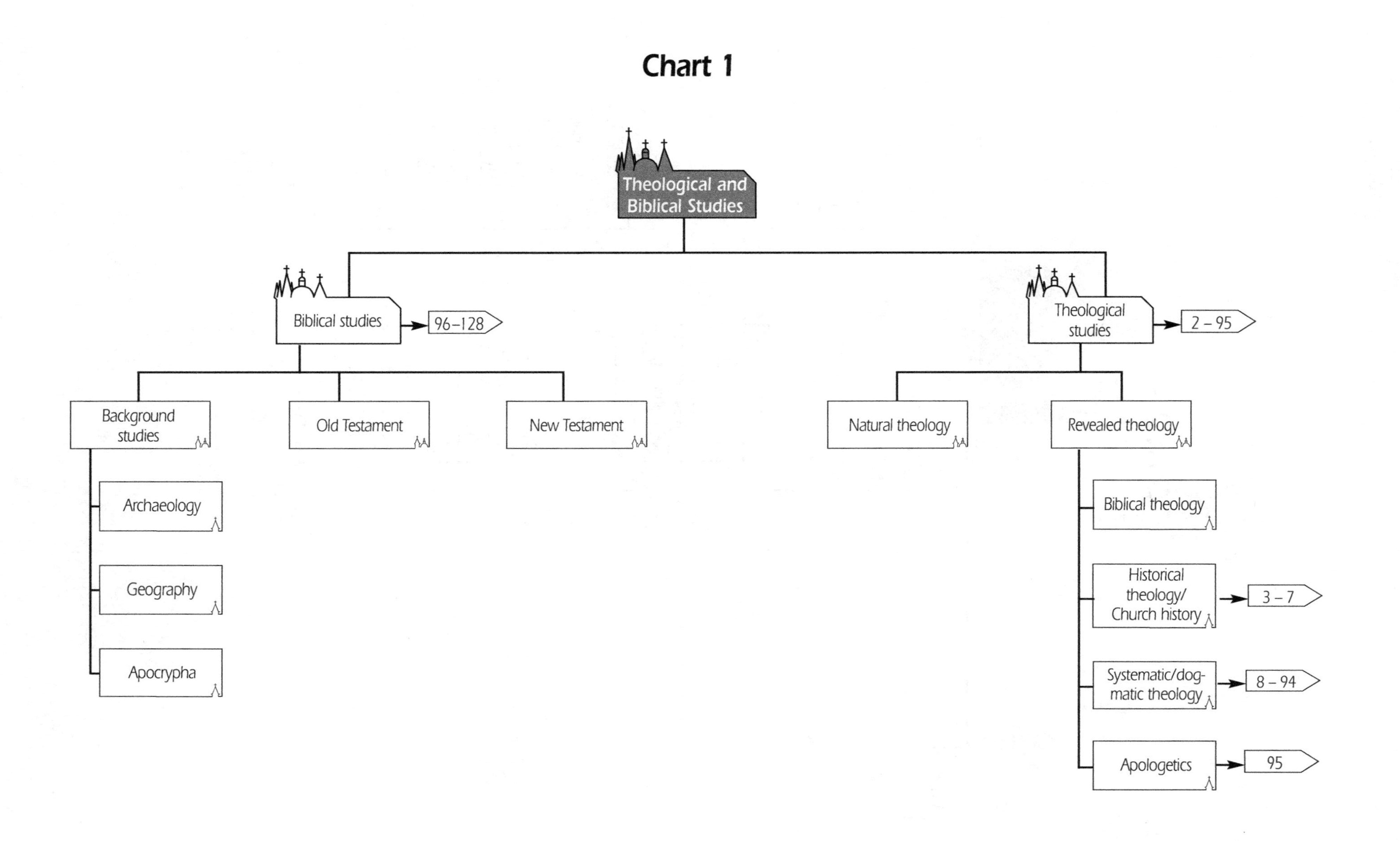
Theological and Biblical Studies
Biblical studies
96–128
Background studies
Archaeology
Geography
Apocrypha
Old Testament
New Testament
Theological studies
2 – 95
Natural theology
Revealed theology
Biblical theology
Historical theology/ Church history
3 – 7
Systematic/dog-matic theology
8 – 94
Apologetics
95

Chart 2

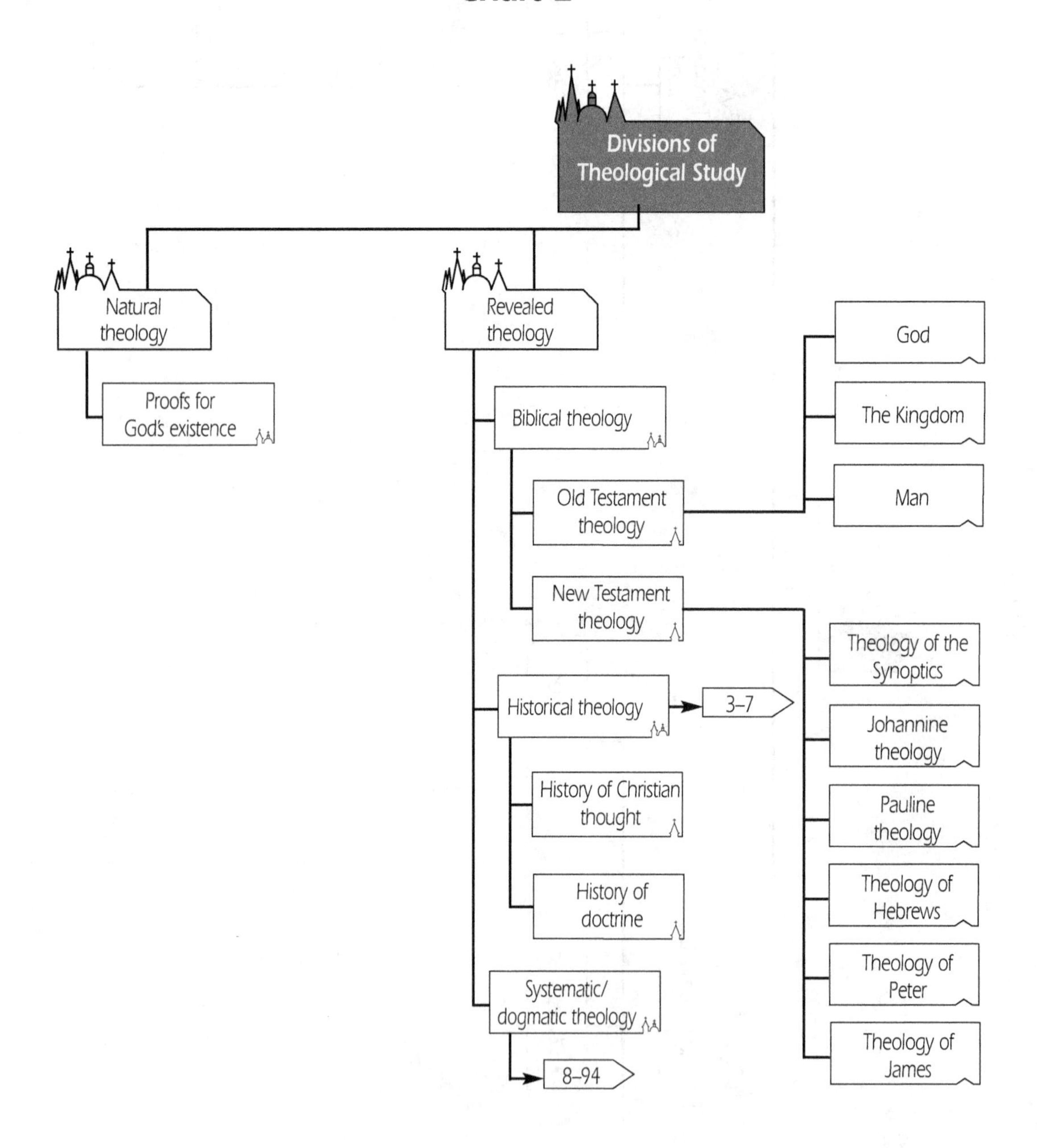

Divisions of Theological Study
Natural theology
Proofs for God's existence
Revealed theology
Biblical theology
Old Testament theology
God
The Kingdom
Man
New Testament theology
Theology of the Synoptics
Johannine theology
Pauline theology
Theology of Hebrews
Theology of Peter
Theology of James
Historical theology
3–7
History of Christian thought
History of doctrine
Systematic/ dogmatic theology
8–94

Chart 3

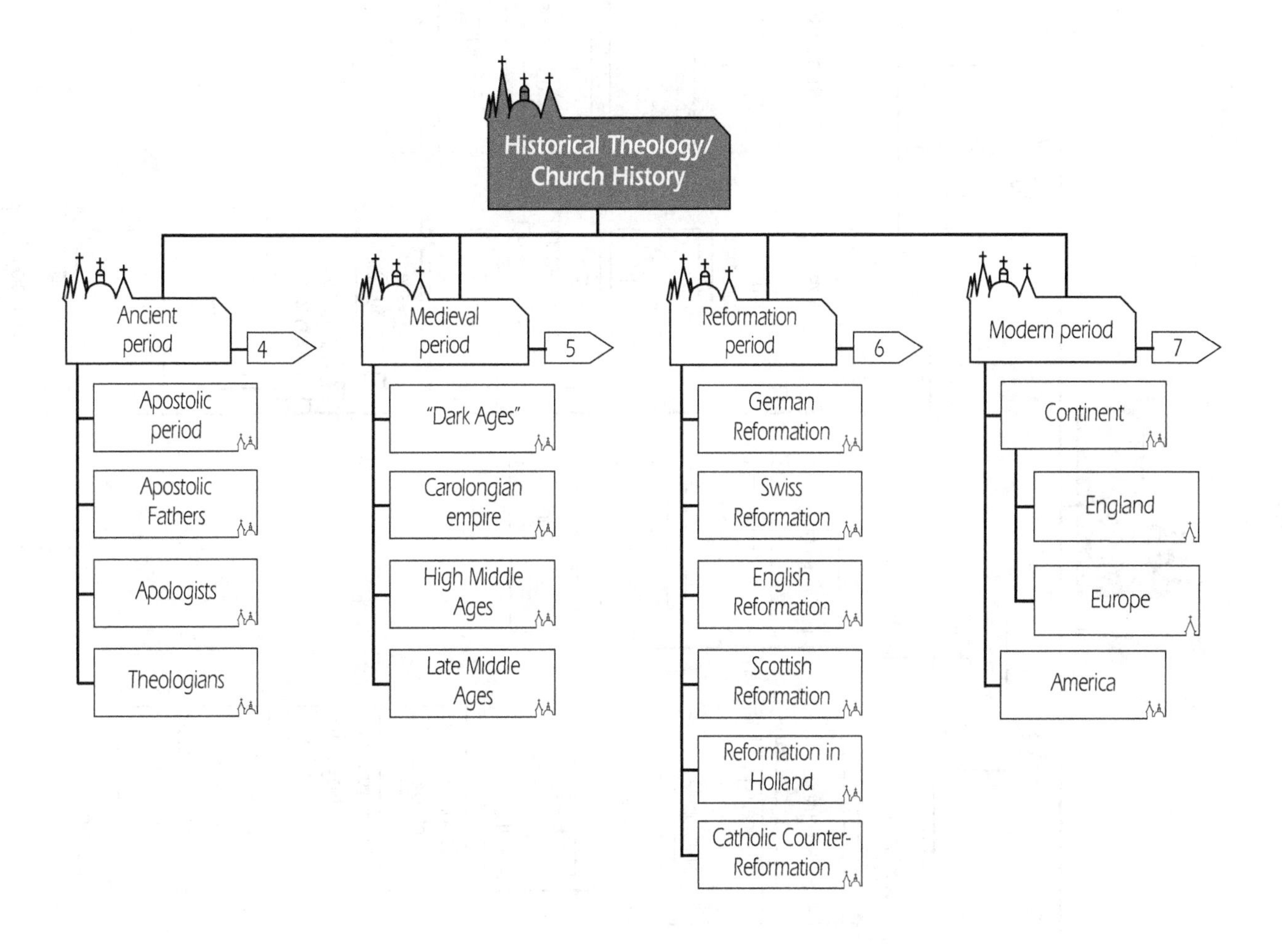

Historical Theology/
Church History
Ancient
period
4
Apostolic
period
Apostolic
Fathers
Apologists
Theologians
Medieval
period
5
"Dark Ages"
Carolongian
empire
High Middle
Ages
Late Middle
Ages
Reformation
period
6
German
Reformation
Swiss
Reformation
English
Reformation
Scottish
Reformation
Reformation in
Holland
Catholic Counter-
Reformation
Modern period
7
Continent
England
Europe
America

Chart 4

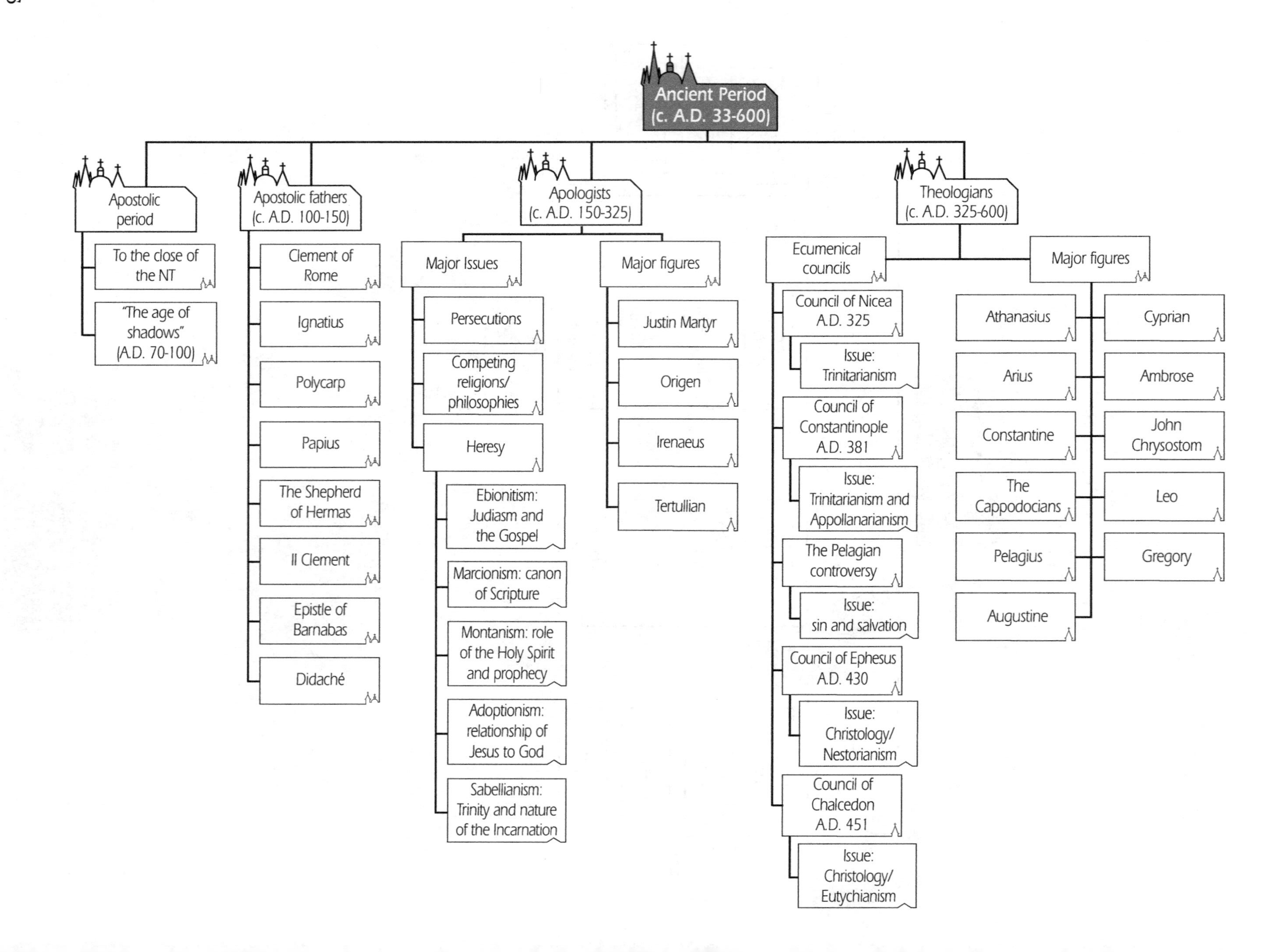

Ancient Period
(c. A.D. 33-600)
Apostolic period
To the close of the NT
"The age of shadows" (A.D. 70-100)
Apostolic fathers (c. A.D. 100-150)
Clement of Rome
Ignatius
Polycarp
Papius
The Shepherd of Hermas
II Clement
Epistle of Barnabas
Didaché
Apologists (c. A.D. 150-325)
Major Issues
Persecutions
Competing religions/ philosophies
Heresy
Ebionitism: Judiasm and the Gospel
Marcionism: canon of Scripture
Montanism: role of the Holy Spirit and prophecy
Adoptionism: relationship of Jesus to God
Sabellianism: Trinity and nature of the Incarnation
Major figures
Justin Martyr
Origen
Irenaeus
Tertullian
Theologians (c. A.D. 325-600)
Ecumenical councils
Council of Nicea A.D. 325
Issue: Trinitarianism
Council of Constantinople A.D. 381
Issue: Trinitarianism and Appollanarianism
The Pelagian controversy
Issue: sin and salvation
Council of Ephesus A.D. 430
Issue: Christology/ Nestorianism
Council of Chalcedon A.D. 451
Issue: Christology/ Eutychianism
Major figures
Athanasius
Arius
Constantine
The Cappodocians
Pelagius
Augustine
Cyprian
Ambrose
John Chrysostom
Leo
Gregory

Chart 5

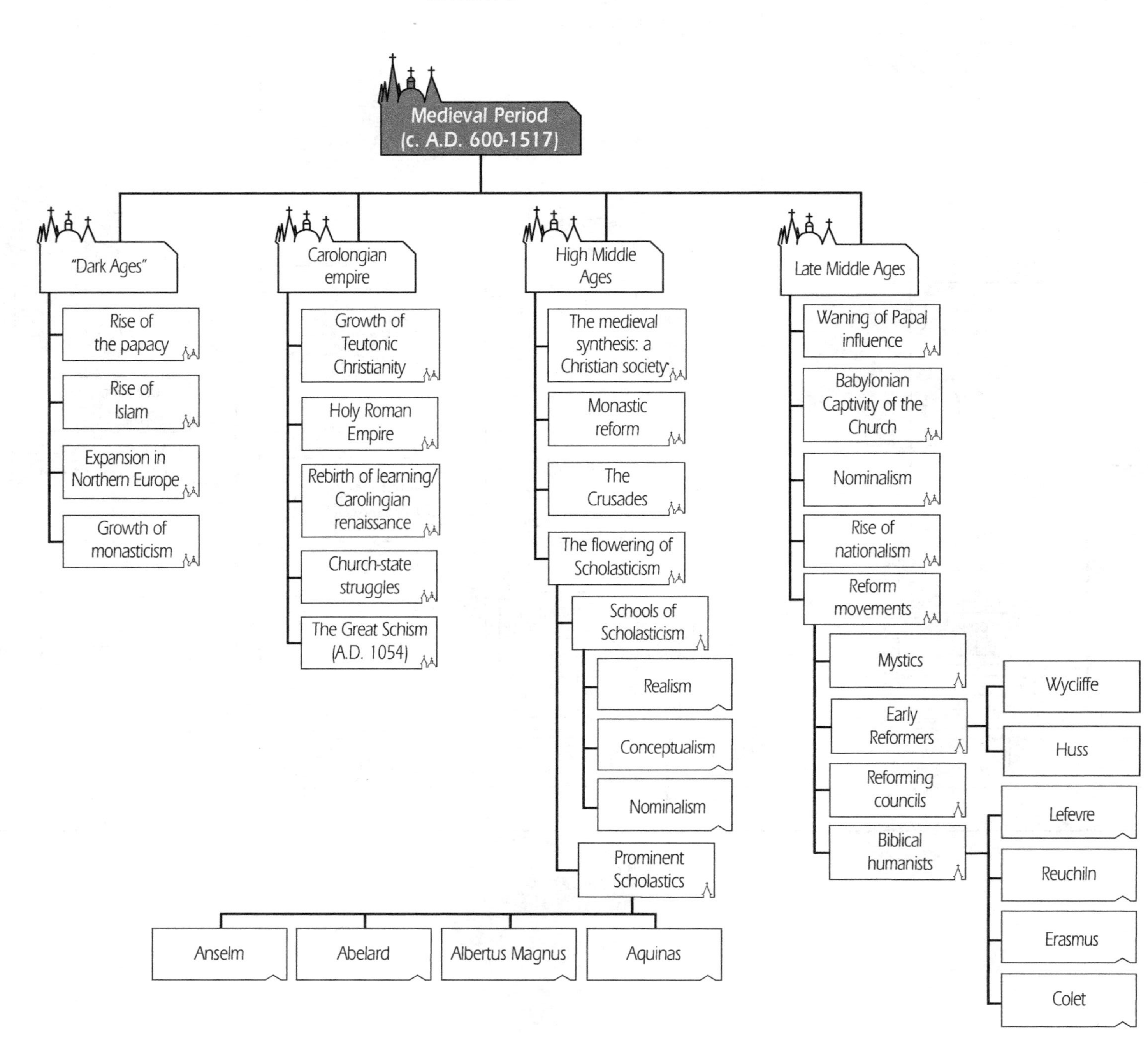

Medieval Period
(c. A.D. 600-1517)
"Dark Ages"
Rise of the papacy
Rise of Islam
Expansion in Northern Europe
Growth of monasticism
Carolongian empire
Growth of Teutonic Christianity
Holy Roman Empire
Rebirth of learning/ Carolingian renaissance
Church-state struggles
The Great Schism (A.D. 1054)
High Middle Ages
The medieval synthesis: a Christian society
Monastic reform
The Crusades
The flowering of Scholasticism
Schools of Scholasticism
Realism
Conceptualism
Nominalism
Prominent Scholastics
Anselm
Abelard
Albertus Magnus
Aquinas
Late Middle Ages
Waning of Papal influence
Babylonian Captivity of the Church
Nominalism
Rise of nationalism
Reform movements
Mystics
Early Reformers
Wycliffe
Huss
Reforming councils
Biblical humanists
Lefevre
Reuchiln
Erasmus
Colet

Chart 6

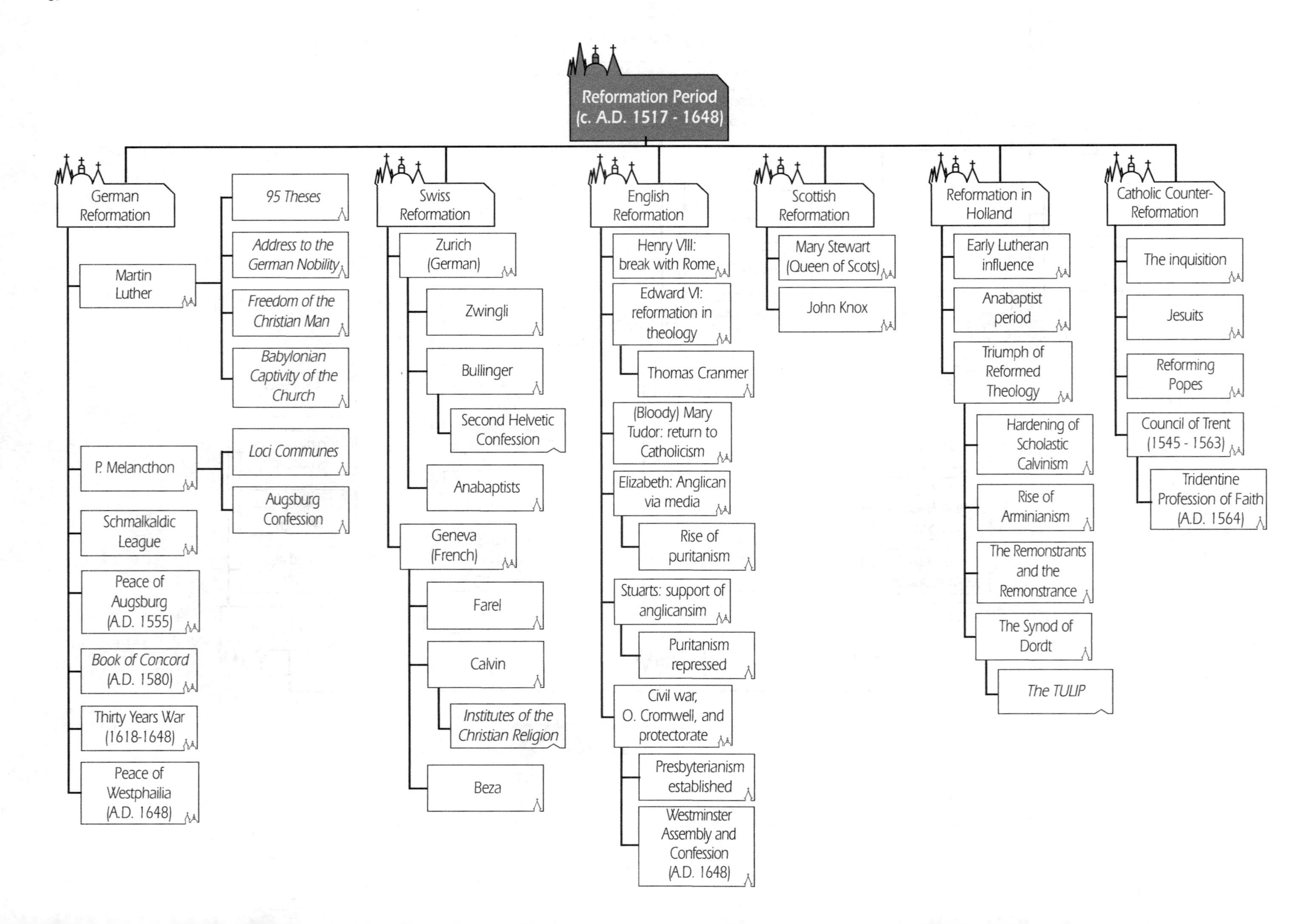
Reformation Period
(c. A.D. 1517 - 1648)
German Reformation
Martin Luther
95 Theses
Address to the German Nobility
Freedom of the Christian Man
Babylonian Captivity of the Church
P. Melancthon
Loci Communes
Augsburg Confession
Schmalkaldic League
Peace of Augsburg (A.D. 1555)
Book of Concord (A.D. 1580)
Thirty Years War (1618-1648)
Peace of Westphailia (A.D. 1648)
Swiss Reformation
Zurich (German)
Zwingli
Bullinger
Second Helvetic Confession
Anabaptists
Geneva (French)
Farel
Calvin
Institutes of the Christian Religion
Beza
English Reformation
Henry VIII: break with Rome
Edward VI: reformation in theology
Thomas Cranmer
(Bloody) Mary Tudor: return to Catholicism
Elizabeth: Anglican via media
Rise of puritanism
Stuarts: support of anglicansim
Puritanism repressed
Civil war, O. Cromwell, and protectorate
Presbyterianism established
Westminster Assembly and Confession (A.D. 1648)
Scottish Reformation
Mary Stewart (Queen of Scots)
John Knox
Reformation in Holland
Early Lutheran influence
Anabaptist period
Triumph of Reformed Theology
Hardening of Scholastic Calvinism
Rise of Arminianism
The Remonstrants and the Remonstrance
The Synod of Dordt
The TULIP
Catholic Counter-Reformation
The inquisition
Jesuits
Reforming Popes
Council of Trent (1545 - 1563)
Tridentine Profession of Faith (A.D. 1564)

Chart 7

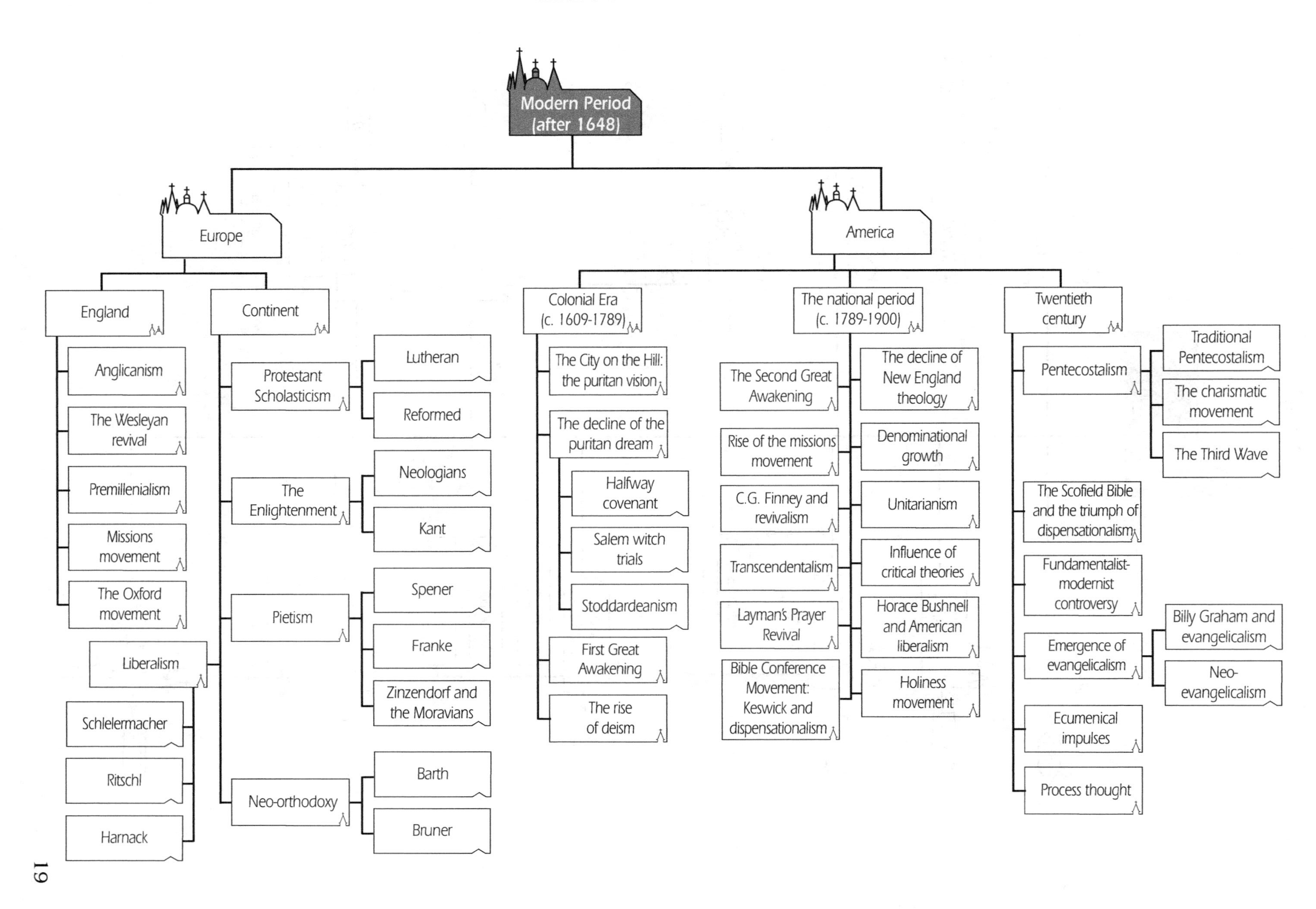

Modern Period
(after 1648)
Europe
England
Anglicanism
The Wesleyan revival
Premillenialism
Missions movement
The Oxford movement
Liberalism
Schlelermacher
Ritschl
Harnack
Continent
Protestant Scholasticism
Lutheran
Reformed
The Enlightenment
Neologians
Kant
Pietism
Spener
Franke
Zinzendorf and the Moravians
Neo-orthodoxy
Barth
Bruner
America
Colonial Era (c. 1609-1789)
The City on the Hill: the puritan vision
The decline of the puritan dream
Halfway covenant
Salem witch trials
Stoddardeanism
First Great Awakening
The rise of deism
The national period (c. 1789-1900)
The Second Great Awakening
Rise of the missions movement
C.G. Finney and revivalism
Transcendentalism
Layman's Prayer Revival
Bible Conference Movement: Keswick and dispensationalism
The decline of New England theology
Denominational growth
Unitarianism
Influence of critical theories
Horace Bushnell and American liberalism
Holiness movement
Twentieth century
Pentecostalism
Traditional Pentecostalism
The charismatic movement
The Third Wave
The Scofield Bible and the triumph of dispensationalism
Fundamentalist-modernist controversy
Emergence of evangelicalism
Billy Graham and evangelicalism
Neo-evangelicalism
Ecumenical impulses
Process thought

Chart 8

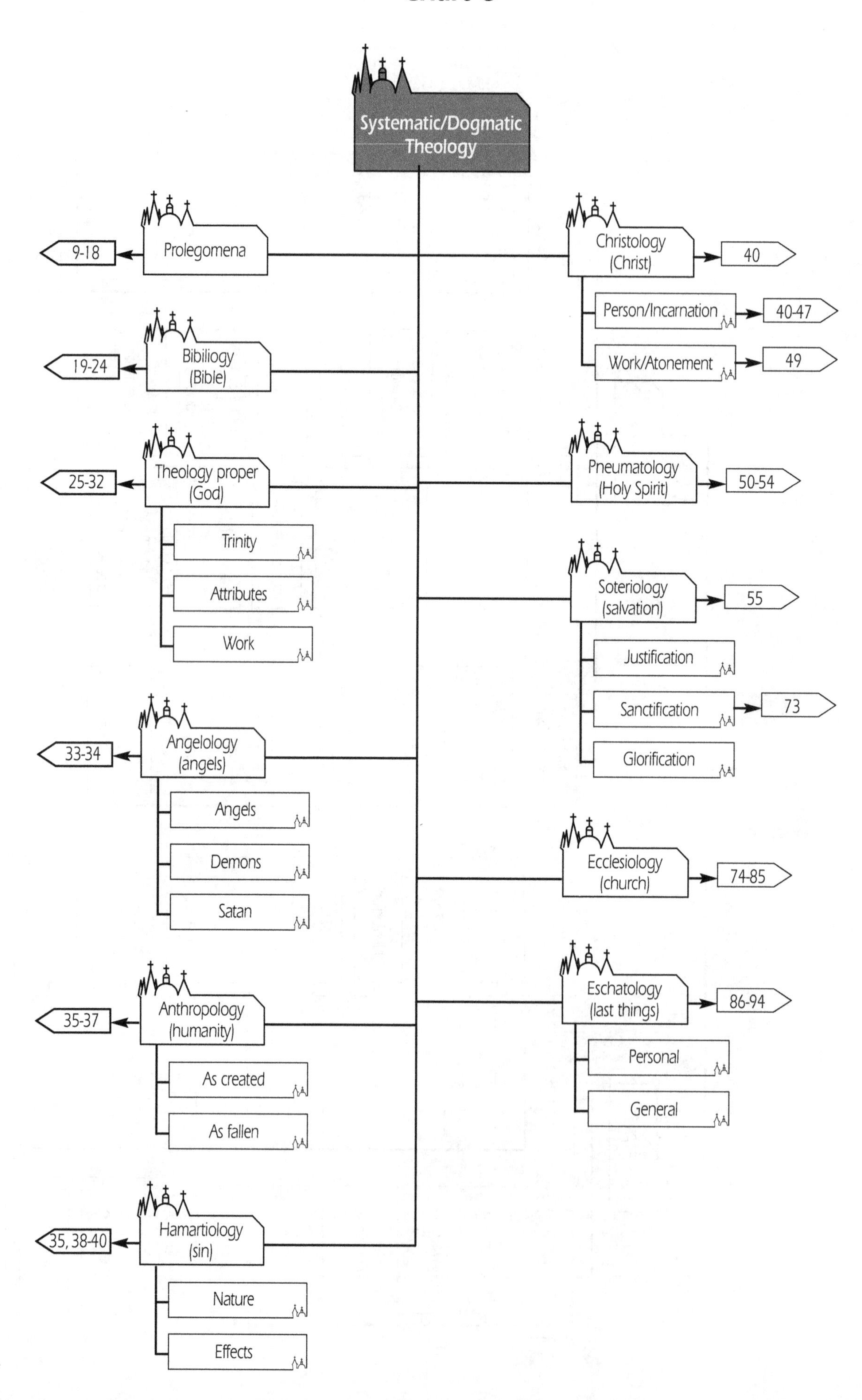
Systematic/Dogmatic Theology
Prolegomena
9-18
Bibiliogy (Bible)
19-24
Theology proper (God)
25-32
Trinity
Attributes
Work
Angelology (angels)
33-34
Angels
Demons
Satan
Anthropology (humanity)
35-37
As created
As fallen
Hamartiology (sin)
35, 38-40
Nature
Effects
Christology (Christ)
40
Person/Incarnation
40-47
Work/Atonement
49
Pneumatology (Holy Spirit)
50-54
Soteriology (salvation)
55
Justification
Sanctification
73
Glorification
Ecclesiology (church)
74-85
Eschatology (last things)
86-94
Personal
General

Chart 9

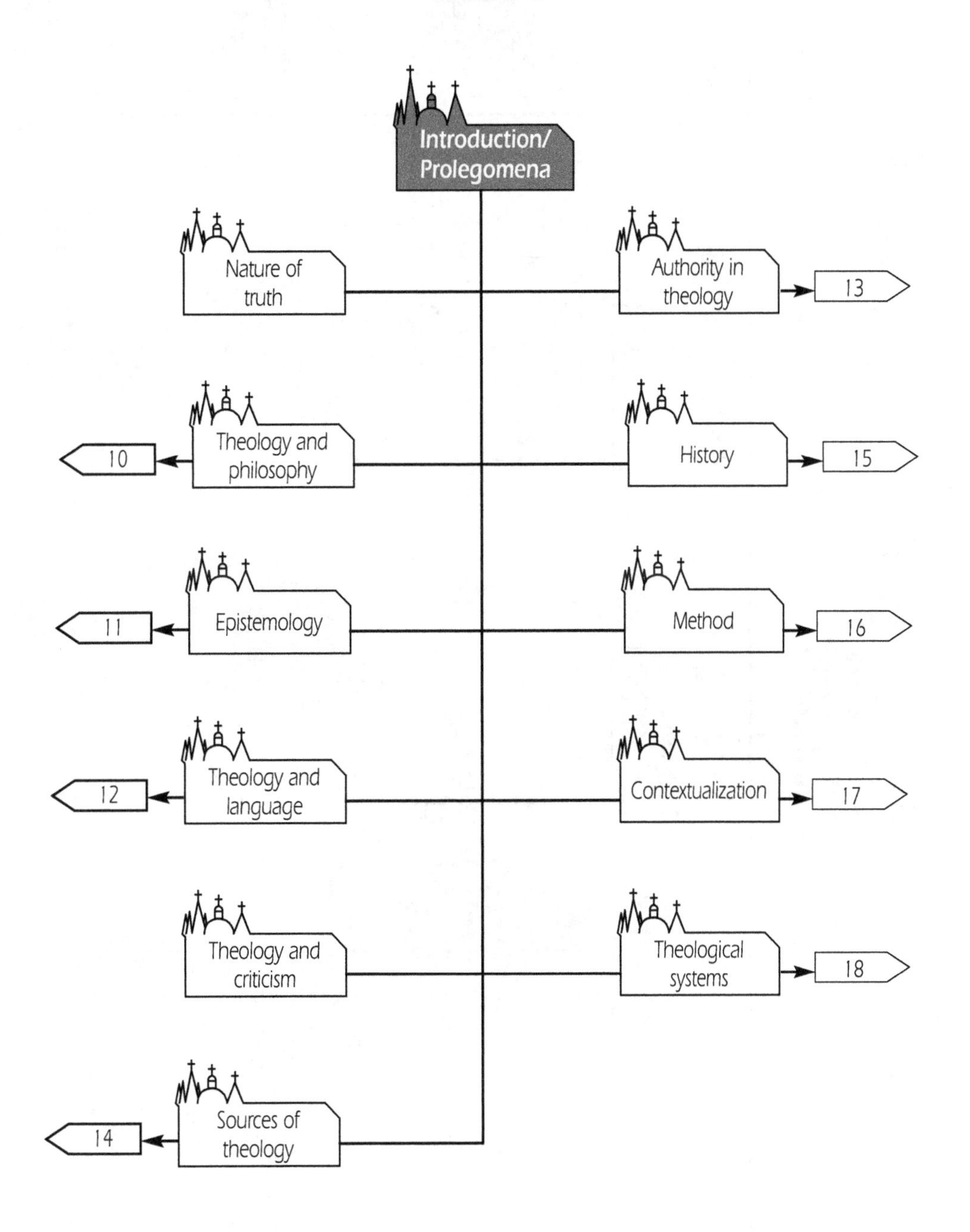

Introduction/ Prolegomena
Nature of truth
Authority in theology
13
Theology and philosophy
10
History
15
Epistemology
11
Method
16
Theology and language
12
Contextualization
17
Theology and criticism
Theological systems
18
Sources of theology
14

Chart 10

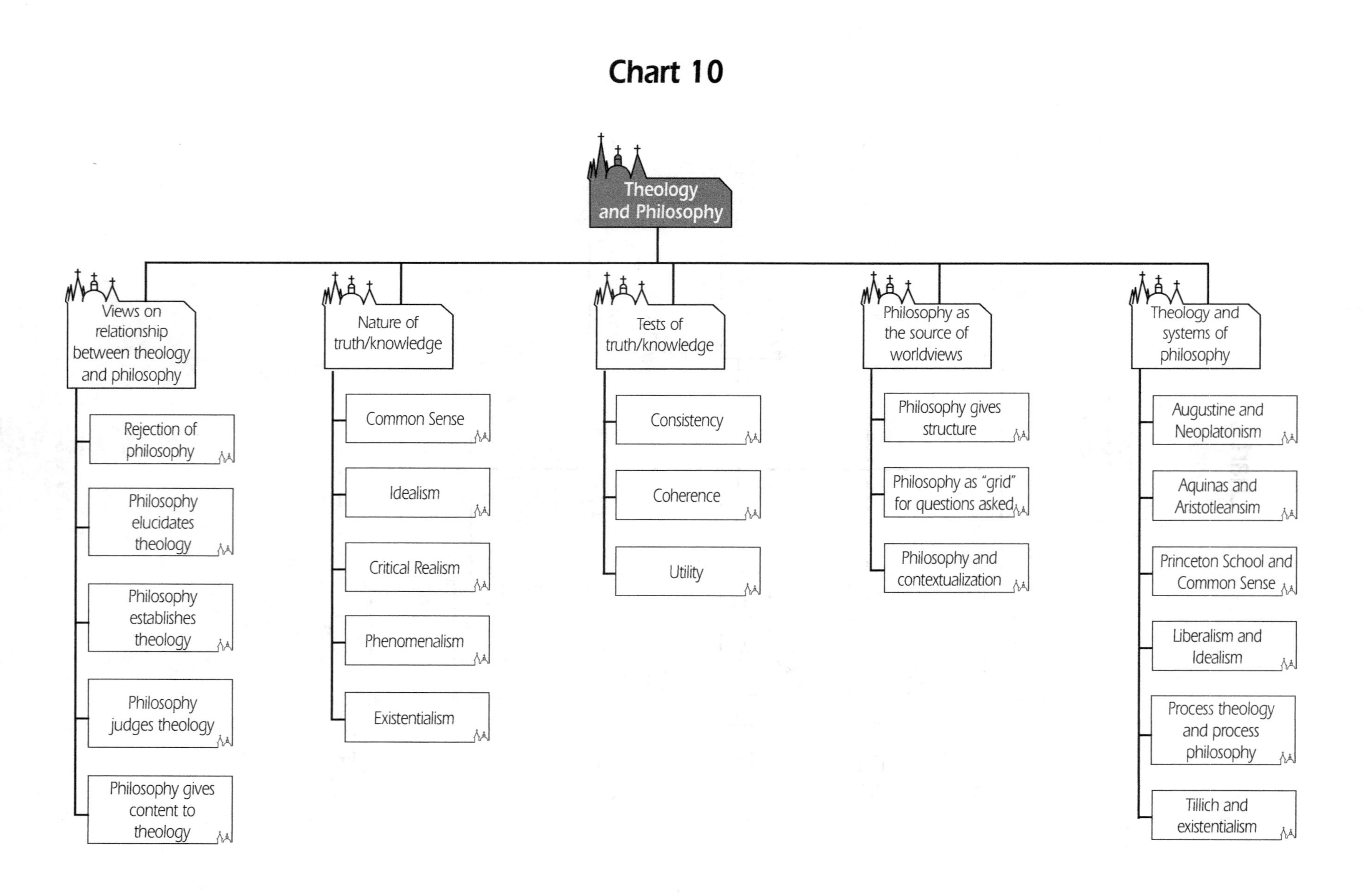
Theology and Philosophy
Views on relationship between theology and philosophy
Rejection of philosophy
Philosophy elucidates theology
Philosophy establishes theology
Philosophy judges theology
Philosophy gives content to theology
Nature of truth/knowledge
Common Sense
Idealism
Critical Realism
Phenomenalism
Existentialism
Tests of truth/knowledge
Consistency
Coherence
Utility
Philosophy as the source of worldviews
Philosophy gives structure
Philosophy as "grid" for questions asked
Philosophy and contextualization
Theology and systems of philosophy
Augustine and Neoplatonism
Aquinas and Aristotleansim
Princeton School and Common Sense
Liberalism and Idealism
Process theology and process philosophy
Tillich and existentialism

Chart 11

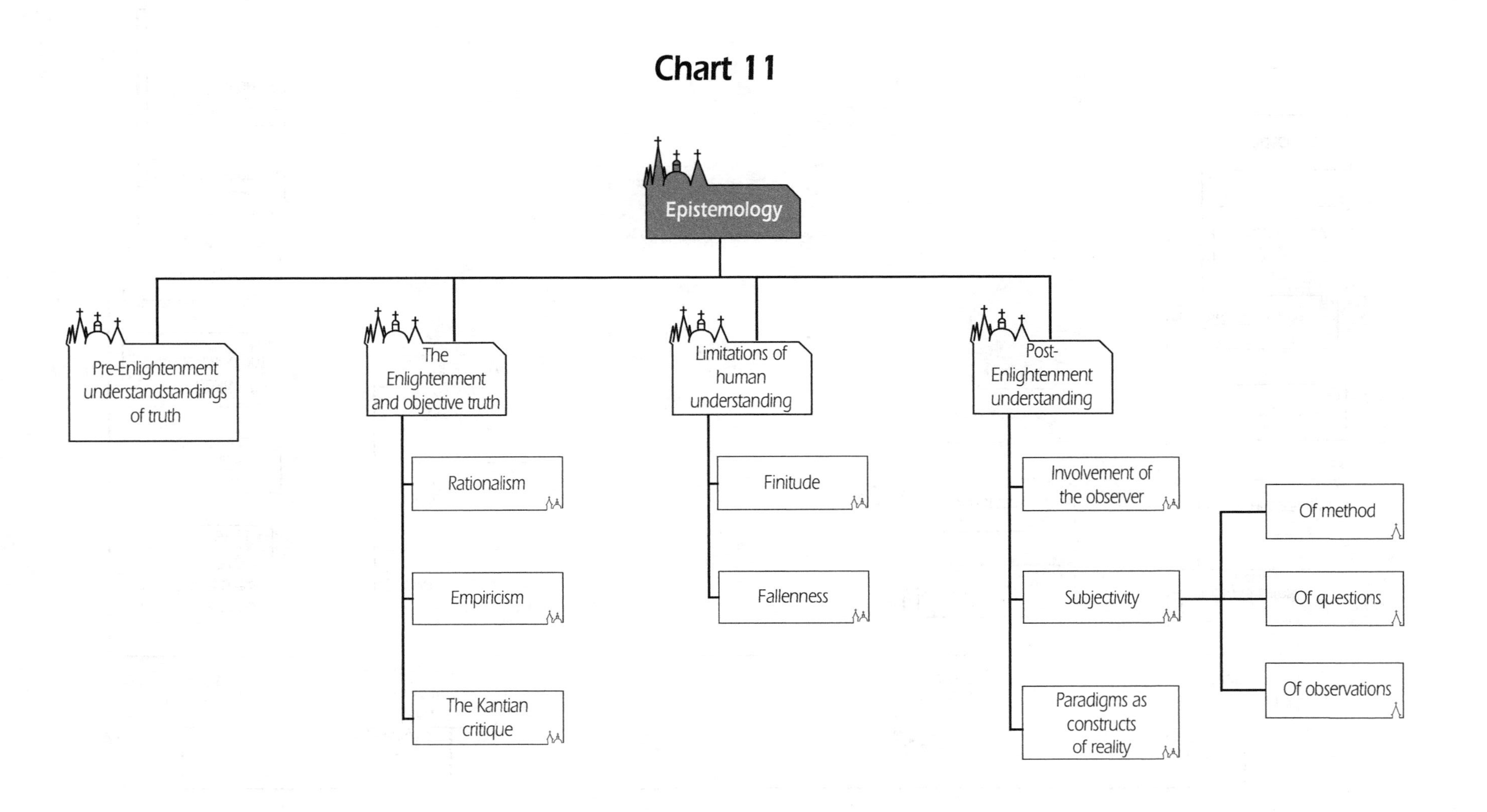

Epistemology
Pre-Enlightenment understandstandings of truth
The Enlightenment and objective truth
Rationalism
Empiricism
The Kantian critique
Limitations of human understanding
Finitude
Fallenness
Post-Enlightenment understanding
Involvement of the observer
Subjectivity
Of method
Of questions
Of observations
Paradigms as constructs of reality

Chart 12

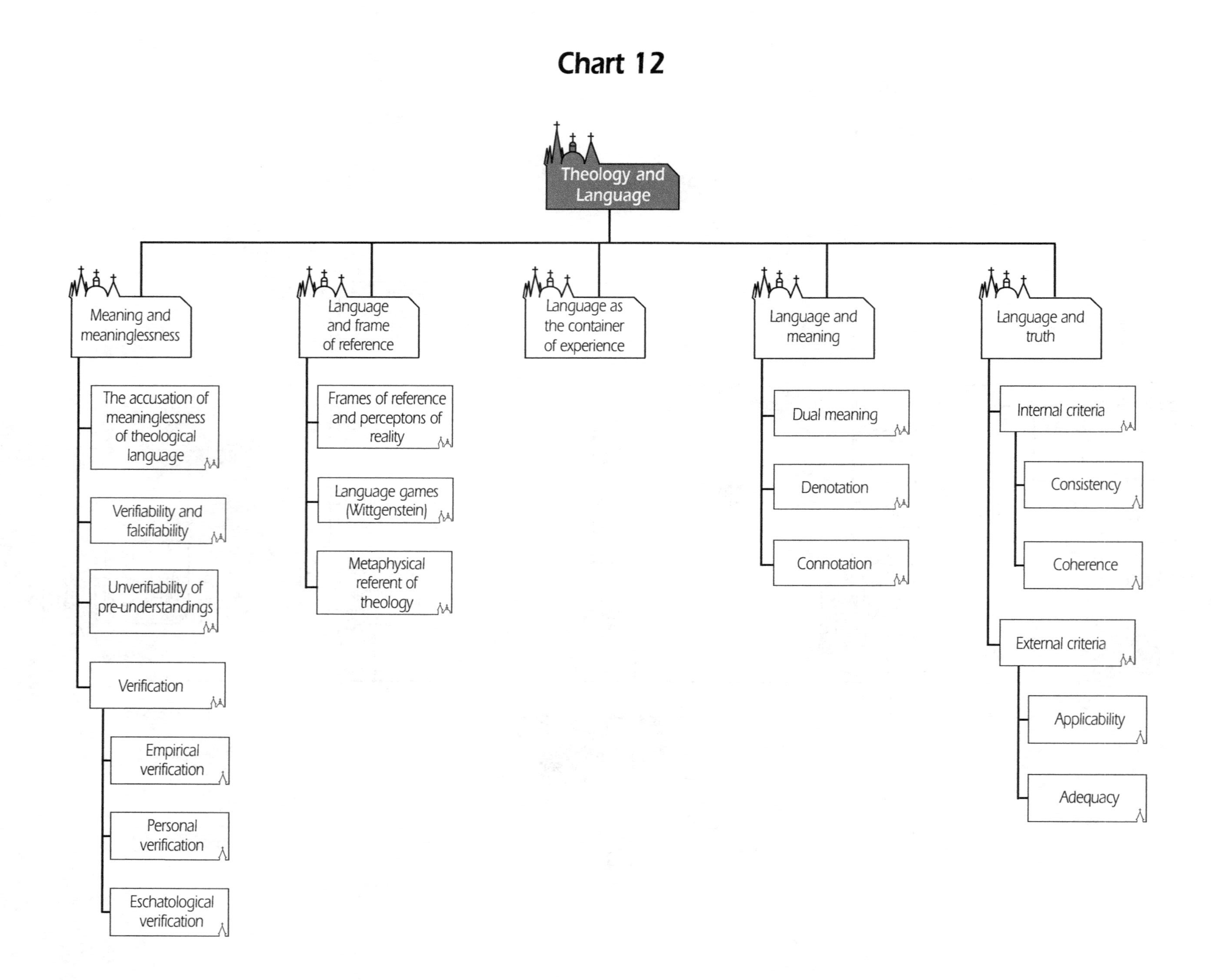
Theology and Language
Meaning and meaninglessness
The accusation of meaninglessness of theological language
Verifiability and falsifiability
Unverifiability of pre-understandings
Verification
Empirical verification
Personal verification
Eschatological verification
Language and frame of reference
Frames of reference and perceptons of reality
Language games (Wittgenstein)
Metaphysical referent of theology
Language as the container of experience
Language and meaning
Dual meaning
Denotation
Connotation
Language and truth
Internal criteria
Consistency
Coherence
External criteria
Applicability
Adequacy

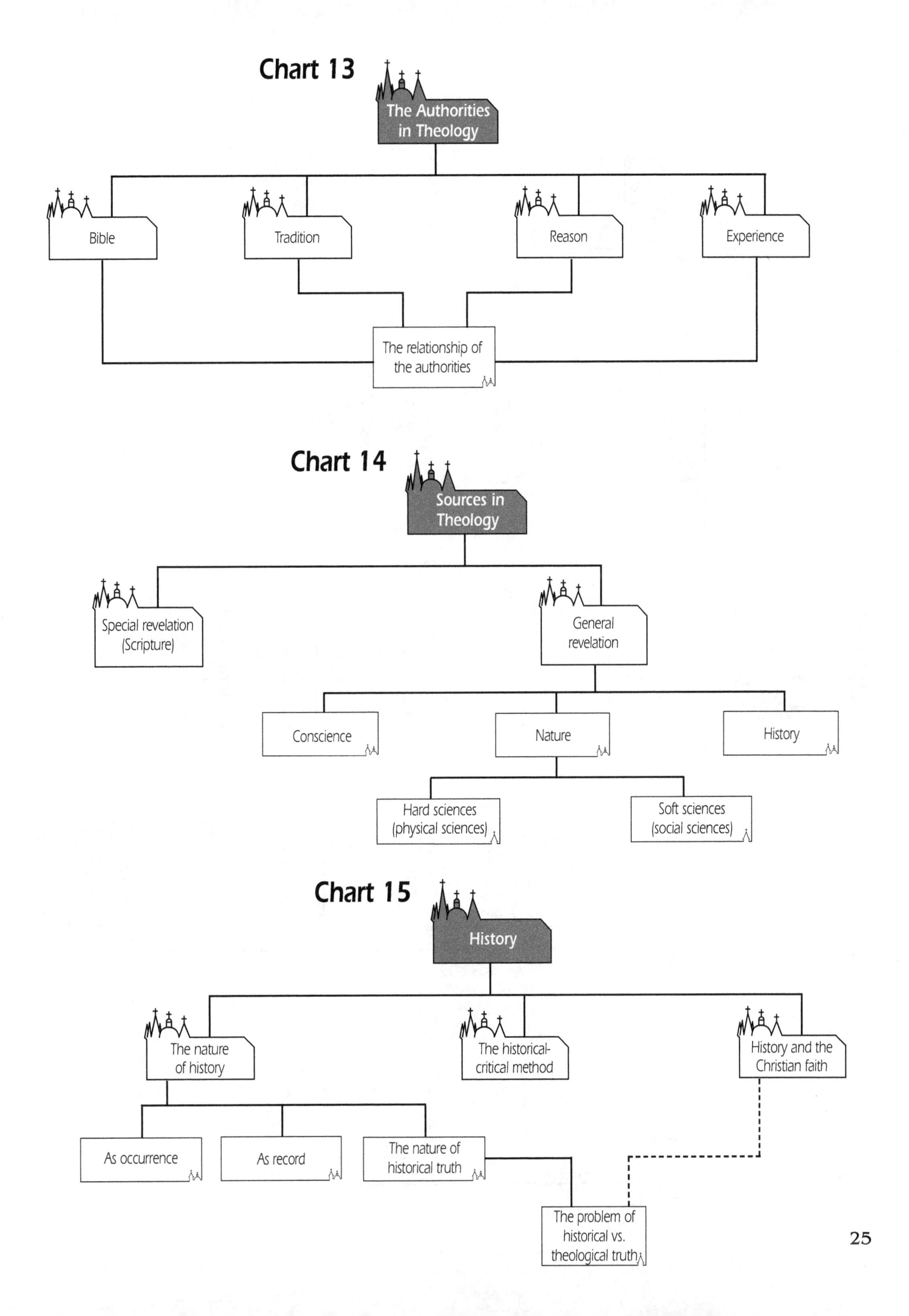
Chart 13
The Authorities in Theology
Bible
Tradition
Reason
Experience
The relationship of the authorities
Chart 14
Sources in Theology
Special revelation (Scripture)
General revelation
Conscience
Nature
History
Hard sciences (physical sciences)
Soft sciences (social sciences)
Chart 15
History
The nature of history
The historical-critical method
History and the Christian faith
As occurrence
As record
The nature of historical truth
The problem of historical vs. theological truth

Chart 16

Theological Method

- The occasional nature of theology
  - Doctrinal formulation and controversy
  - The truth of doctrines
    - Formal truth (words)
    - Material truth (intrinsic)
  - Theologies and theological statements reflect underlying philosophies
- Doing theology
  - The priority of Scripture
    - Collection of biblical material
    - Exegesis of relevant passages
    - Correlation of biblical theology
  - Historical treatments of the topic
  - Distillation of the essence of the doctrine
  - Insight from extra-biblical sources (general revelation)
  - Contemporary, contextualized expression of the doctrine
    - Correlation with contemporary questions
- Degrees of authority in theological conclusions
  - Direct statements of Scripture
  - Direct implication
  - Probable implications
  - Inductive conclusions
  - Conclusions based on general revelation
  - Conclusions based on inference from a system
  - Speculations
- Establishing a theological taxonomy
  - The importance of ranking doctrines
  - Methods of determination
  - Dangers in failing to rank doctrines
  - The centrality of the consensus of the Christian tradition
- Determining a central motif
  - The need for a central motif
  - Motifs vary with theologians
  - Factors in determining a motif

Chart 17

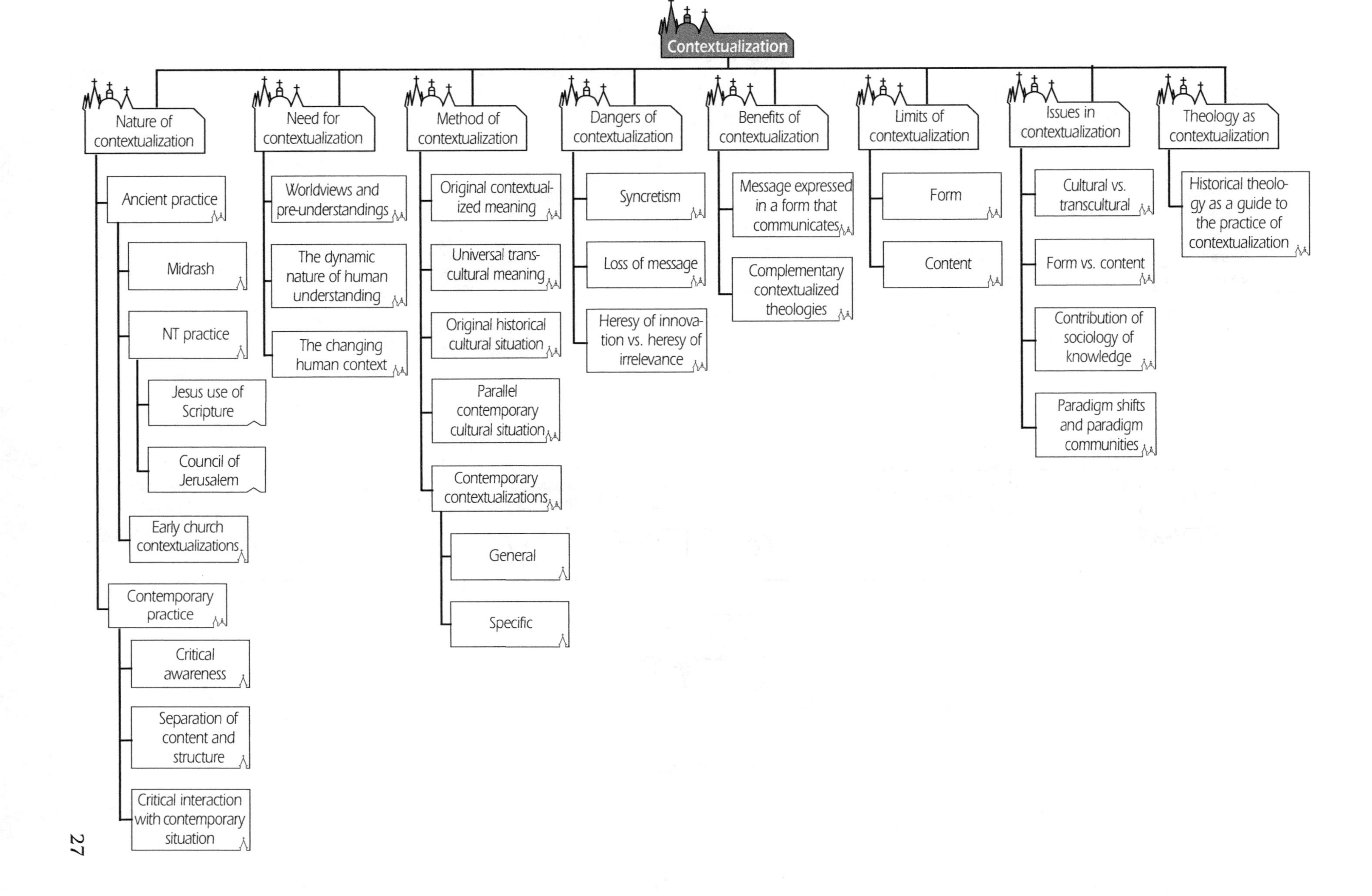

Contextualization
Nature of contextualization
Ancient practice
Midrash
NT practice
Jesus use of Scripture
Council of Jerusalem
Early church contextualizations
Contemporary practice
Critical awareness
Separation of content and structure
Critical interaction with contemporary situation
Need for contextualization
Worldviews and pre-understandings
The dynamic nature of human understanding
The changing human context
Method of contextualization
Original contextual-ized meaning
Universal trans-cultural meaning
Original historical cultural situation
Parallel contemporary cultural situation
Contemporary contextualizations
General
Specific
Dangers of contextualization
Syncretism
Loss of message
Heresy of innova-tion vs. heresy of irrelevance
Benefits of contextualization
Message expressed in a form that communicates
Complementary contextualized theologies
Limits of contextualization
Form
Content
Issues in contextualization
Cultural vs. transcultural
Form vs. content
Contribution of sociology of knowledge
Paradigm shifts and paradigm communities
Theology as contextualization
Historical theolo-gy as a guide to the practice of contextualization

Chart 18

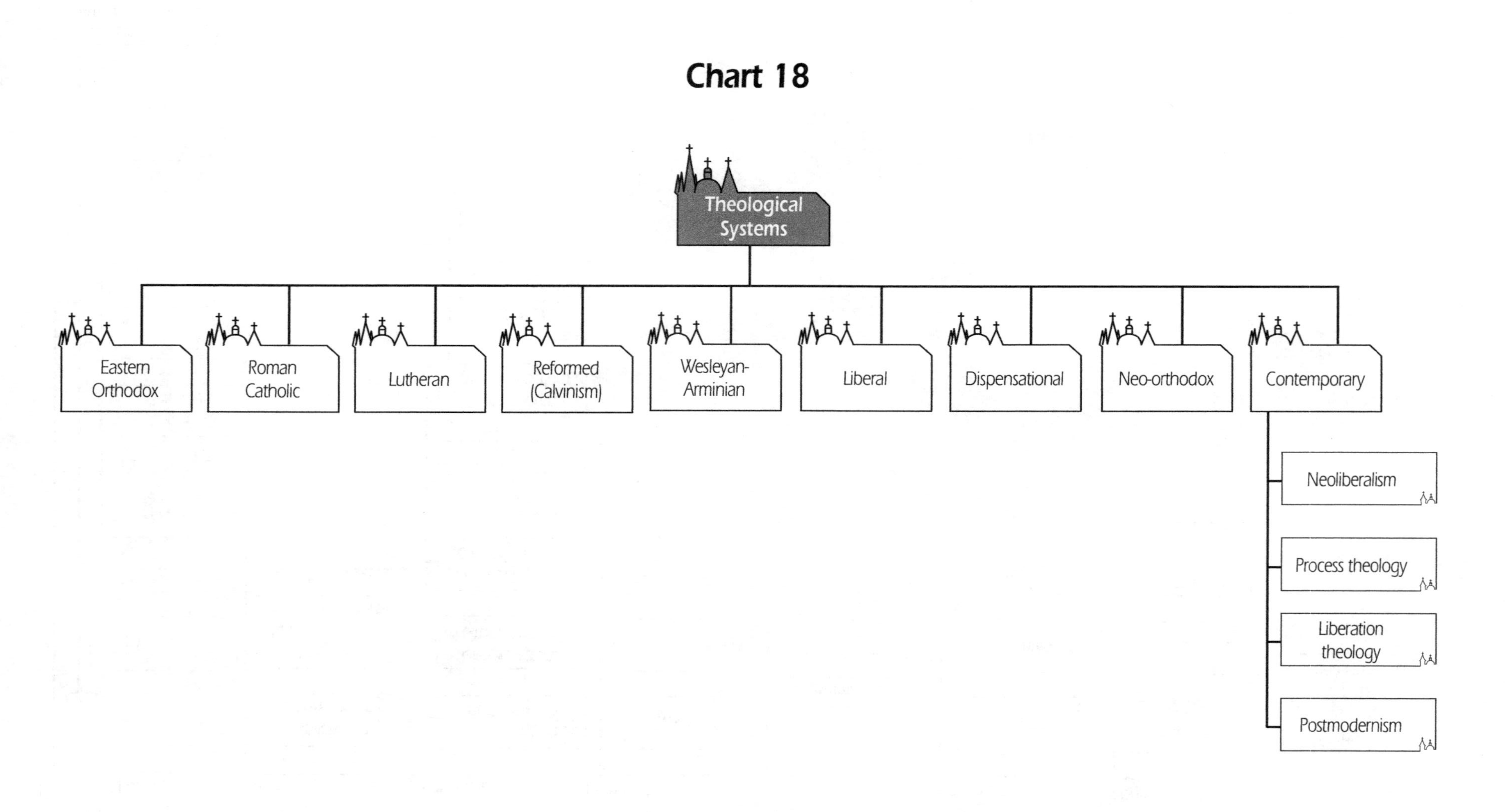
Theological Systems
Eastern Orthodox
Roman Catholic
Lutheran
Reformed (Calvinism)
Wesleyan-Arminian
Liberal
Dispensational
Neo-orthodox
Contemporary
Neoliberalism
Process theology
Liberation theology
Postmodernism

Chart 19

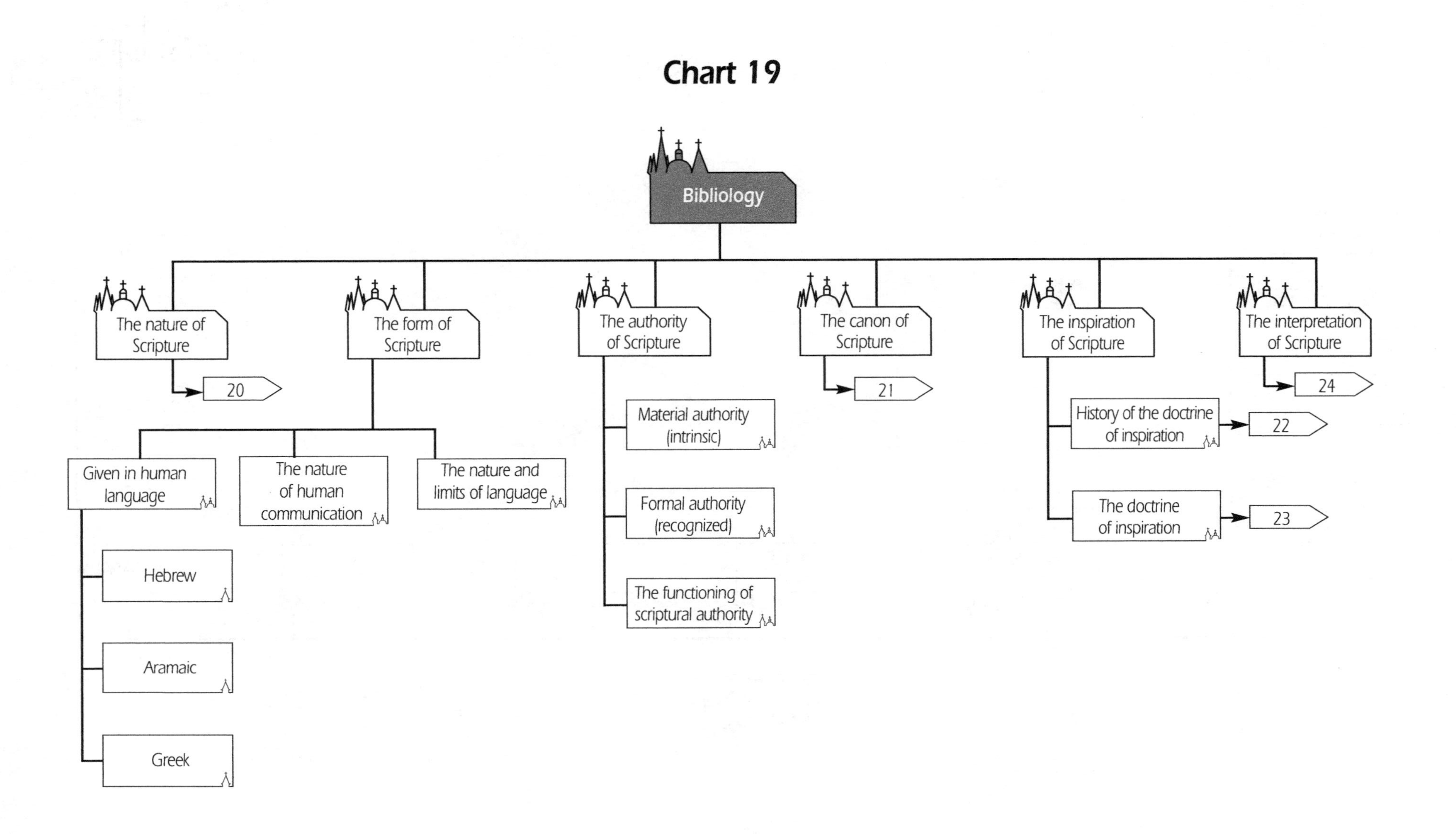

Bibliology
The nature of Scripture
20
The form of Scripture
Given in human language
Hebrew
Aramaic
Greek
The nature of human communication
The nature and limits of language
The authority of Scripture
Material authority (intrinsic)
Formal authority (recognized)
The functioning of scriptural authority
The canon of Scripture
21
The inspiration of Scripture
History of the doctrine of inspiration
22
The doctrine of inspiration
23
The interpretation of Scripture
24

Chart 20

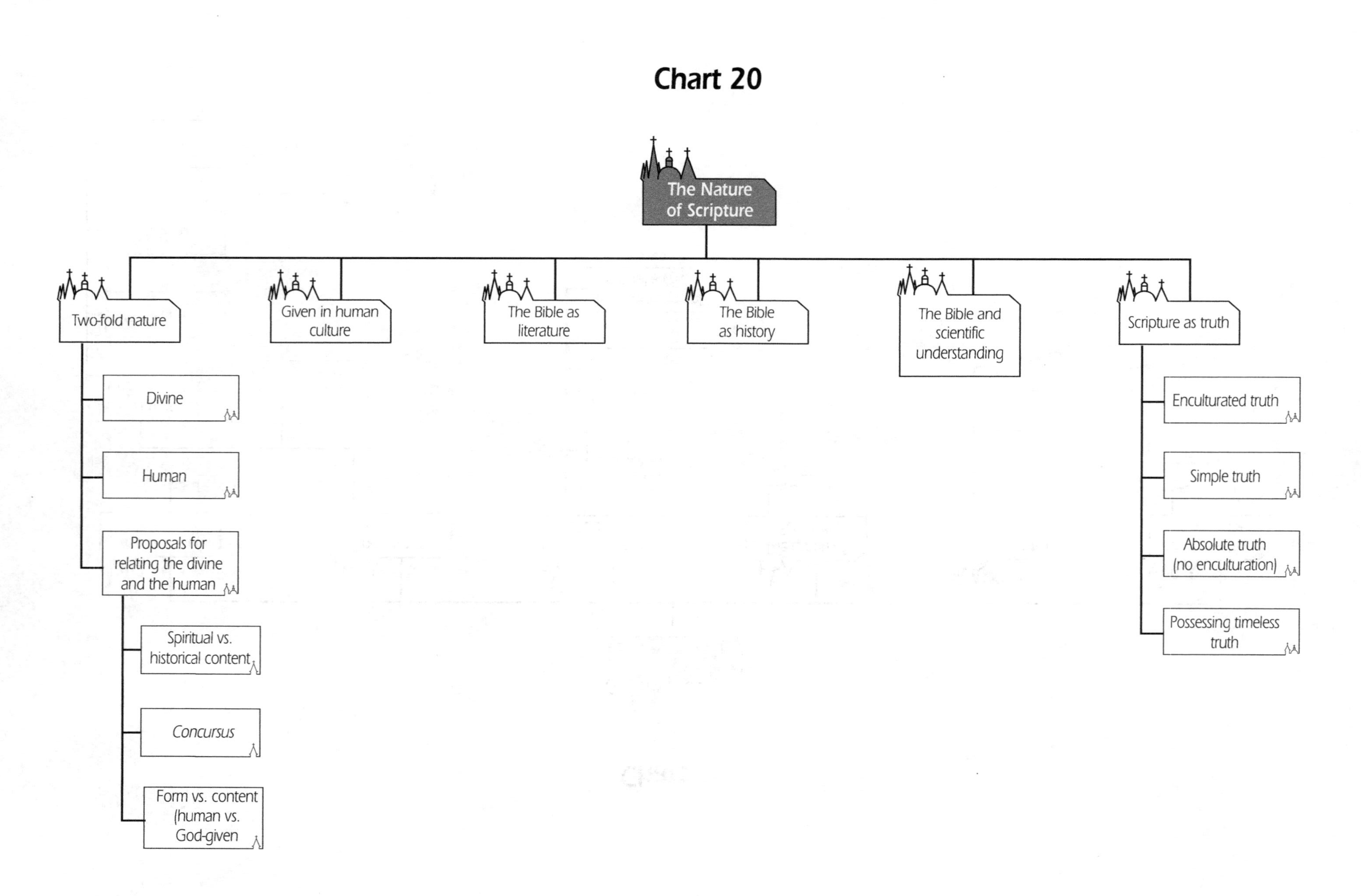
The Nature of Scripture
Two-fold nature
Divine
Human
Proposals for relating the divine and the human
Spiritual vs. historical content
Concursus
Form vs. content (human vs. God-given
Given in human culture
The Bible as literature
The Bible as history
The Bible and scientific understanding
Scripture as truth
Enculturated truth
Simple truth
Absolute truth (no enculturation)
Possessing timeless truth

Chart 21

- The Canon of Scripture
  - The concept of canon
    - Definition of canon
      - Material canon (intrinsic)
      - Formal canon (recognized)
    - Canonicity as an early concept
      - ANE psychology of canonicity (closure)
      - ANE treaties and covenant documents
  - The canon of the Old Testament
    - The critical conception: 3 phase canonization
      - Law
      - Prophets
      - Writings
    - The Bible defines its contents
      - Implicit claims of the biblical books
        - Law code
        - Prophetic voice of Yahweh
      - Jewish recognition
        - Very words of God
        - Prophetic authorship
        - Cessation of prophecy
      - Christ as the final authority
  - The canon of the New Testament
    - Development of the canon
      - The early church and the Jewish canon
      - The Lord as canon
      - The Apostles as canon
      - Apostolic tradition in the post-apostolic church
      - Canonicity and the gnostic challenge
      - Catholicity and canonicity
      - Canonicity and Marcion
      - Canonicity and the public reading
      - Fourth-century consensus
      - Medieval discussions
      - The Reformation: formal closure of the NT canon
    - Factors in recognizing canonicity
      - Intrinsic content
      - Apostolicity
      - Antiquity

Chart 22

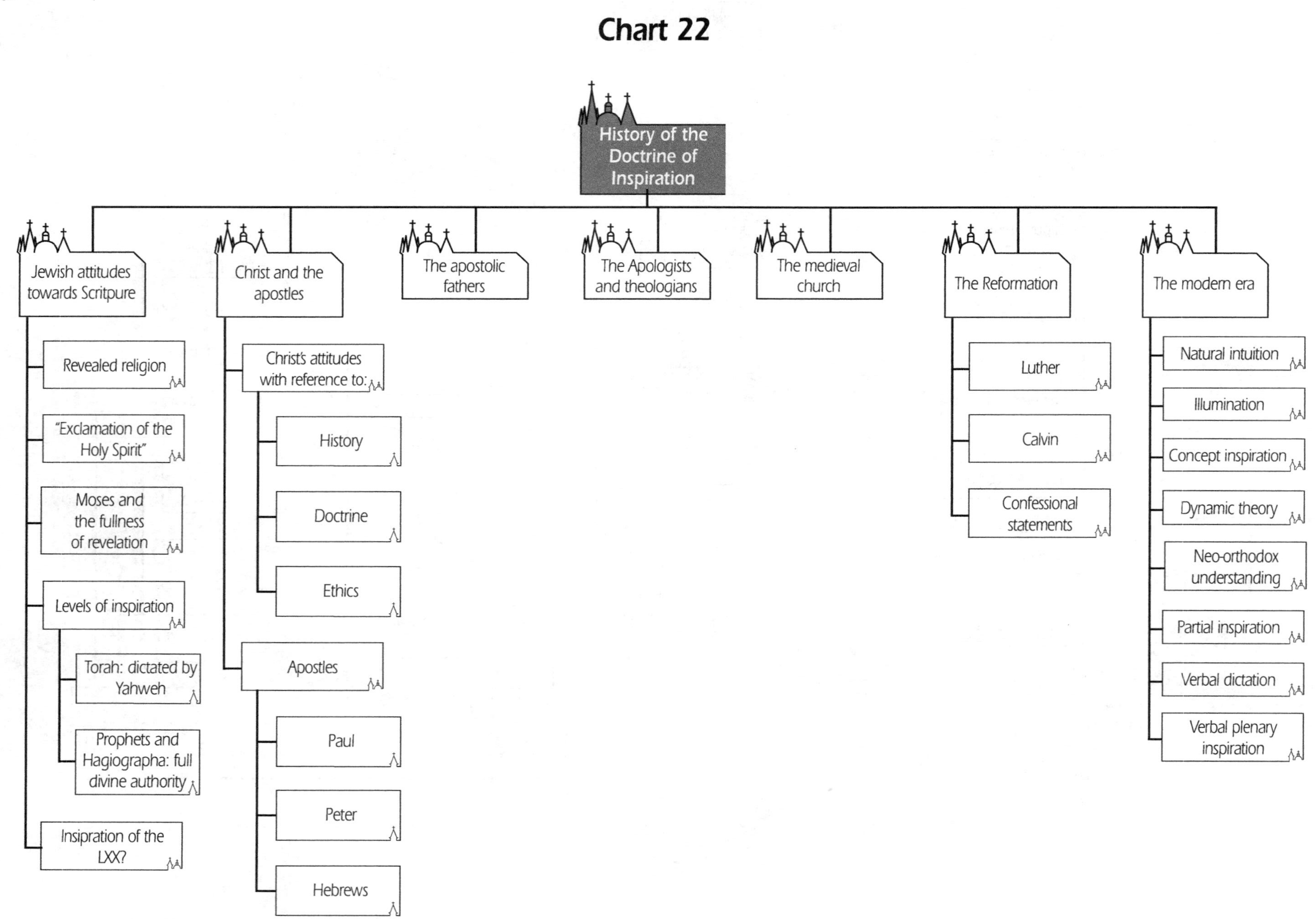
History of the Doctrine of Inspiration
Jewish attitudes towards Scritpure
Revealed religion
"Exclamation of the Holy Spirit"
Moses and the fullness of revelation
Levels of inspiration
Torah: dictated by Yahweh
Prophets and Hagiographa: full divine authority
Insipration of the LXX?
Christ and the apostles
Christ's attitudes with reference to:
History
Doctrine
Ethics
Apostles
Paul
Peter
Hebrews
The apostolic fathers
The Apologists and theologians
The medieval church
The Reformation
Luther
Calvin
Confessional statements
The modern era
Natural intuition
Illumination
Concept inspiration
Dynamic theory
Neo-orthodox understanding
Partial inspiration
Verbal dictation
Verbal plenary inspiration

Chart 23

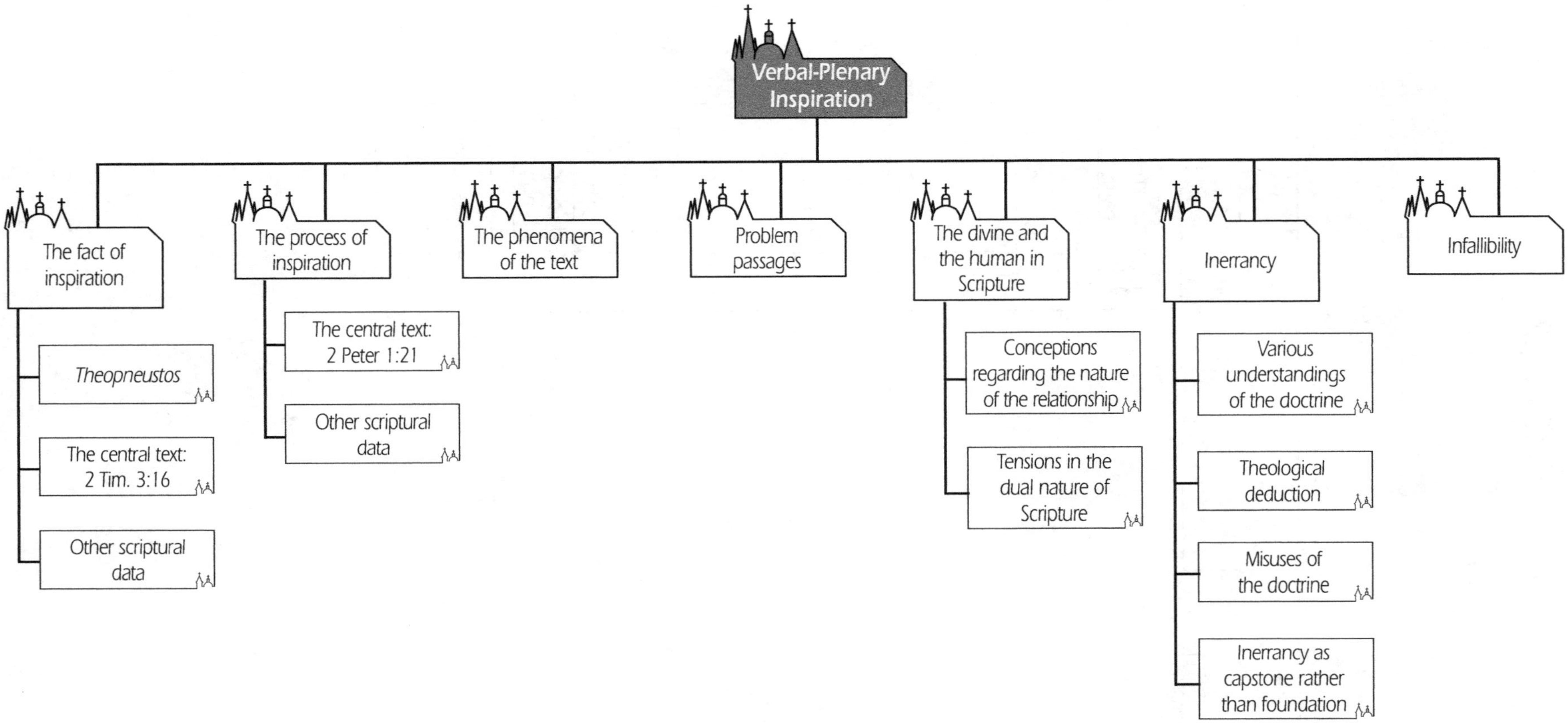

Verbal-Plenary Inspiration

- The fact of inspiration
  - *Theopneustos*
  - The central text: 2 Tim. 3:16
  - Other scriptural data
- The process of inspiration
  - The central text: 2 Peter 1:21
  - Other scriptural data
- The phenomena of the text
- Problem passages
- The divine and the human in Scripture
  - Conceptions regarding the nature of the relationship
  - Tensions in the dual nature of Scripture
- Inerrancy
  - Various understandings of the doctrine
  - Theological deduction
  - Misuses of the doctrine
  - Inerrancy as capstone rather than foundation
- Infallibility

Chart 24

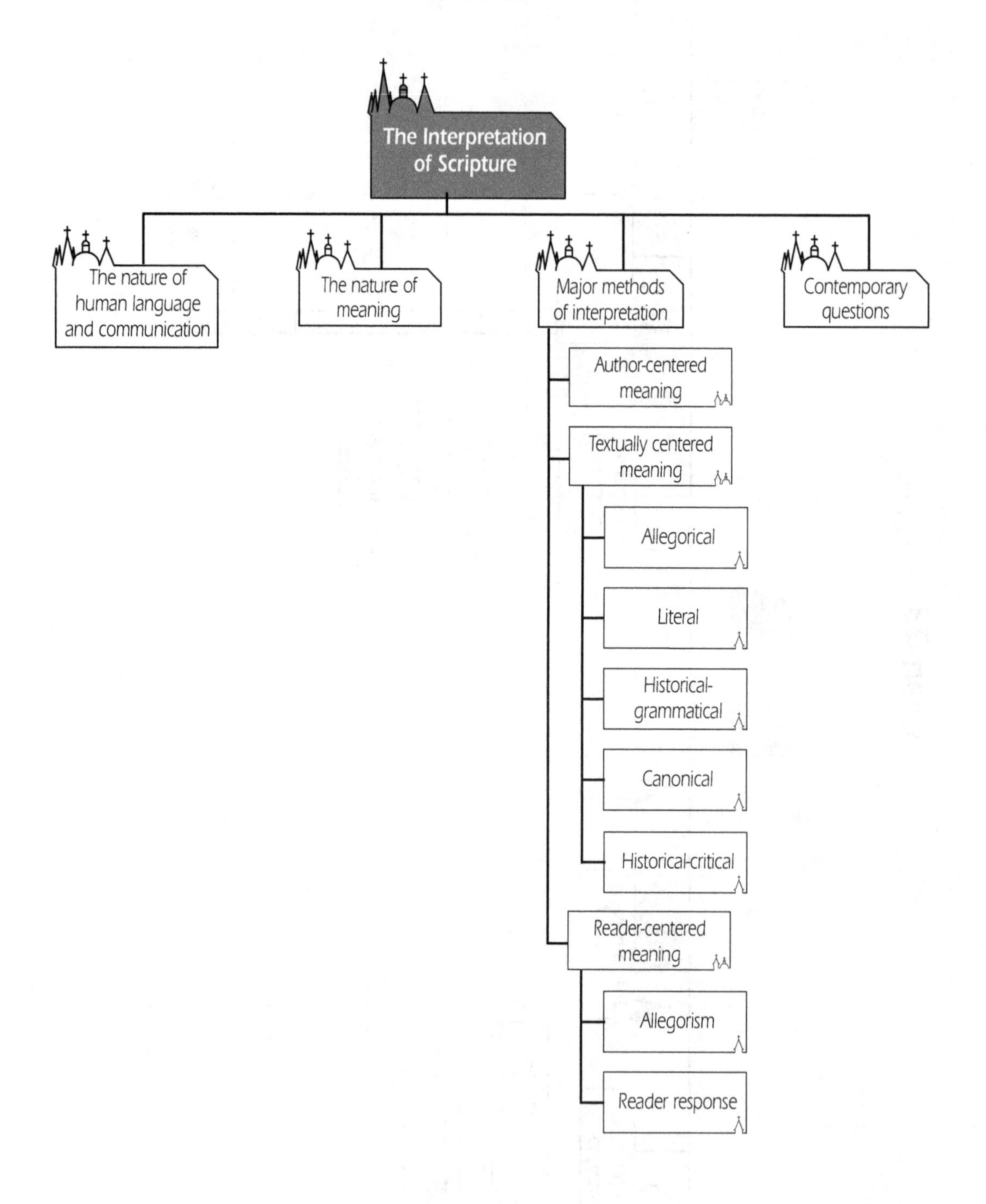

The Interpretation of Scripture
The nature of human language and communication
The nature of meaning
Major methods of interpretation
Contemporary questions
Author-centered meaning
Textually centered meaning
Allegorical
Literal
Historical-grammatical
Canonical
Historical-critical
Reader-centered meaning
Allegorism
Reader response

Chart 25

Theology Proper

- Sources of knowledge of God
  - General revelation
  - Human conception
  - Self-revelation
    - The development of the understanding of God
    - General revelation
    - Special revelation
- Rival understandings of God
  - Judaism
  - Islam
  - Unitarianism
  - Process
  - Classical theism (the God of the philosophers)
- God as Trinity → 26
- Immanence and transcendence
- The nature of God
  - The essence of God
  - How is God known?
    - Rationally and cataphatically
    - Mystically and apophatically
    - By his works
    - Personally and relationally
- God as Person
  - The primacy of personhood
  - The names of God → 28
  - God as Father → 27
- Attributes of God → 30-31
- Works of God
  - Creation
  - Providence (all-inclusive)
- Biblical Presentation of God → 29
- Philosophical proofs → 32

Chart 26

God as Trinity

- The origin of the doctrine
  - See glossary, "Trinity"
- Unitarianism
  - Judaism
  - Islam
  - Heterodox Christian Unitariansim
    - Early Christian forms
    - Later rejection of Trinitarianism
      - Socinianism
      - Deism
      - Liberalism
- Biblical Evidence
  - OT presentation of God
  - Hints of the Trinity in the OT
  - The Trinity as seen in the NT
    - The centrality of Jesus in Trinitarian understanding
- The development of Trinitarian theology
  - Implicit, naive Trinitarianism
  - Monarchianism
    - Dynamic
    - Modalistic
  - Arianism
  - Nicea
    - *Homoousia*
  - Constantinople
    - The full deity of the Spirit
- Trinitarian explanations
  - Eastern Cappadocian
  - Augustinitian
  - The *Filioque*
  - Contribution of the Reformers
  - Economic and ontic Trinitarian understanding
- Issues involved in a Trinitarian understanding of God
  - Unity and diversity in the Godhead
  - Implications for salvation

Chart 27

God as Father

- Old Testament
  - Uniqueness of concept in ANE
  - Yahweh as Father
  - Yahweh's son: Davidic king; Israel
  - The meaning of fatherhood (relational vs. legal)
- New Testament
  - Use of the term
  - God as the Father of Jesus
  - Limited scope of divine fatherhood
  - Comfort of God's fatherhood
- History of the doctrine
  - Ante-Nicene period
    - The Father as God
    - Early confessional statements
    - Early writings
    - The Gnostic challenge
    - Orthodox answer
    - Tertullian and Hyppolytus
    - Novatian and Origen
  - The Nicene period
    - Modalism
    - Adoption
    - Arianism
    - The Nicene Creed
    - Augustine and Cyril of Jerusalem
  - Modern period
    - Orthodoxy
    - Unitarianism
    - Liberalism
    - Women's liberation
- Issues
  - Is God male?

Chart 28

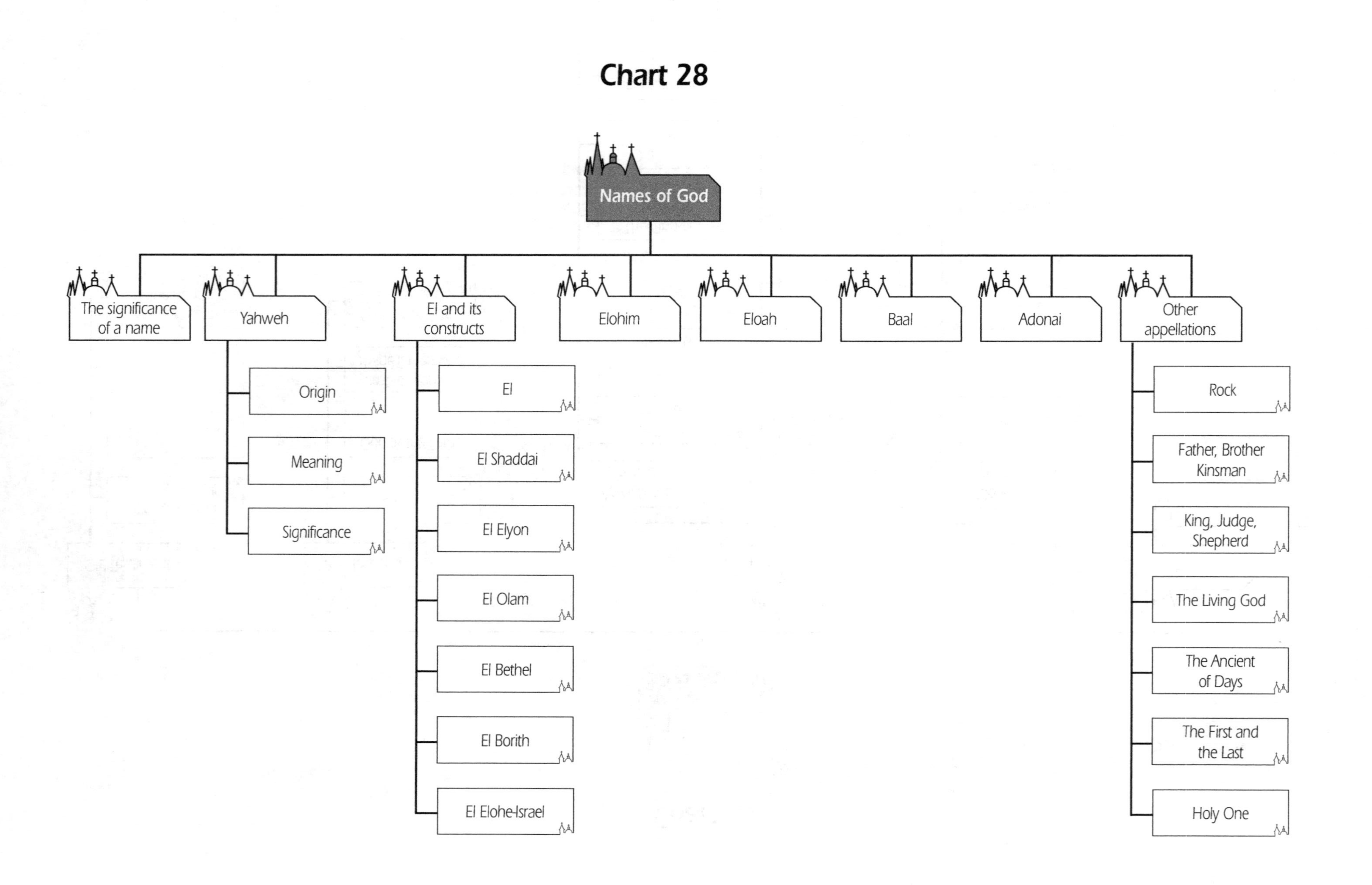
Names of God
The significance of a name
Yahweh
Origin
Meaning
Significance
El and its constructs
El
El Shaddai
El Elyon
El Olam
El Bethel
El Borith
El Elohe-Israel
Elohim
Eloah
Baal
Adonai
Other appellations
Rock
Father, Brother Kinsman
King, Judge, Shepherd
The Living God
The Ancient of Days
The First and the Last
Holy One

Chart 29

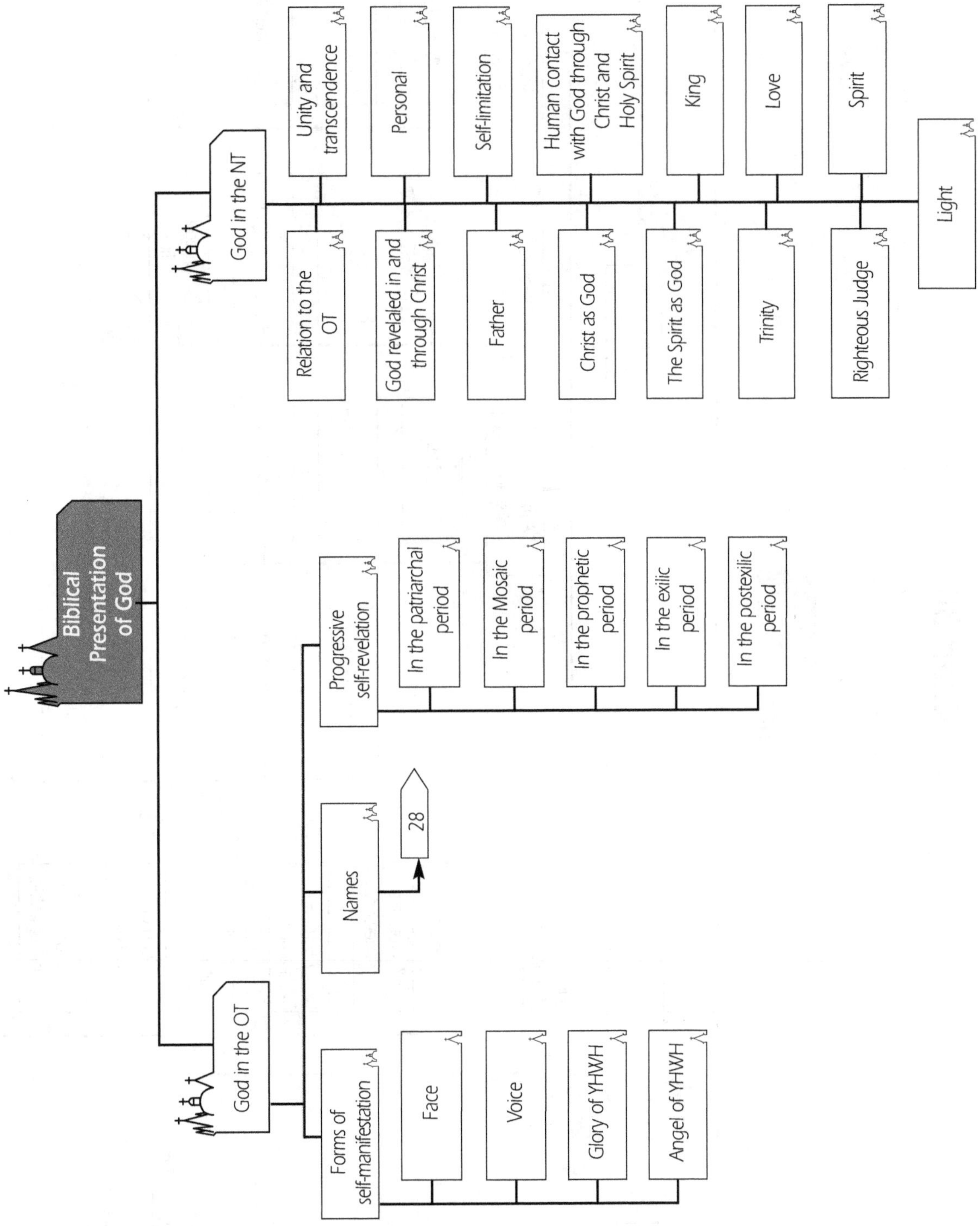

Biblical Presentation of God

- God in the OT
  - Forms of self-manifestation
    - Face
    - Voice
    - Glory of YHWH
    - Angel of YHWH
  - Names
    - 28
  - Progressive self-revelation
    - In the patriarchal period
    - In the Mosaic period
    - In the prophetic period
    - In the exilic period
    - In the postexilic period
- God in the NT
  - Relation to the OT
  - Unity and transcendence
  - God revealed in and through Christ
  - Personal
  - Father
  - Self-limitation
  - Christ as God
  - Human contact with God through Christ and Holy Spirit
  - The Spirit as God
  - King
  - Trinity
  - Love
  - Righteous Judge
  - Spirit
  - Light

Chart 30

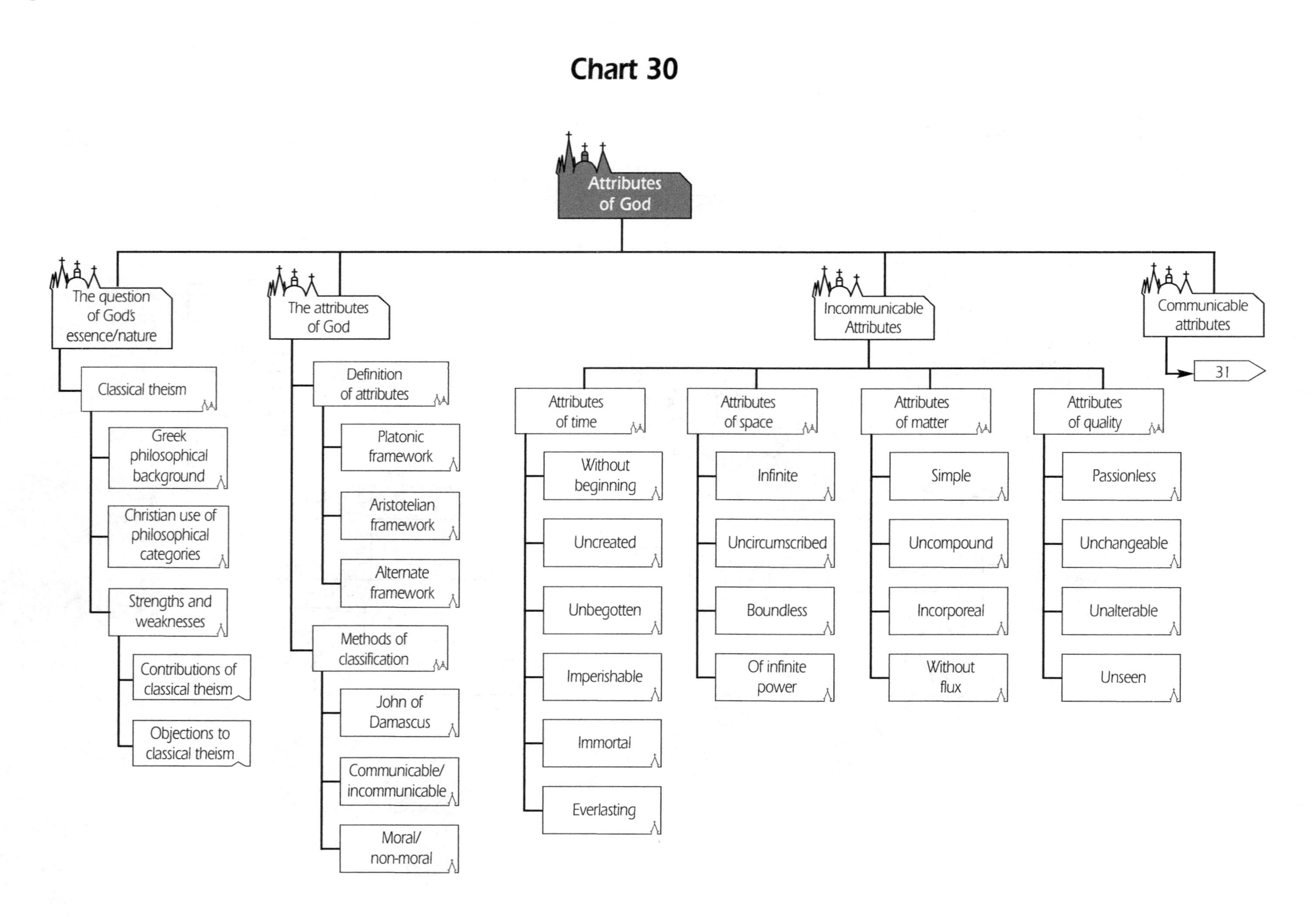

Attributes of God
The question of God's essence/nature
Classical theism
Greek philosophical background
Christian use of philosophical categories
Strengths and weaknesses
Contributions of classical theism
Objections to classical theism
The attributes of God
Definition of attributes
Platonic framework
Aristotelian framework
Alternate framework
Methods of classification
John of Damascus
Communicable/ incommunicable
Moral/ non-moral
Incommunicable Attributes
Attributes of time
Without beginning
Uncreated
Unbegotten
Imperishable
Immortal
Everlasting
Attributes of space
Infinite
Uncircumscribed
Boundless
Of infinite power
Attributes of matter
Simple
Uncompound
Incorporeal
Without flux
Attributes of quality
Passionless
Unchangeable
Unalterable
Unseen
Communicable attributes
31

Chart 31

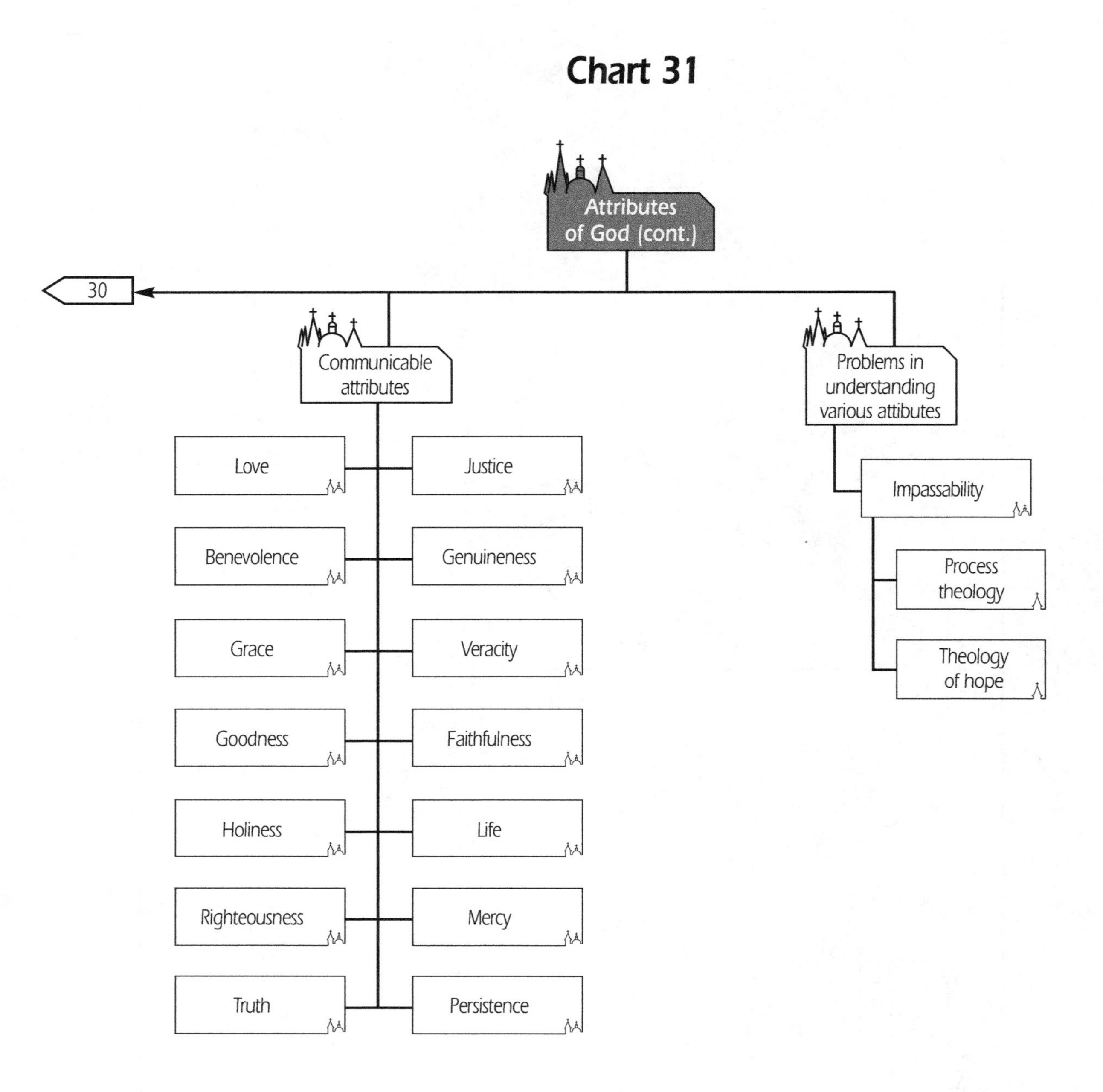
Attributes of God (cont.)
30
Communicable attributes
Love
Justice
Benevolence
Genuineness
Grace
Veracity
Goodness
Faithfulness
Holiness
Life
Righteousness
Mercy
Truth
Persistence
Problems in understanding various attibutes
Impassability
Process theology
Theology of hope

Chart 32

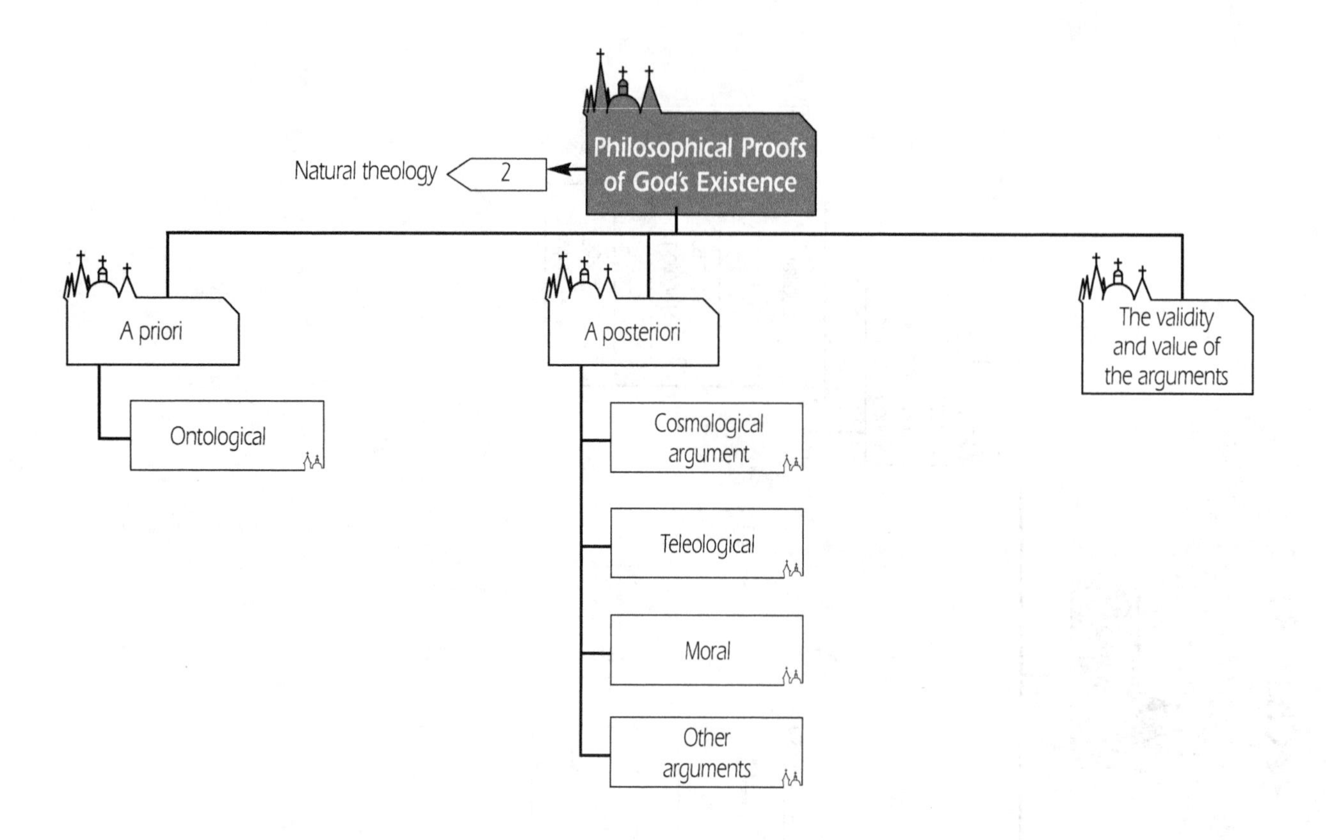
Philosophical Proofs of God's Existence
Natural theology
2
A priori
Ontological
A posteriori
Cosmological argument
Teleological
Moral
Other arguments
The validity and value of the arguments

Chart 33

- Angelology
  - Angelology
    - The origin of angels
    - The nature of angels
      - The creation of angels
      - Types of angels
      - The personality of angels
      - Modes of angelic existence
      - Angelic power and authority
      - Angels and humanity
    - The function of angels
      - As ministering spirits
      - As agents of judgment
      - In worship of God
  - Demonology
    - Demons
      - The nature of demons
      - The activity of demons
      - Genesis 6: demonic and human joining?
    - Satan → 34
    - Issues affecting human existence
      - Demon possession
        - Outer personal possession
        - Collective possession
        - Demons and the demonic
      - Superstition
      - The occult
  - The spiritual world and the structures of human existence

Chart 34

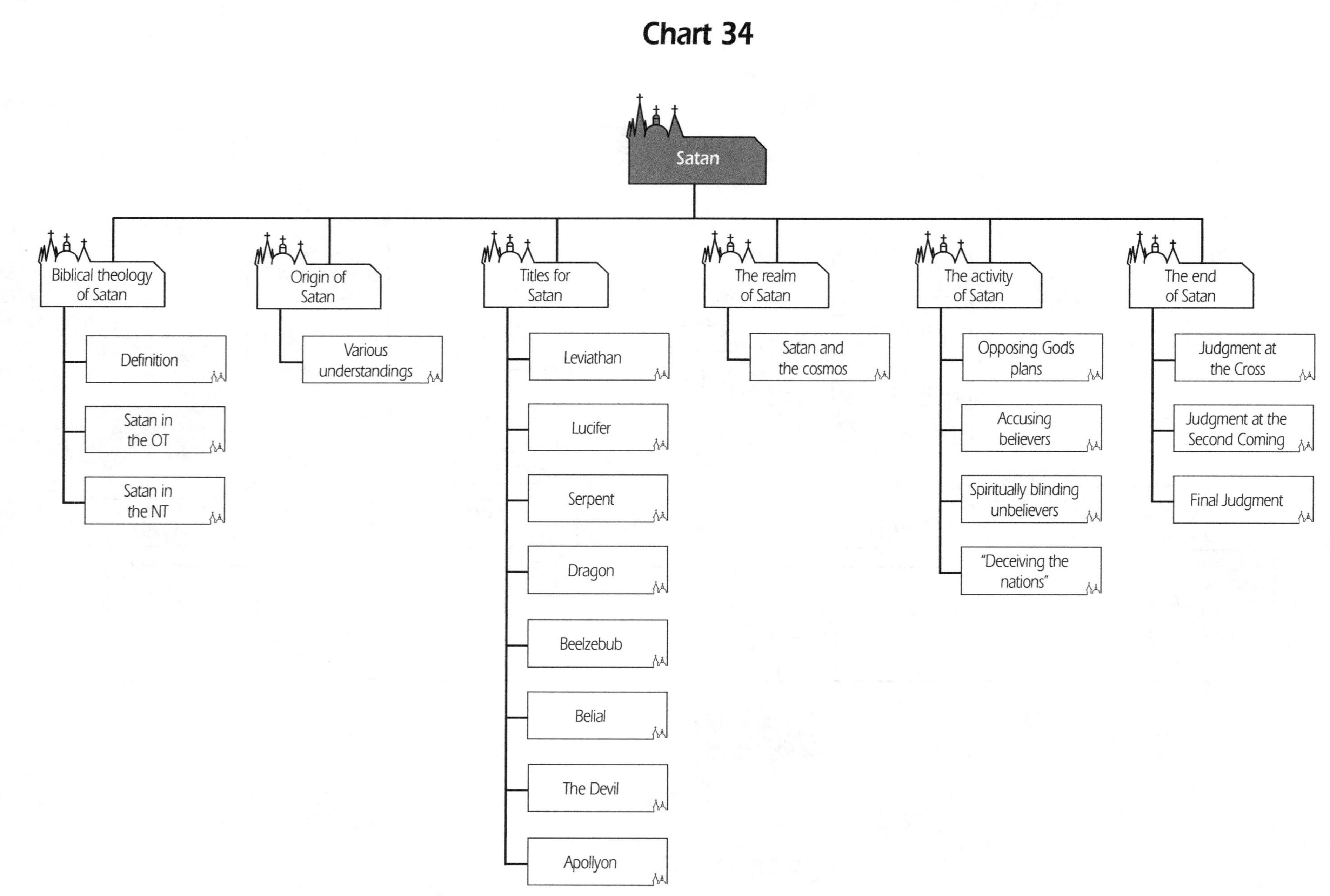

Satan
Biblical theology of Satan
Definition
Satan in the OT
Satan in the NT
Origin of Satan
Various understandings
Titles for Satan
Leviathan
Lucifer
Serpent
Dragon
Beelzebub
Belial
The Devil
Apollyon
The realm of Satan
Satan and the cosmos
The activity of Satan
Opposing God's plans
Accusing believers
Spiritually blinding unbelievers
"Deceiving the nations"
The end of Satan
Judgment at the Cross
Judgment at the Second Coming
Final Judgment

Chart 35

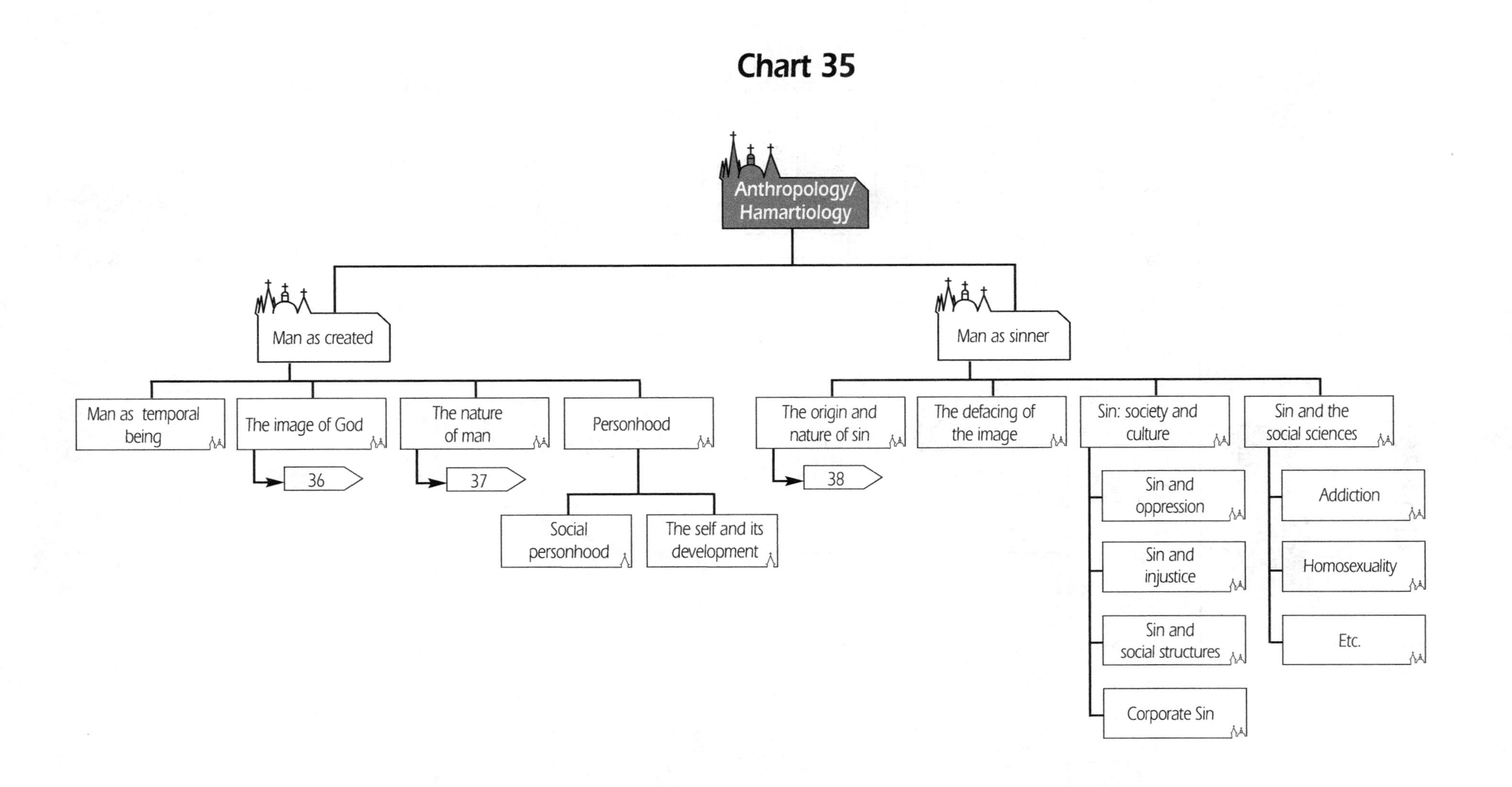

Anthropology/
Hamartiology
Man as created
Man as temporal being
The image of God
36
The nature of man
37
Personhood
Social personhood
The self and its development
Man as sinner
The origin and nature of sin
38
The defacing of the image
Sin: society and culture
Sin and oppression
Sin and injustice
Sin and social structures
Corporate Sin
Sin and the social sciences
Addiction
Homosexuality
Etc.

Chart 36

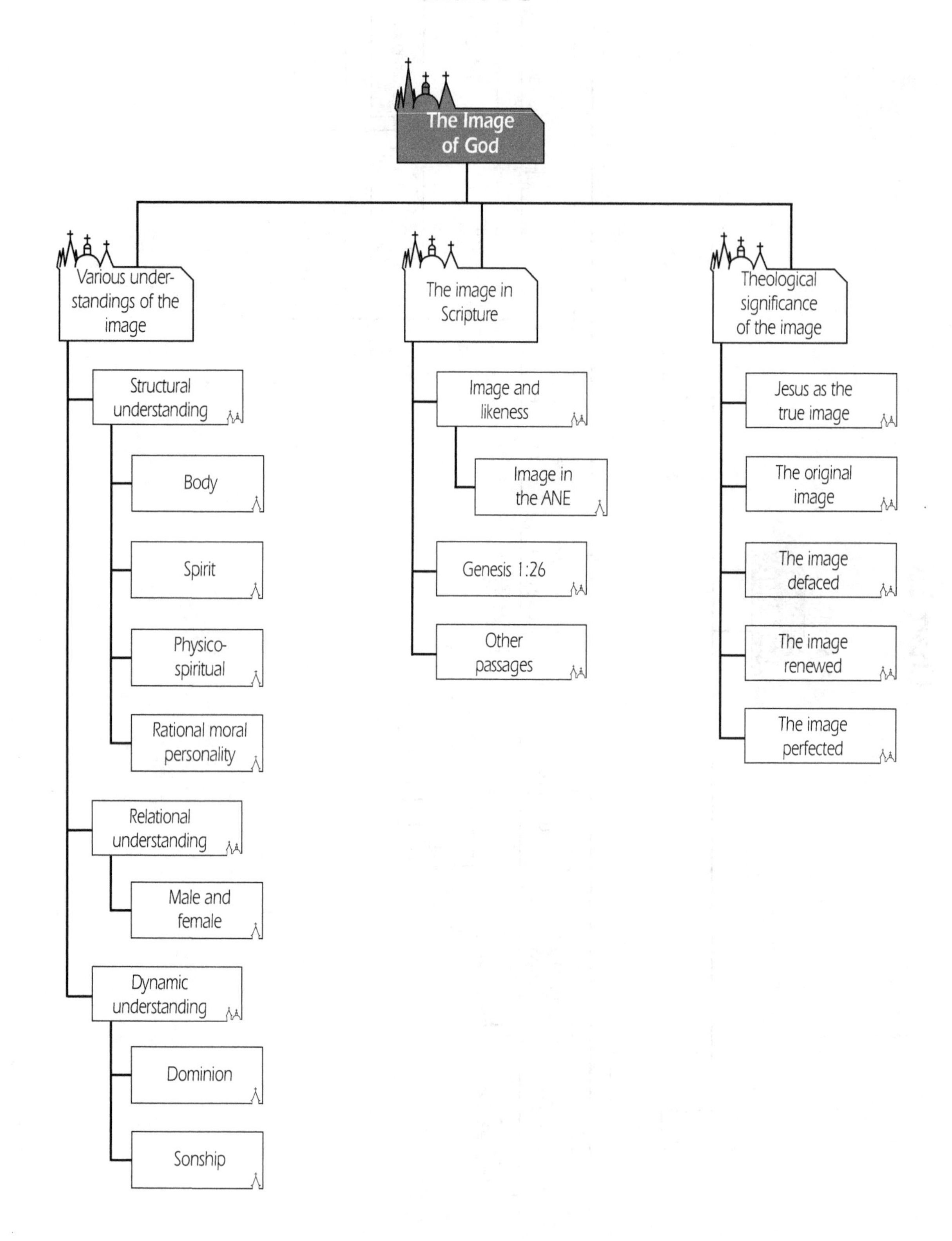
The Image of God
Various understandings of the image
Structural understanding
Body
Spirit
Physico-spiritual
Rational moral personality
Relational understanding
Male and female
Dynamic understanding
Dominion
Sonship
The image in Scripture
Image and likeness
Image in the ANE
Genesis 1:26
Other passages
Theological significance of the image
Jesus as the true image
The original image
The image defaced
The image renewed
The image perfected

Chart 37

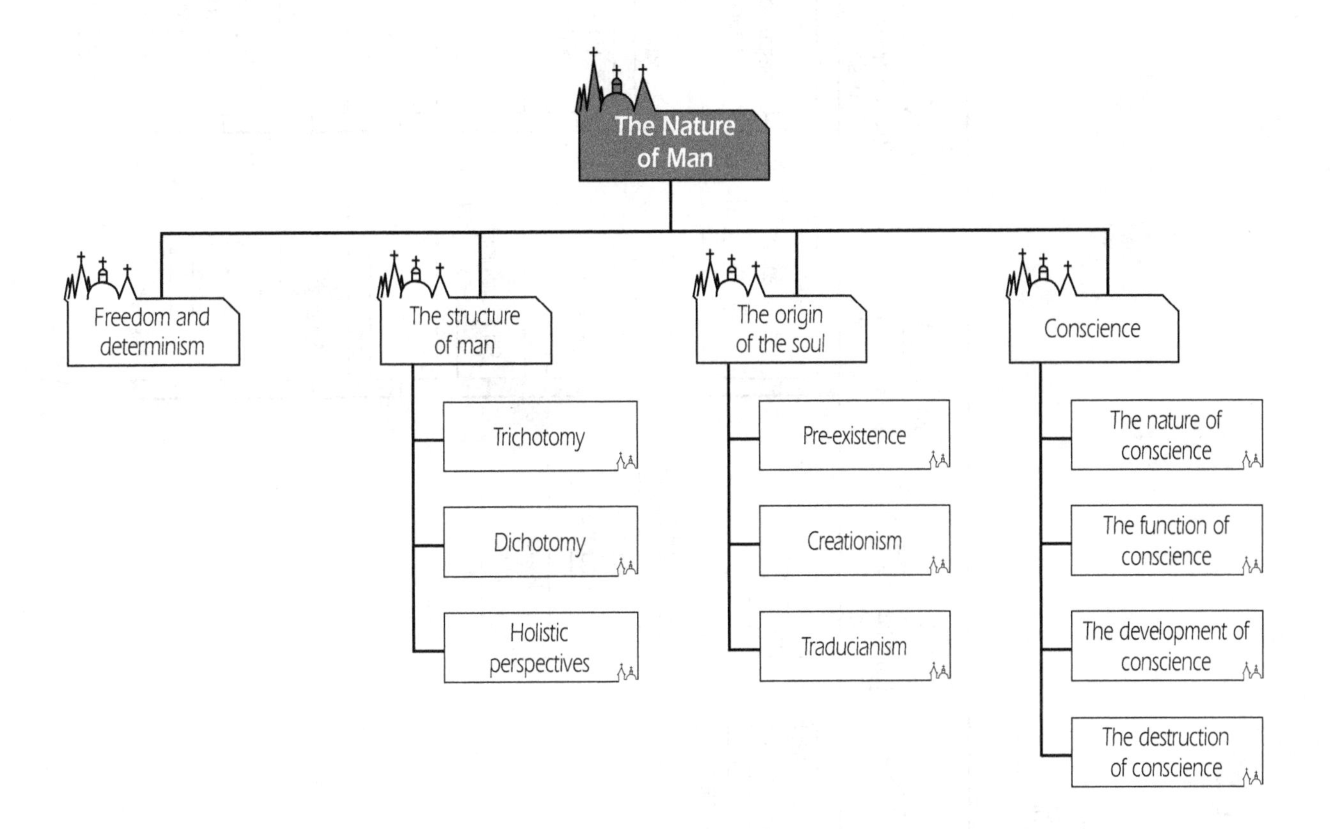

The Nature of Man
Freedom and determinism
The structure of man
The origin of the soul
Conscience
Trichotomy
Dichotomy
Holistic perspectives
Pre-existence
Creationism
Traducianism
The nature of conscience
The function of conscience
The development of conscience
The destruction of conscience

Chart 38

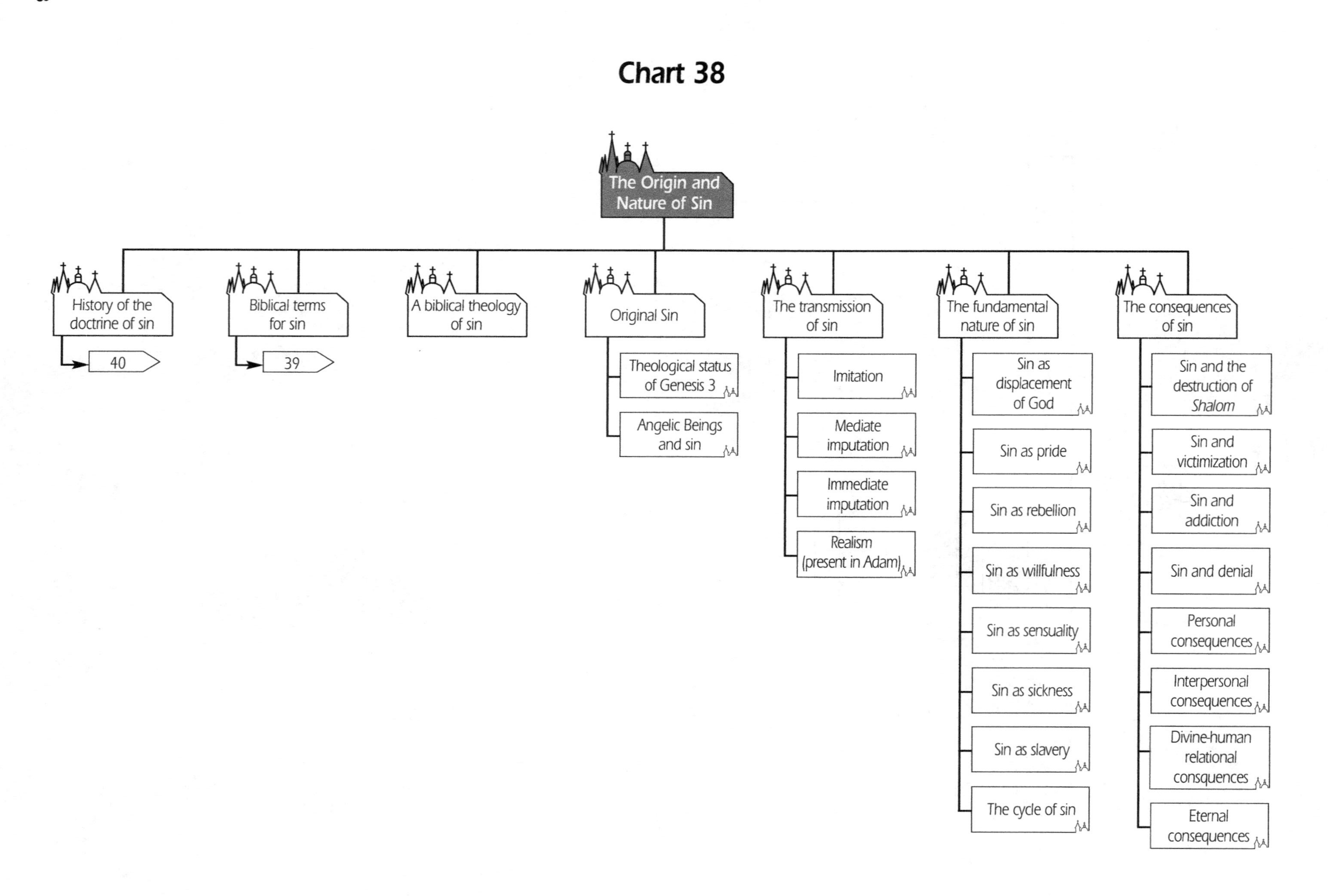
The Origin and Nature of Sin
History of the doctrine of sin
40
Biblical terms for sin
39
A biblical theology of sin
Original Sin
Theological status of Genesis 3
Angelic Beings and sin
The transmission of sin
Imitation
Mediate imputation
Immediate imputation
Realism (present in Adam)
The fundamental nature of sin
Sin as displacement of God
Sin as pride
Sin as rebellion
Sin as willfulness
Sin as sensuality
Sin as sickness
Sin as slavery
The cycle of sin
The consequences of sin
Sin and the destruction of Shalom
Sin and victimization
Sin and addiction
Sin and denial
Personal consequences
Interpersonal consequences
Divine-human relational consquences
Eternal consequences

Chart 39

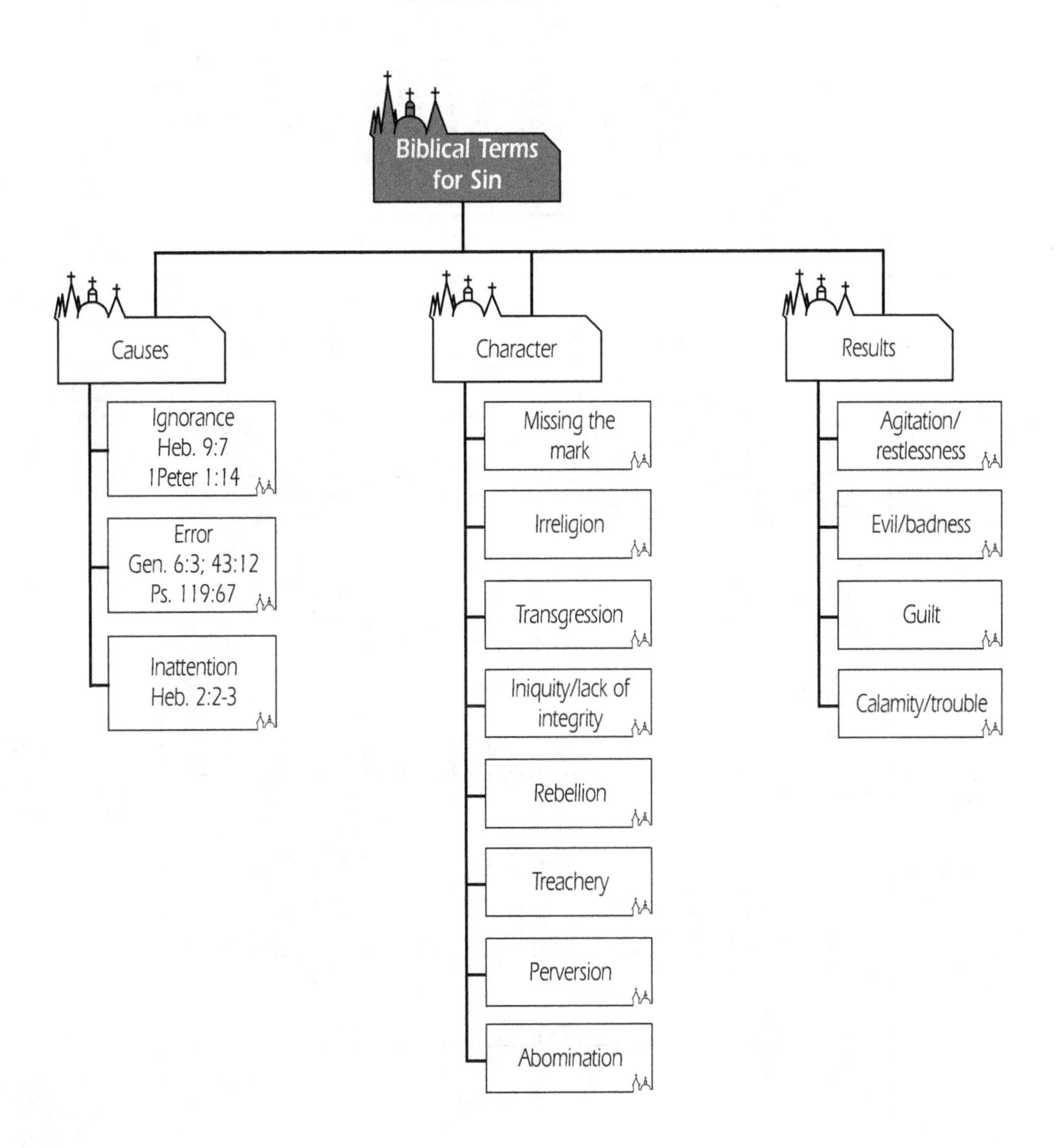

Biblical Terms for Sin
Causes
Ignorance
Heb. 9:7
1Peter 1:14
Error
Gen. 6:3; 43:12
Ps. 119:67
Inattention
Heb. 2:2-3
Character
Missing the mark
Irreligion
Transgression
Iniquity/lack of integrity
Rebellion
Treachery
Perversion
Abomination
Results
Agitation/ restlessness
Evil/badness
Guilt
Calamity/trouble

Chart 40

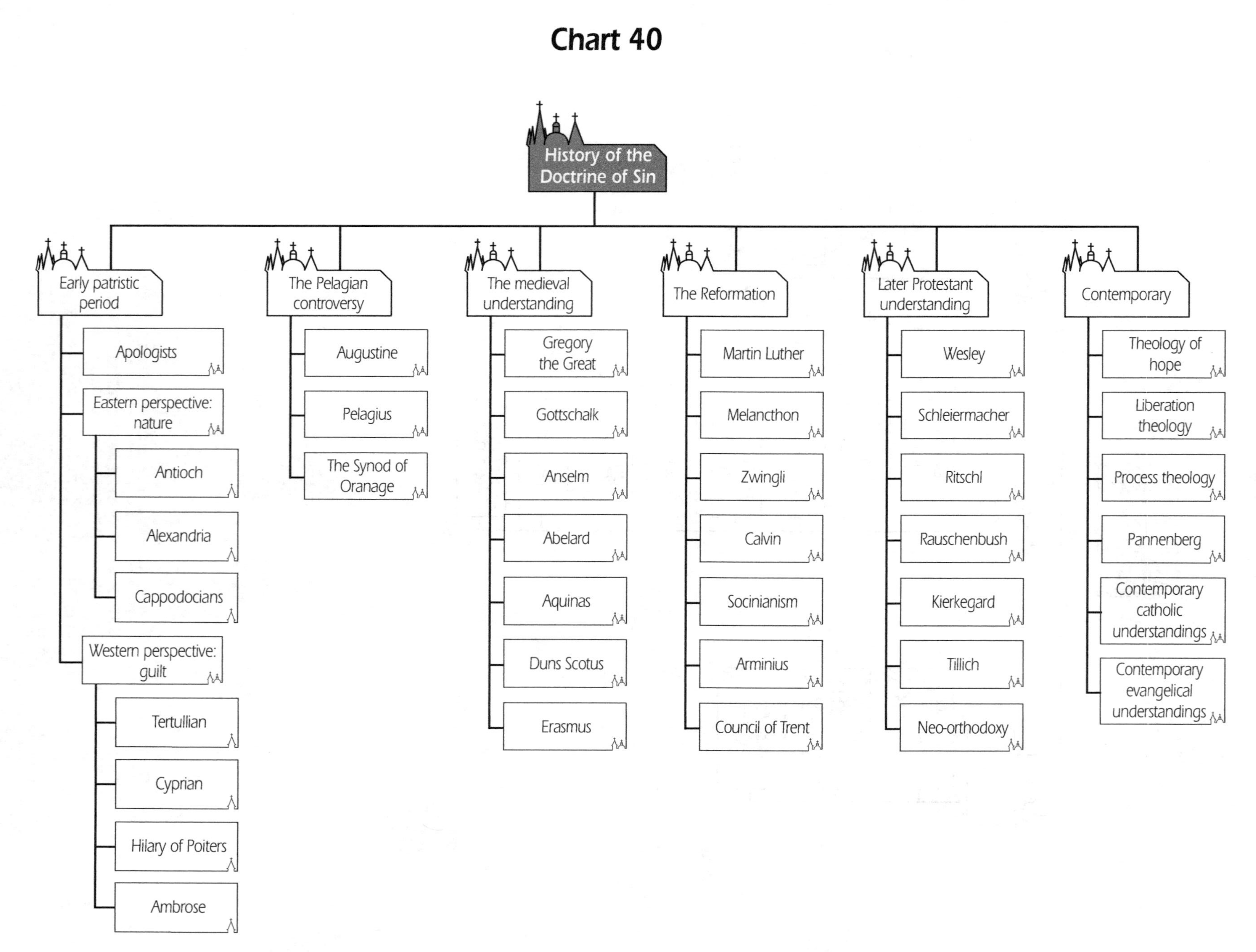

History of the Doctrine of Sin
Early patristic period
Apologists
Eastern perspective: nature
Antioch
Alexandria
Cappodocians
Western perspective: guilt
Tertullian
Cyprian
Hilary of Poiters
Ambrose
The Pelagian controversy
Augustine
Pelagius
The Synod of Oranage
The medieval understanding
Gregory the Great
Gottschalk
Anselm
Abelard
Aquinas
Duns Scotus
Erasmus
The Reformation
Martin Luther
Melancthon
Zwingli
Calvin
Socinianism
Arminius
Council of Trent
Later Protestant understanding
Wesley
Schleiermacher
Ritschl
Rauschenbush
Kierkegard
Tillich
Neo-orthodoxy
Contemporary
Theology of hope
Liberation theology
Process theology
Pannenberg
Contemporary catholic understandings
Contemporary evangelical understandings

Chart 41

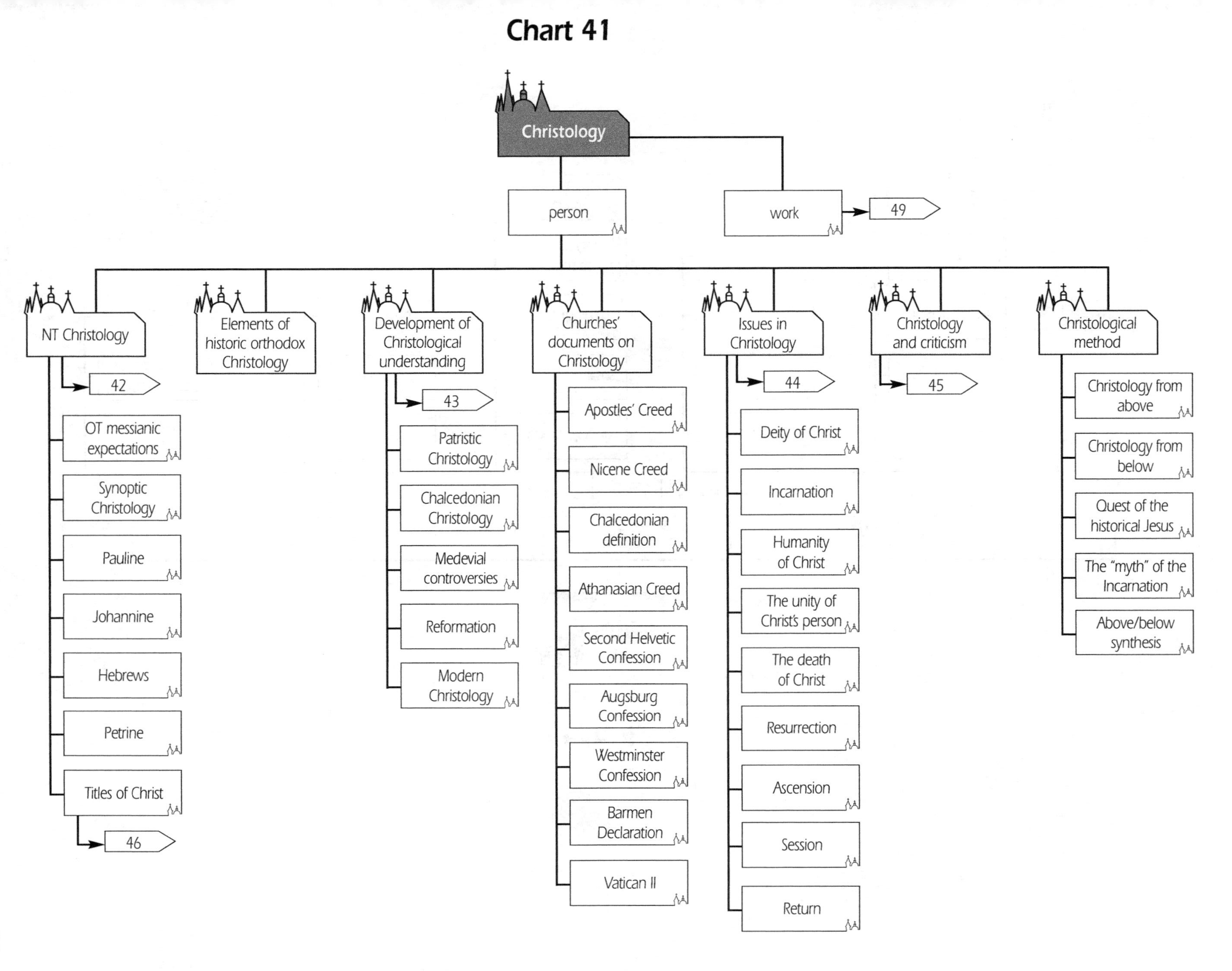

Christology
person
work
49
NT Christology
42
OT messianic expectations
Synoptic Christology
Pauline
Johannine
Hebrews
Petrine
Titles of Christ
46
Elements of historic orthodox Christology
Development of Christological understanding
43
Patristic Christology
Chalcedonian Christology
Medevial controversies
Reformation
Modern Christology
Churches' documents on Christology
Apostles' Creed
Nicene Creed
Chalcedonian definition
Athanasian Creed
Second Helvetic Confession
Augsburg Confession
Westminster Confession
Barmen Declaration
Vatican II
Issues in Christology
44
Deity of Christ
Incarnation
Humanity of Christ
The unity of Christ's person
The death of Christ
Resurrection
Ascension
Session
Return
Christology and criticism
45
Christological method
Christology from above
Christology from below
Quest of the historical Jesus
The "myth" of the Incarnation
Above/below synthesis

Chart 42

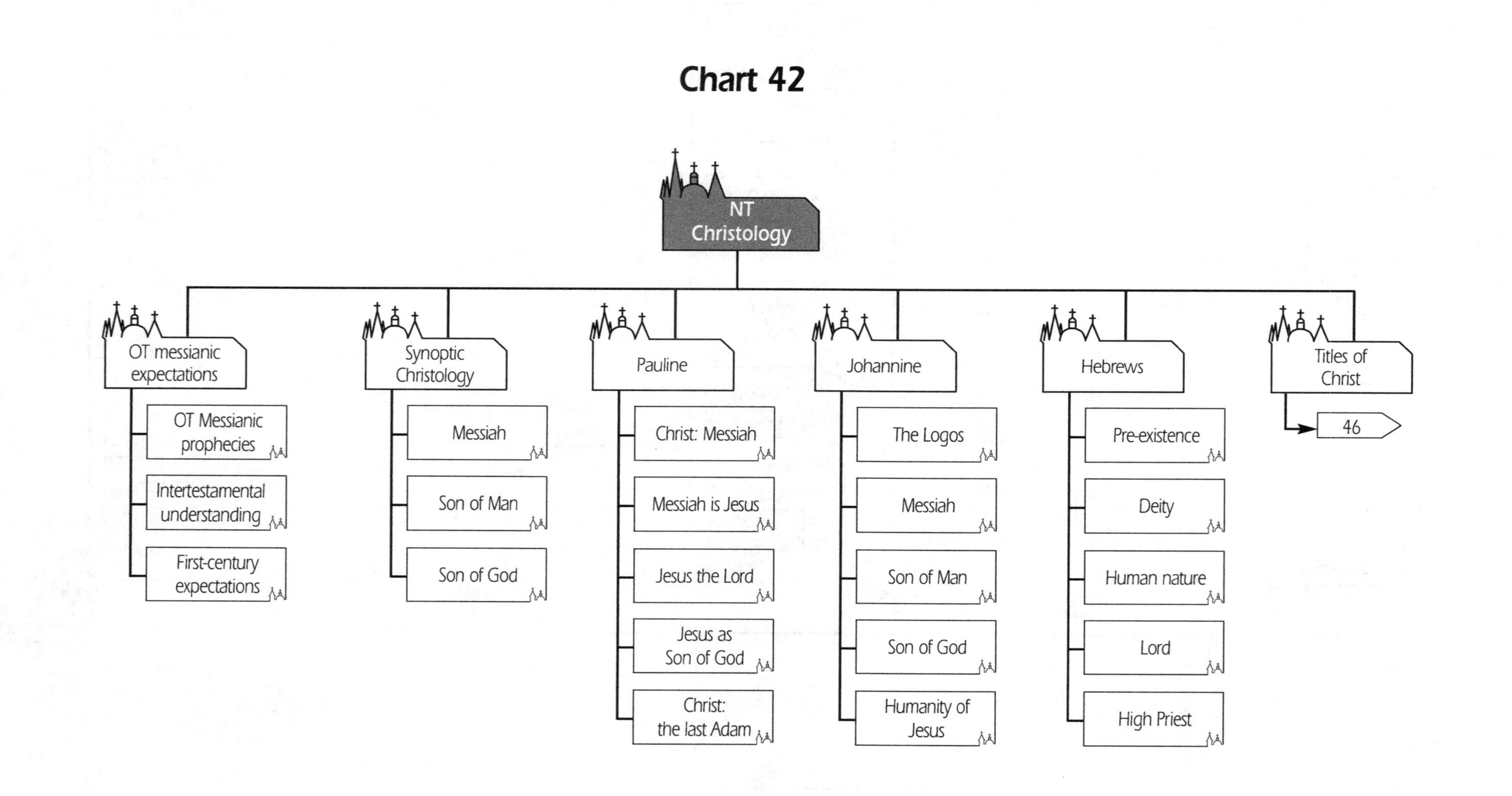
NT Christology
OT messianic expectations
OT Messianic prophecies
Intertestamental understanding
First-century expectations
Synoptic Christology
Messiah
Son of Man
Son of God
Pauline
Christ: Messiah
Messiah is Jesus
Jesus the Lord
Jesus as Son of God
Christ: the last Adam
Johannine
The Logos
Messiah
Son of Man
Son of God
Humanity of Jesus
Hebrews
Pre-existence
Deity
Human nature
Lord
High Priest
Titles of Christ
46

Chart 43

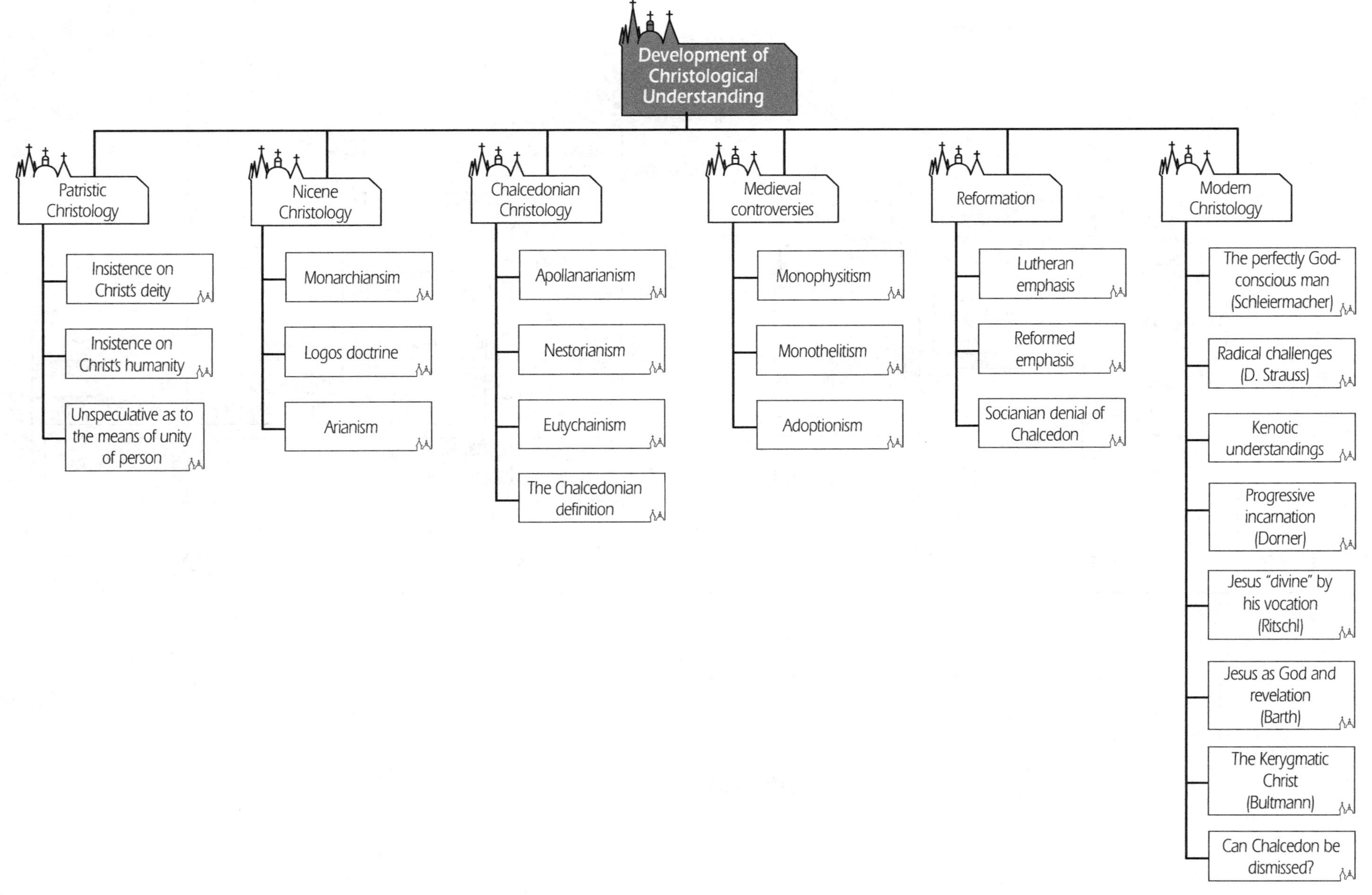

Development of Christological Understanding
Patristic Christology
Insistence on Christ's deity
Insistence on Christ's humanity
Unspeculative as to the means of unity of person
Nicene Christology
Monarchiansim
Logos doctrine
Arianism
Chalcedonian Christology
Apollanarianism
Nestorianism
Eutychainism
The Chalcedonian definition
Medieval controversies
Monophysitism
Monothelitism
Adoptionism
Reformation
Lutheran emphasis
Reformed emphasis
Socianian denial of Chalcedon
Modern Christology
The perfectly God-conscious man (Schleiermacher)
Radical challenges (D. Strauss)
Kenotic understandings
Progressive incarnation (Dorner)
Jesus "divine" by his vocation (Ritschl)
Jesus as God and revelation (Barth)
The Kerygmatic Christ (Bultmann)
Can Chalcedon be dismissed?

Chart 44

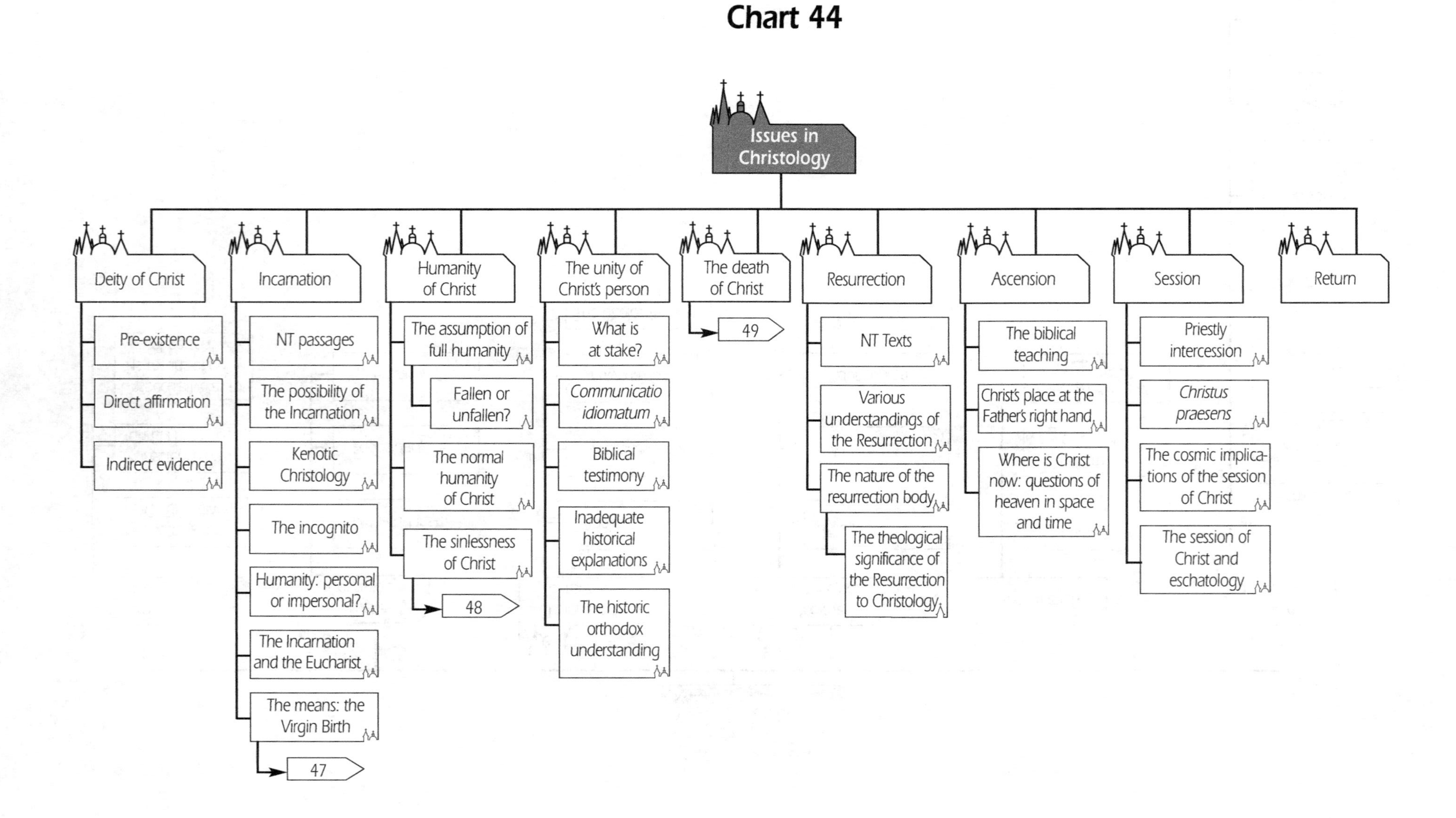
Issues in Christology
Deity of Christ
Pre-existence
Direct affirmation
Indirect evidence
Incarnation
NT passages
The possibility of the Incarnation
Kenotic Christology
The incognito
Humanity: personal or impersonal?
The Incarnation and the Eucharist
The means: the Virgin Birth
47
Humanity of Christ
The assumption of full humanity
Fallen or unfallen?
The normal humanity of Christ
The sinlessness of Christ
48
The unity of Christ's person
What is at stake?
Communicatio idiomatum
Biblical testimony
Inadequate historical explanations
The historic orthodox understanding
The death of Christ
49
Resurrection
NT Texts
Various understandings of the Resurrection
The nature of the resurrection body
The theological significance of the Resurrection to Christology
Ascension
The biblical teaching
Christ's place at the Father's right hand
Where is Christ now: questions of heaven in space and time
Session
Priestly intercession
Christus praesens
The cosmic implications of the session of Christ
The session of Christ and eschatology
Return

Chart 45

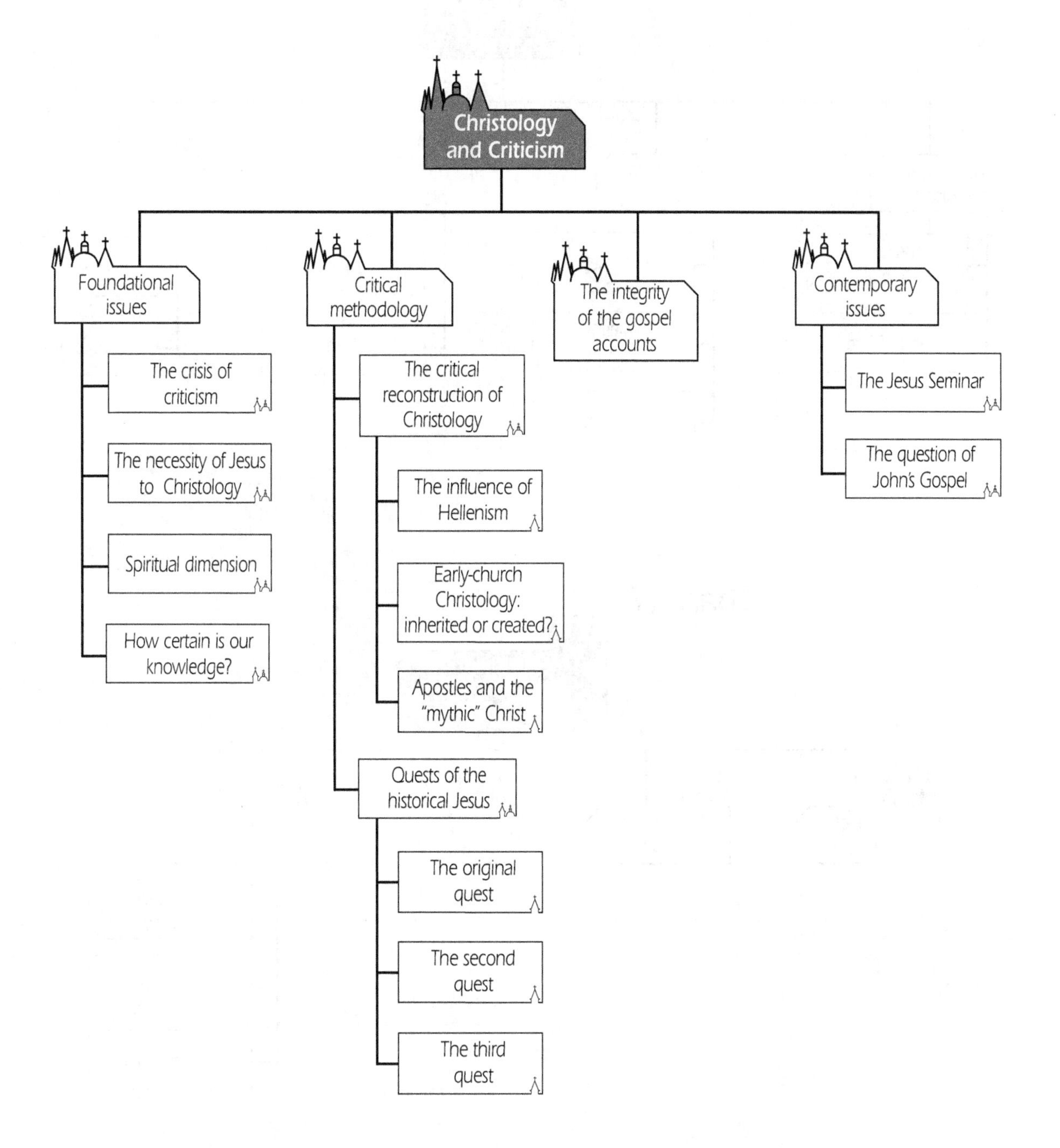

Christology and Criticism
Foundational issues
The crisis of criticism
The necessity of Jesus to Christology
Spiritual dimension
How certain is our knowledge?
Critical methodology
The critical reconstruction of Christology
The influence of Hellenism
Early-church Christology: inherited or created?
Apostles and the "mythic" Christ
Quests of the historical Jesus
The original quest
The second quest
The third quest
The integrity of the gospel accounts
Contemporary issues
The Jesus Seminar
The question of John's Gospel

Chart 46

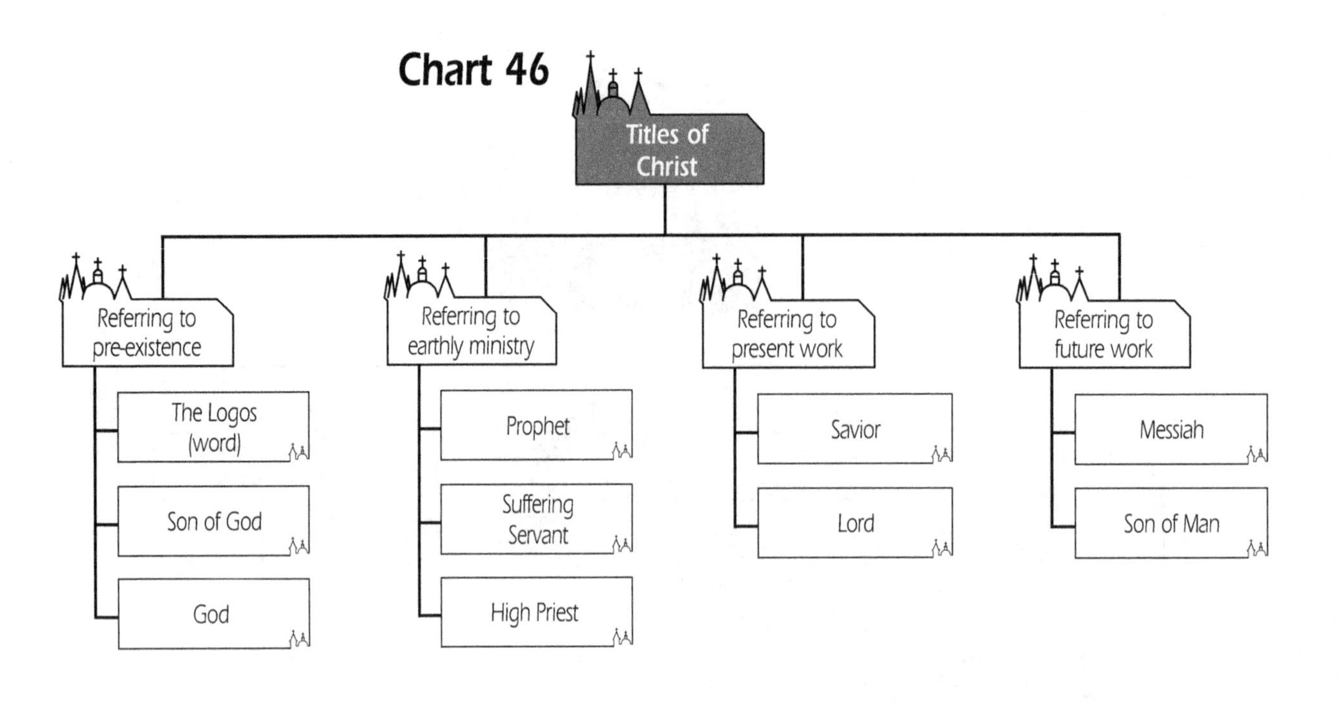

Chart 47

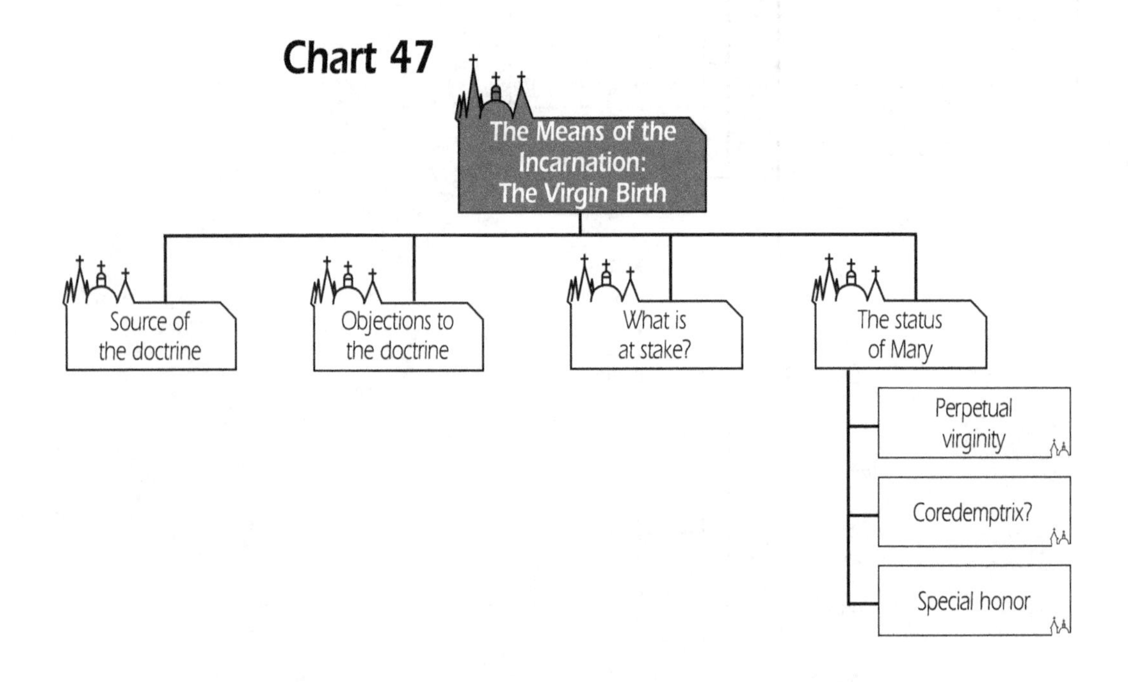

Chart 48

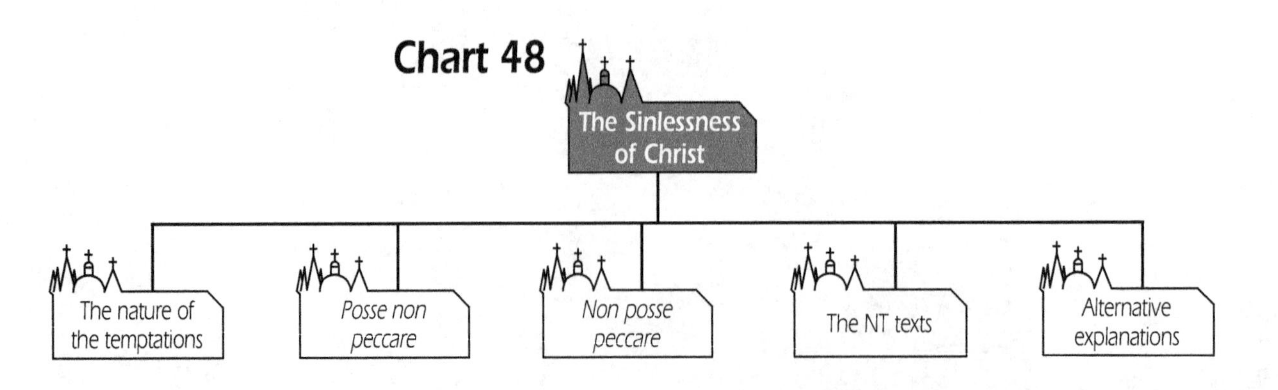

Chart 49

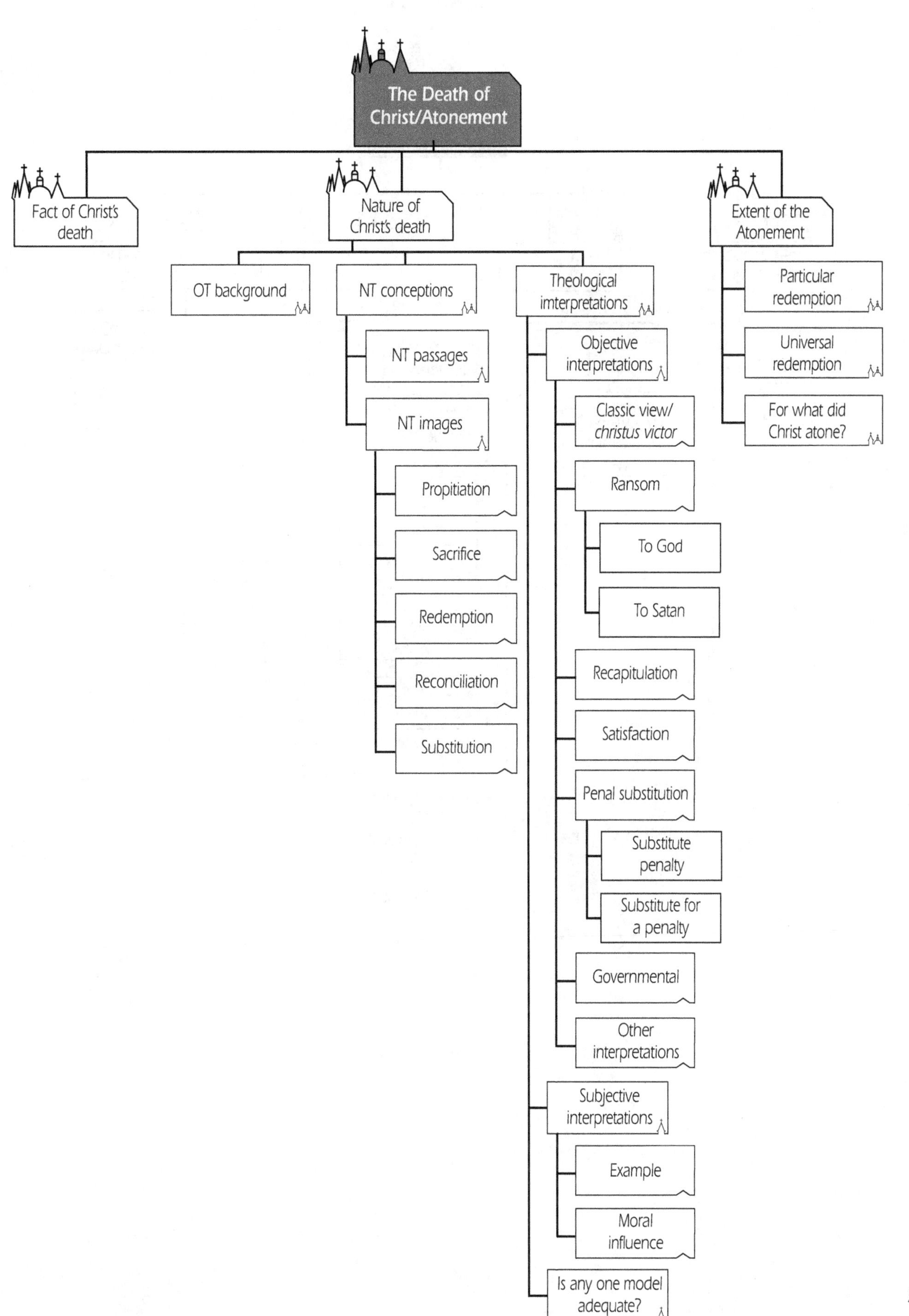

The Death of Christ/Atonement
Fact of Christ's death
Nature of Christ's death
Extent of the Atonement
OT background
NT conceptions
Theological imterpretations
NT passages
NT images
Propitiation
Sacrifice
Redemption
Reconciliation
Substitution
Objective interpretations
Classic view/ *christus victor*
Ransom
To God
To Satan
Recapitulation
Satisfaction
Penal substitution
Substitute penalty
Substitute for a penalty
Governmental
Other interpretations
Subjective interpretations
Example
Moral influence
Is any one model adequate?
Particular redemption
Universal redemption
For what did Christ atone?

Chart 50

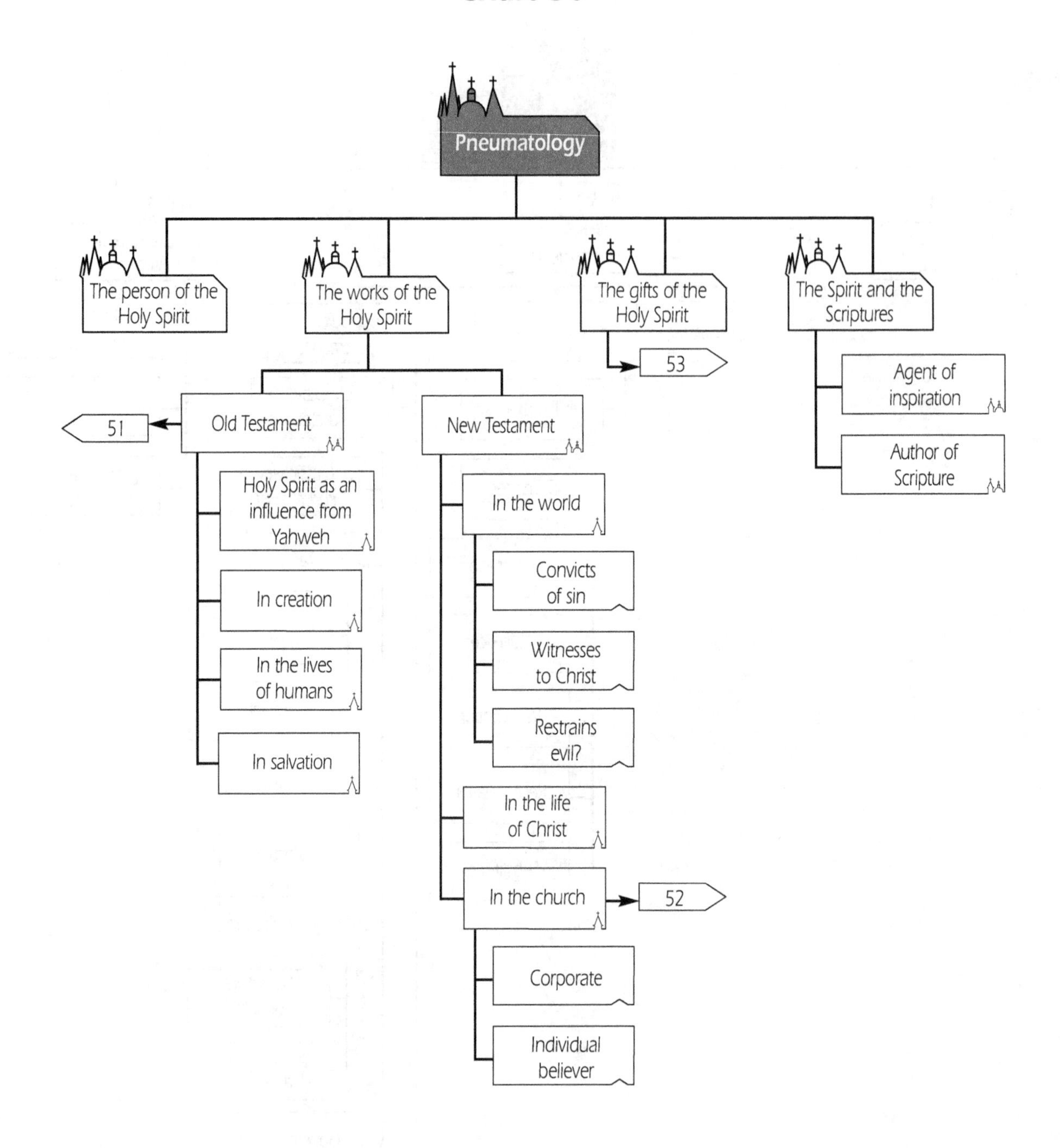

Pneumatology
The person of the Holy Spirit
The works of the Holy Spirit
The gifts of the Holy Spirit
53
The Spirit and the Scriptures
Agent of inspiration
Author of Scripture
51
Old Testament
Holy Spirit as an influence from Yahweh
In creation
In the lives of humans
In salvation
New Testament
In the world
Convicts of sin
Witnesses to Christ
Restrains evil?
In the life of Christ
In the church
52
Corporate
Individual believer

Chart 51

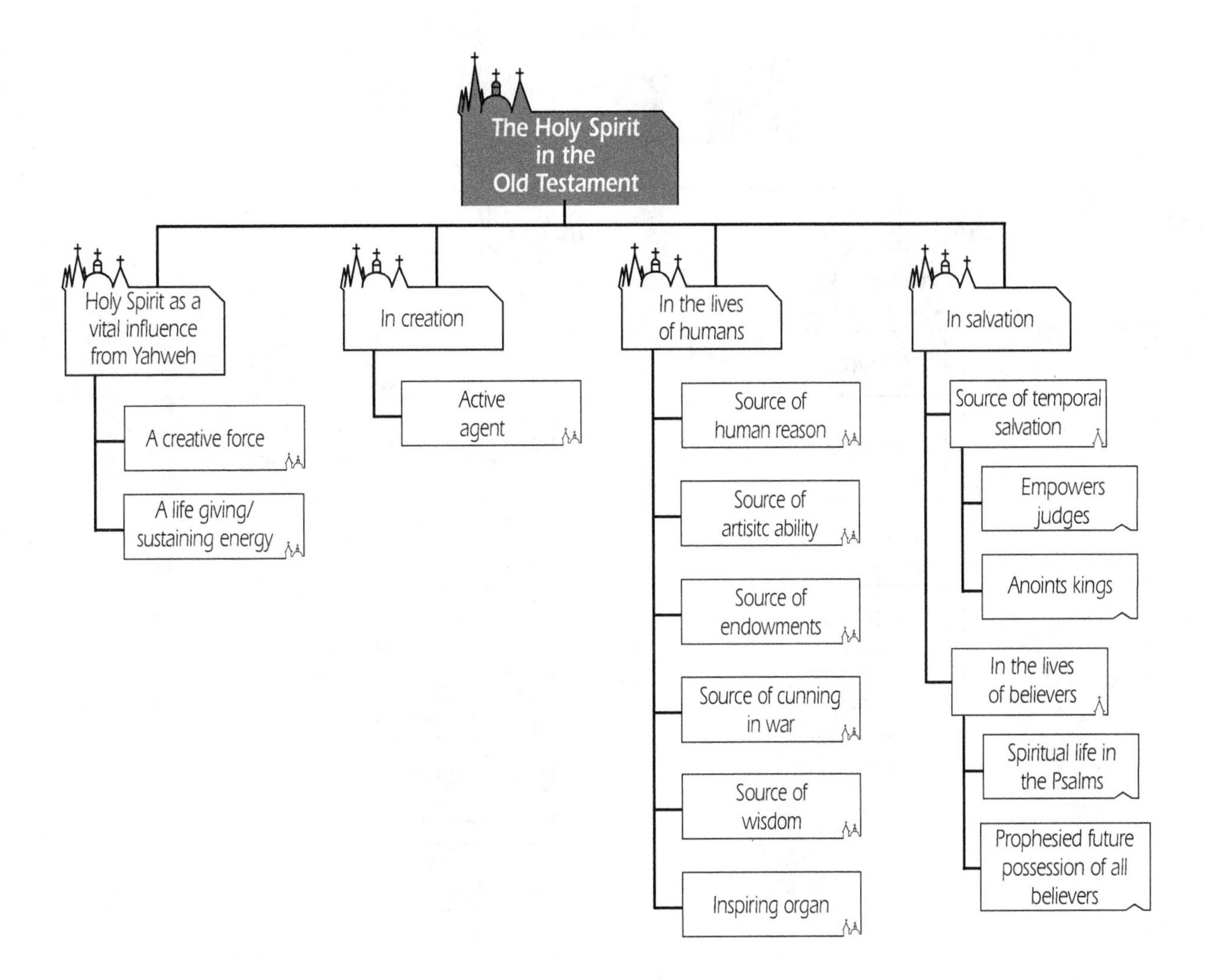

The Holy Spirit in the Old Testament
Holy Spirit as a vital influence from Yahweh
A creative force
A life giving/ sustaining energy
In creation
Active agent
In the lives of humans
Source of human reason
Source of artisitc ability
Source of endowments
Source of cunning in war
Source of wisdom
Inspiring organ
In salvation
Source of temporal salvation
Empowers judges
Anoints kings
In the lives of believers
Spiritual life in the Psalms
Prophesied future possession of all believers

Chart 52

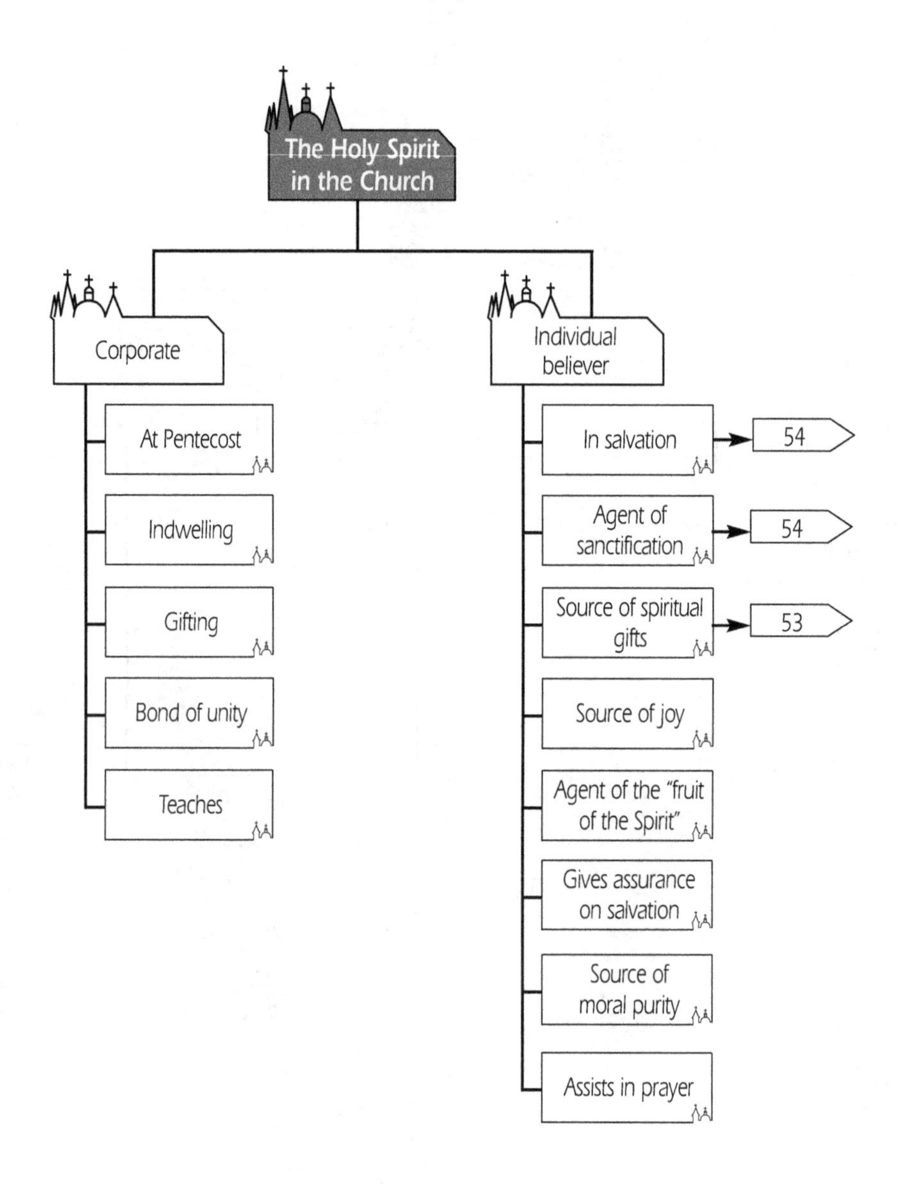

The Holy Spirit in the Church
Corporate
At Pentecost
Indwelling
Gifting
Bond of unity
Teaches
Individual believer
In salvation
54
Agent of sanctification
54
Source of spiritual gifts
53
Source of joy
Agent of the "fruit of the Spirit"
Gives assurance on salvation
Source of moral purity
Assists in prayer

Chart 53

The Gifts of the Holy Spirit

- Types of gifts
  - "Charismatic"
    - Apostleship
    - Prophecy
    - Miracles
    - Tongues
    - Discerning spirits
  - "Noncharismatic"
    - Speaking gifts
      - Teaching
      - Evangelism
    - Serving gifts
      - Ministering/serving/helps
      - Faith
      - Exhortation
      - Giving
      - Showing mercy
- Purpose of the gifts
  - Sign
    - To believers
    - To unbelievers
  - Corporate edification
  - Personal edification?
- New Testament lists of gifts
  - Romans 12
  - 1 Corinthians 11
  - 1 Peter
- Special questions
  - Cessation of the charistmata?
    - Biblical arguments
    - Historical arguments
  - Reception of the gifts

Chart 54

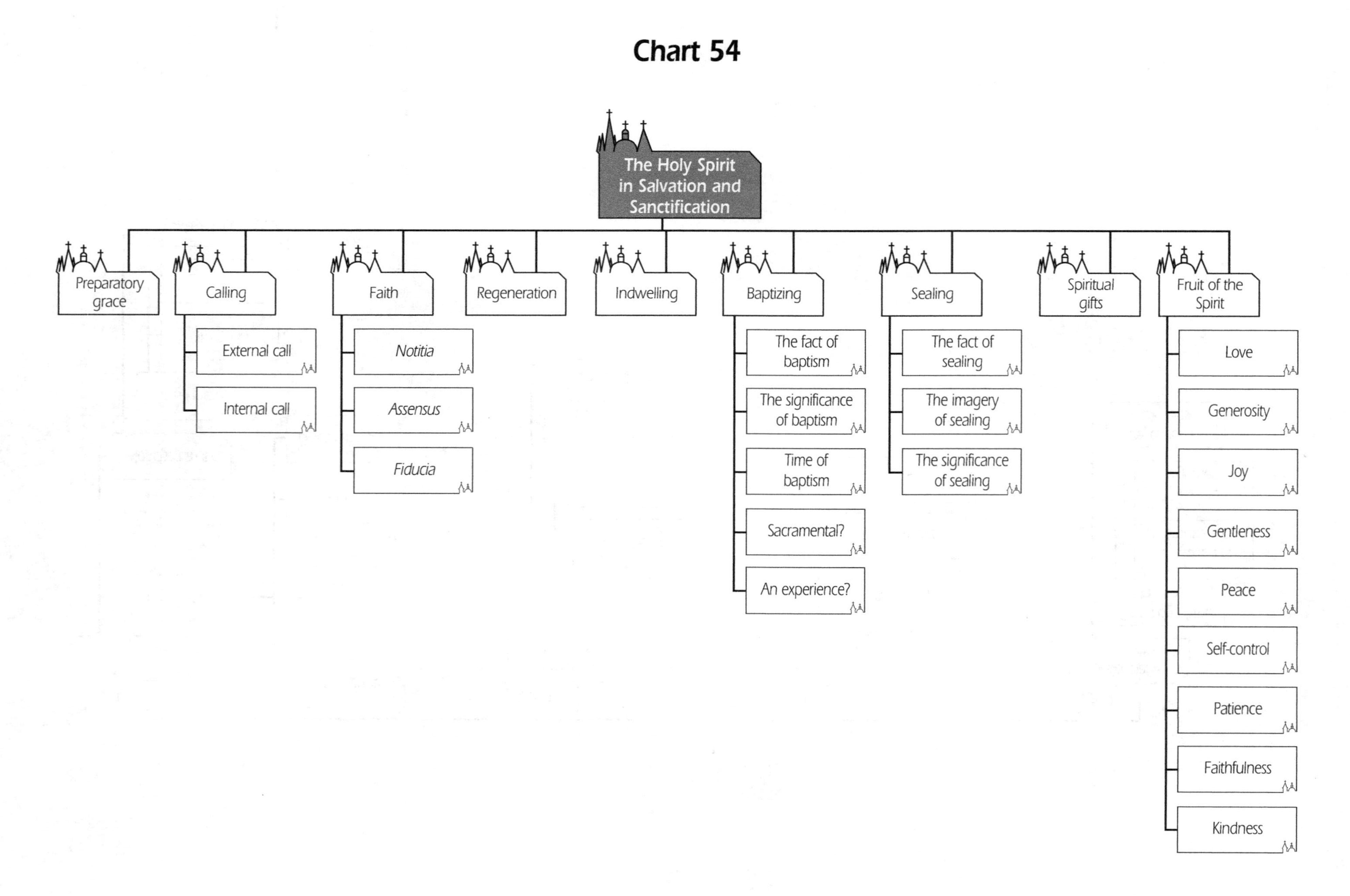
The Holy Spirit in Salvation and Sanctification
Preparatory grace
Calling
External call
Internal call
Faith
Notitia
Assensus
Fiducia
Regeneration
Indwelling
Baptizing
The fact of baptism
The significance of baptism
Time of baptism
Sacramental?
An experience?
Sealing
The fact of sealing
The imagery of sealing
The significance of sealing
Spiritual gifts
Fruit of the Spirit
Love
Generosity
Joy
Gentleness
Peace
Self-control
Patience
Faithfulness
Kindness

Chart 55

Soteriology

- Need for salvation → 56
- Biblical theology of salvation → 57
- History of the doctrine of salvation
- Models of salvation → 58
- Aspects of initial salvation → 59
  - Objective aspects
    - Redemption
    - Sealed unto redemption
    - Reconciliation
    - Sanctified
    - Justification
    - Adoption
    - Predestination
    - Peace
    - Forgiveness
  - Subjective aspects
    - Preparatory aspects
      - Conviction of sin
      - Calling
        - General
        - Efficacious
    - Conversion
    - Regeneration
    - Sonship
    - Peace
    - Hope
    - Indwelling Spirit
- Atonement → 60
- Sanctification → 65-73
- Glorification
  - Nature of glorification
  - Eternal life
  - Freedom from death
  - Freedom from sin
  - Reflection of image of Christ
  - Perfect body
  - Totality of being

Chart 56

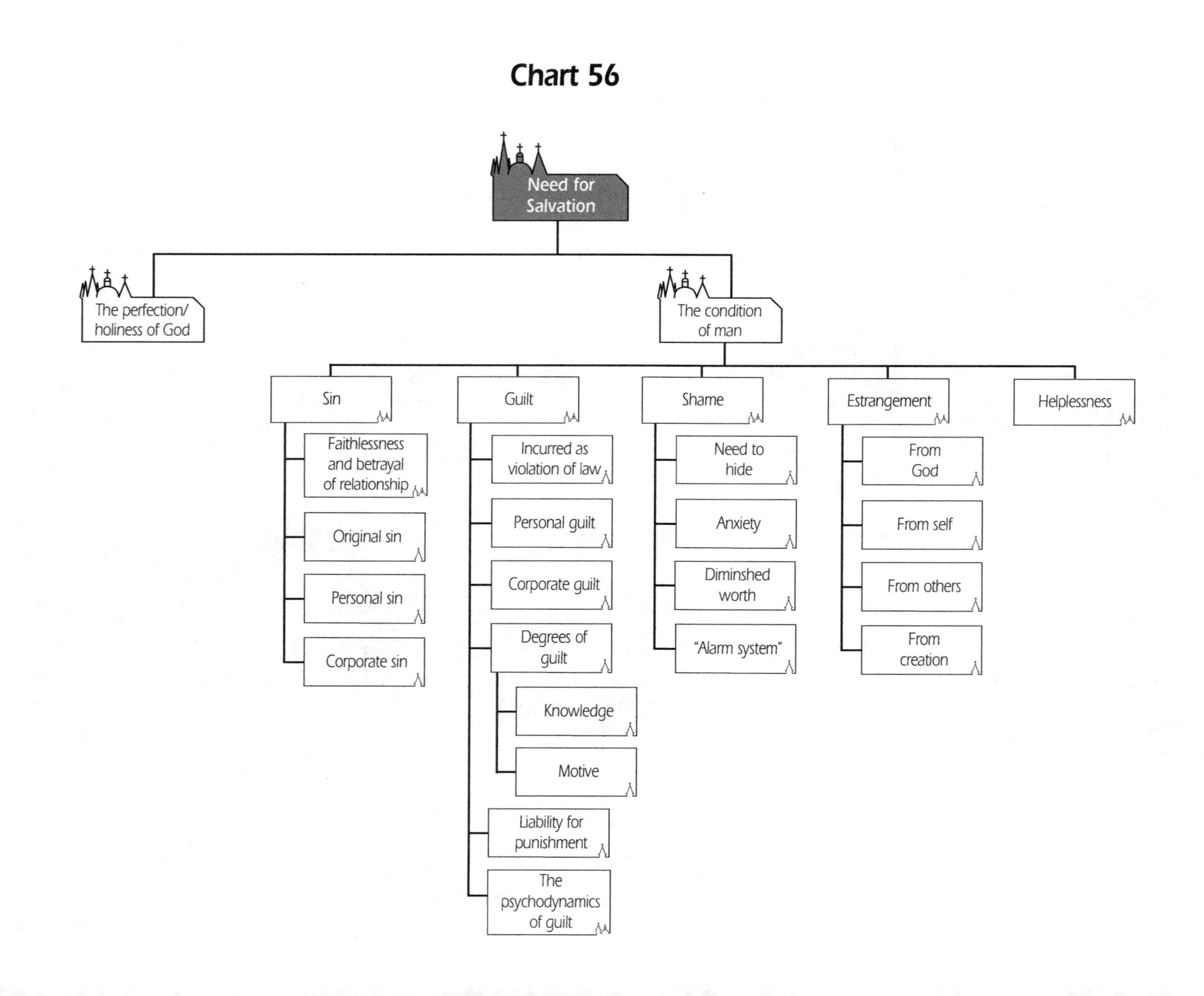
Need for Salvation
The perfection/ holiness of God
The condition of man
Sin
Faithlessness and betrayal of relationship
Original sin
Personal sin
Corporate sin
Guilt
Incurred as violation of law
Personal guilt
Corporate guilt
Degrees of guilt
Knowledge
Motive
Liability for punishment
The psychodynamics of guilt
Shame
Need to hide
Anxiety
Diminshed worth
"Alarm system"
Estrangement
From God
From self
From others
From creation
Helplessness

Chart 57

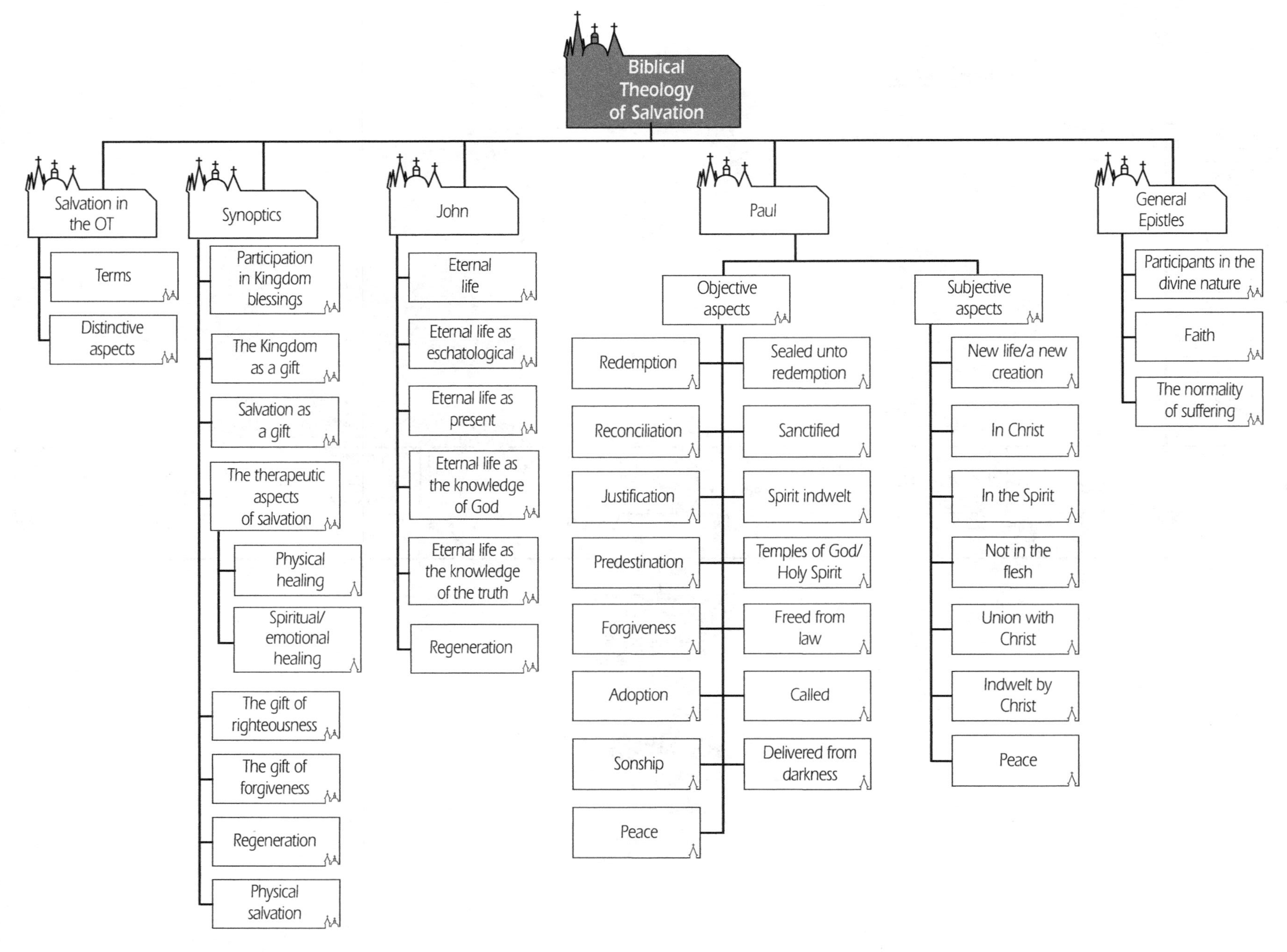

Biblical Theology of Salvation
Salvation in the OT
Terms
Distinctive aspects
Synoptics
Participation in Kingdom blessings
The Kingdom as a gift
Salvation as a gift
The therapeutic aspects of salvation
Physical healing
Spiritual/ emotional healing
The gift of righteousness
The gift of forgiveness
Regeneration
Physical salvation
John
Eternal life
Eternal life as eschatological
Eternal life as present
Eternal life as the knowledge of God
Eternal life as the knowledge of the truth
Regeneration
Paul
Objective aspects
Redemption
Reconciliation
Justification
Predestination
Forgiveness
Adoption
Sonship
Peace
Sealed unto redemption
Sanctified
Spirit indwelt
Temples of God/ Holy Spirit
Freed from law
Called
Delivered from darkness
Subjective aspects
New life/a new creation
In Christ
In the Spirit
Not in the flesh
Union with Christ
Indwelt by Christ
Peace
General Epistles
Participants in the divine nature
Faith
The normality of suffering

Chart 58

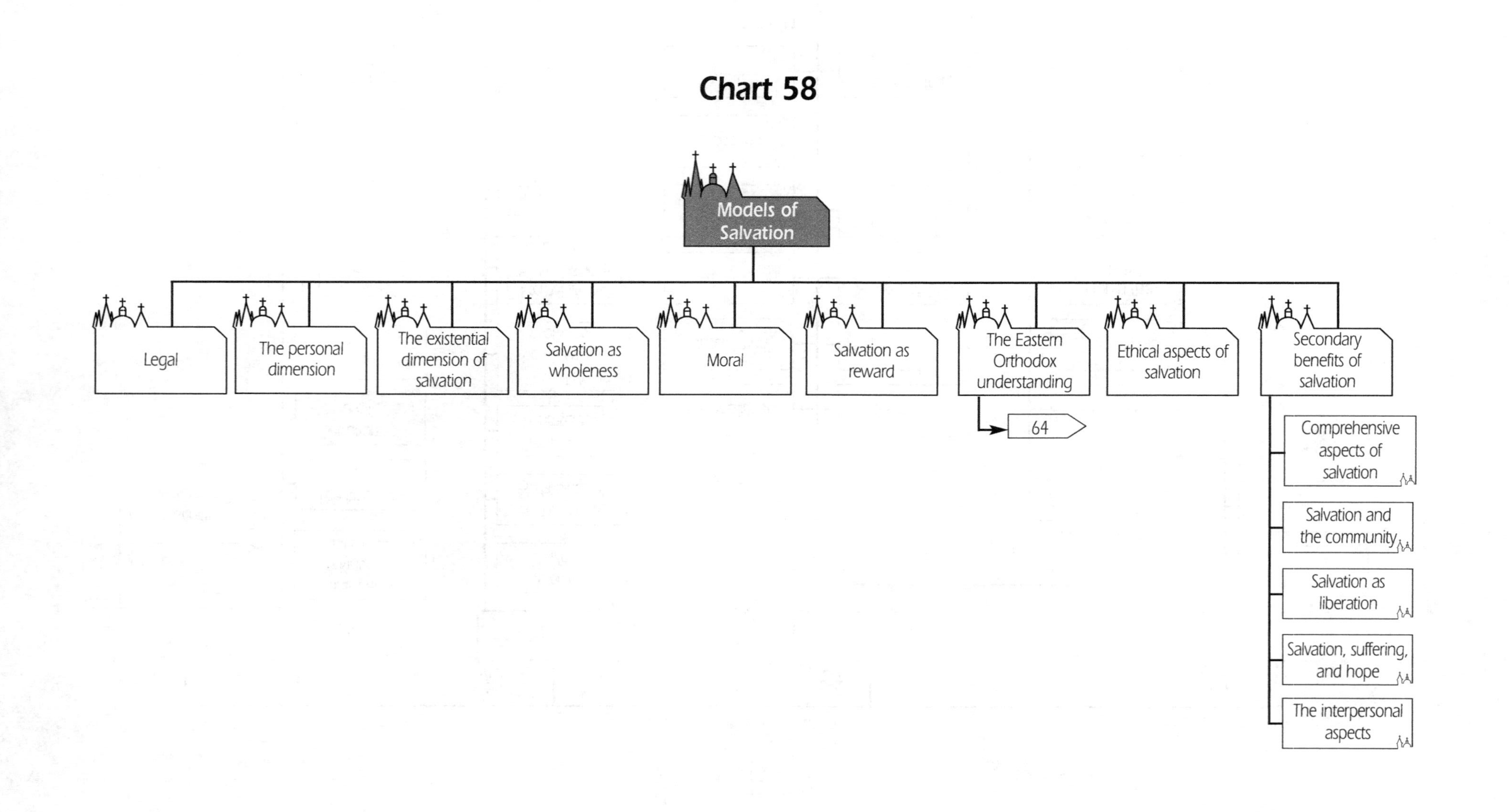

Models of Salvation
Legal
The personal dimension
The existential dimension of salvation
Salvation as wholeness
Moral
Salvation as reward
The Eastern Orthodox understanding
64
Ethical aspects of salvation
Secondary benefits of salvation
Comprehensive aspects of salvation
Salvation and the community
Salvation as liberation
Salvation, suffering, and hope
The interpersonal aspects

Chart 59

- Aspects of Salvation
  - Conversion
  - Calling
    - General calling
    - Officacious calling?
  - The nature of saving faith
    - → 61
  - Predestination/election
    - → 63
  - Adoption
    - The status of children in the ancient world
    - The practice of adoption
      - Jewish
      - Greek
      - Roman
    - The biblical terminology
    - Theological implications
    - The time of adoption
    - The status of the adopted one
  - Regeneration
  - Repentance
    - The nature of repentance
    - The object of repentance
    - Contemporary disputes over repentance
  - Eternal security
    - Biblical images and passages
    - The issues involved
      - The Reformed perspective
      - The Arminian perspective
      - The evangelical perspective
      - Lordship salvation
    - The problem of apostasy
    - Perseverance of the saints
    - Compared with perseverance of the saints
  - Justification
    - → 62

Chart 60

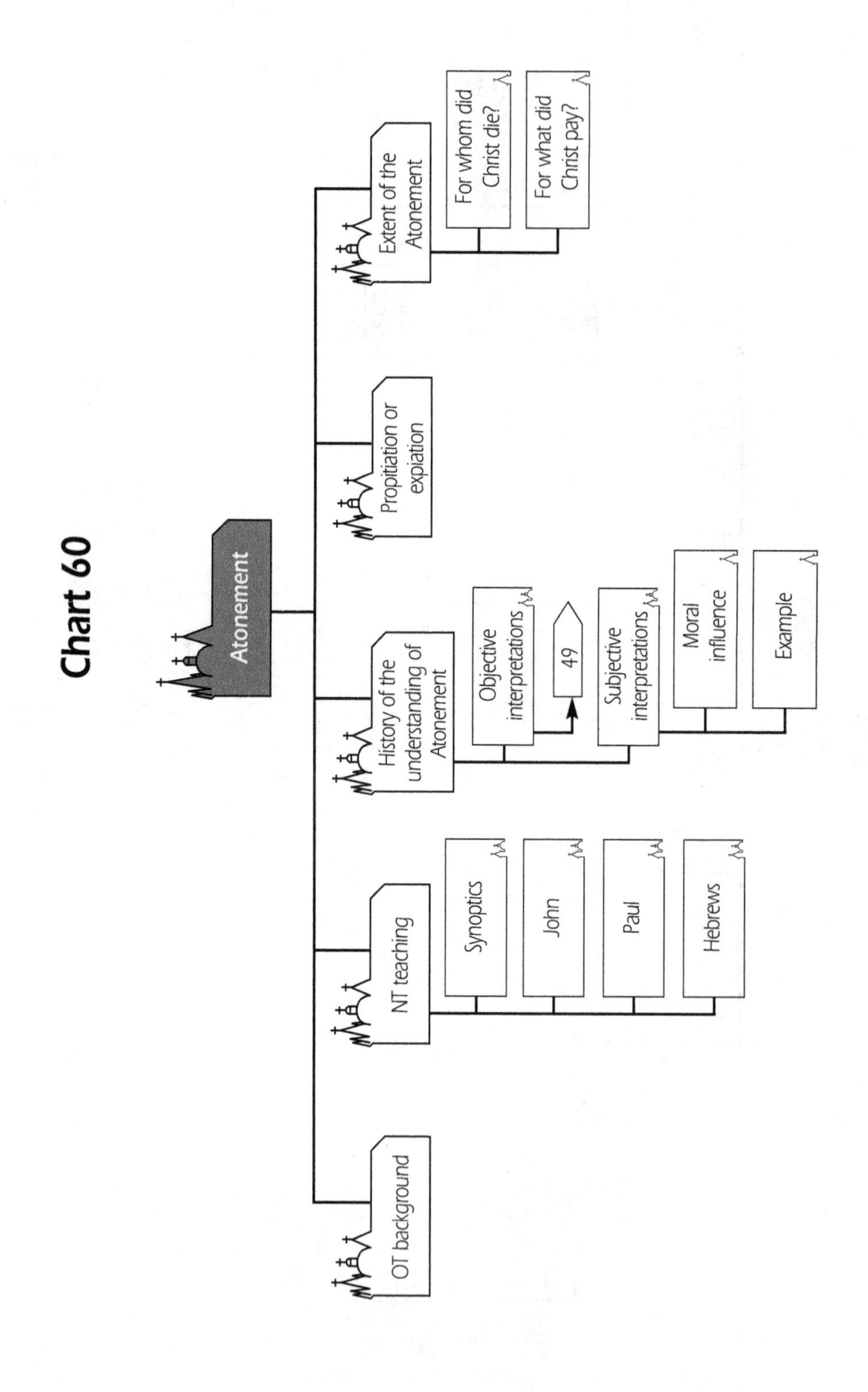

Atonement
OT background
NT teaching
Synoptics
John
Paul
Hebrews
History of the understanding of Atonement
Objective interpretations
49
Subjective interpretations
Moral influence
Example
Propitiation or expiation
Extent of the Atonement
For whom did Christ die?
For what did Christ pay?

Chart 61

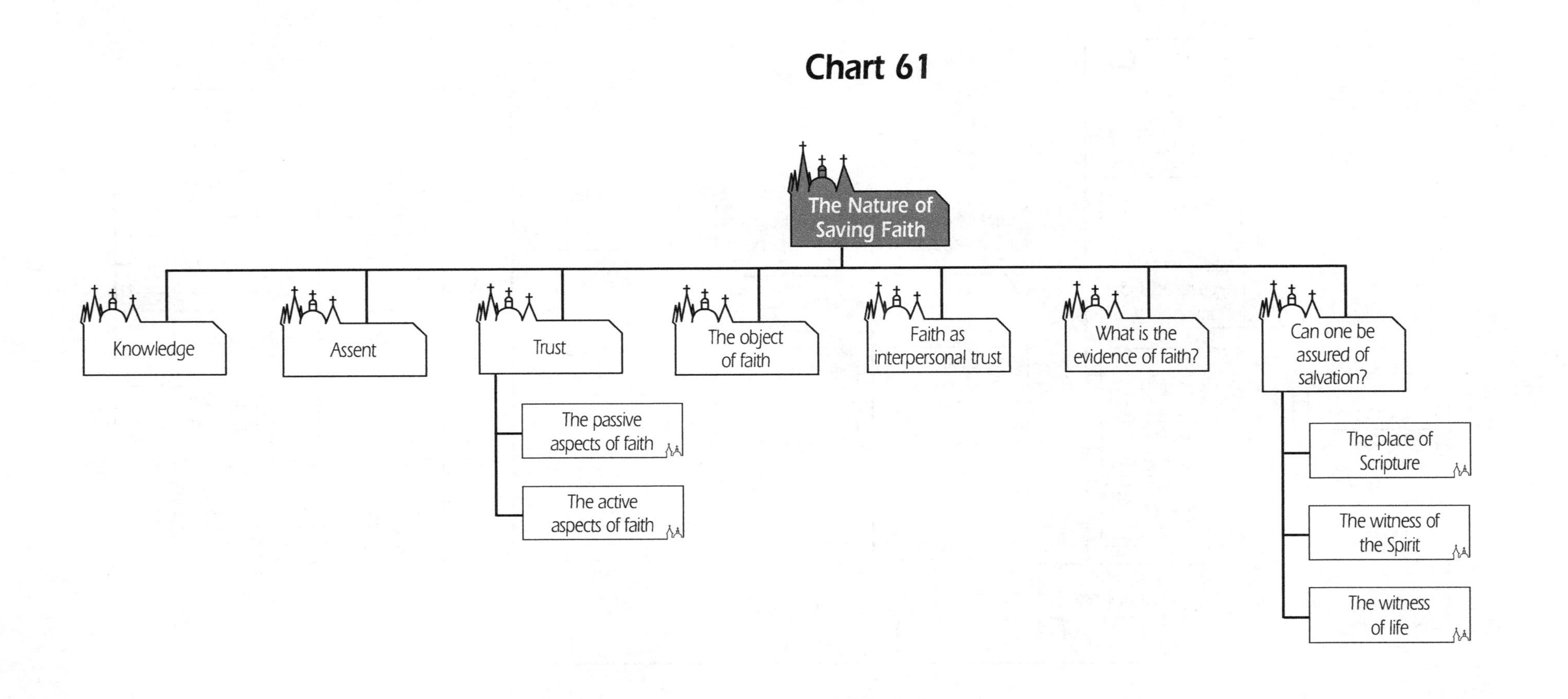
The Nature of Saving Faith
Knowledge
Assent
Trust
The passive aspects of faith
The active aspects of faith
The object of faith
Faith as interpersonal trust
What is the evidence of faith?
Can one be assured of salvation?
The place of Scripture
The witness of the Spirit
The witness of life

Chart 62

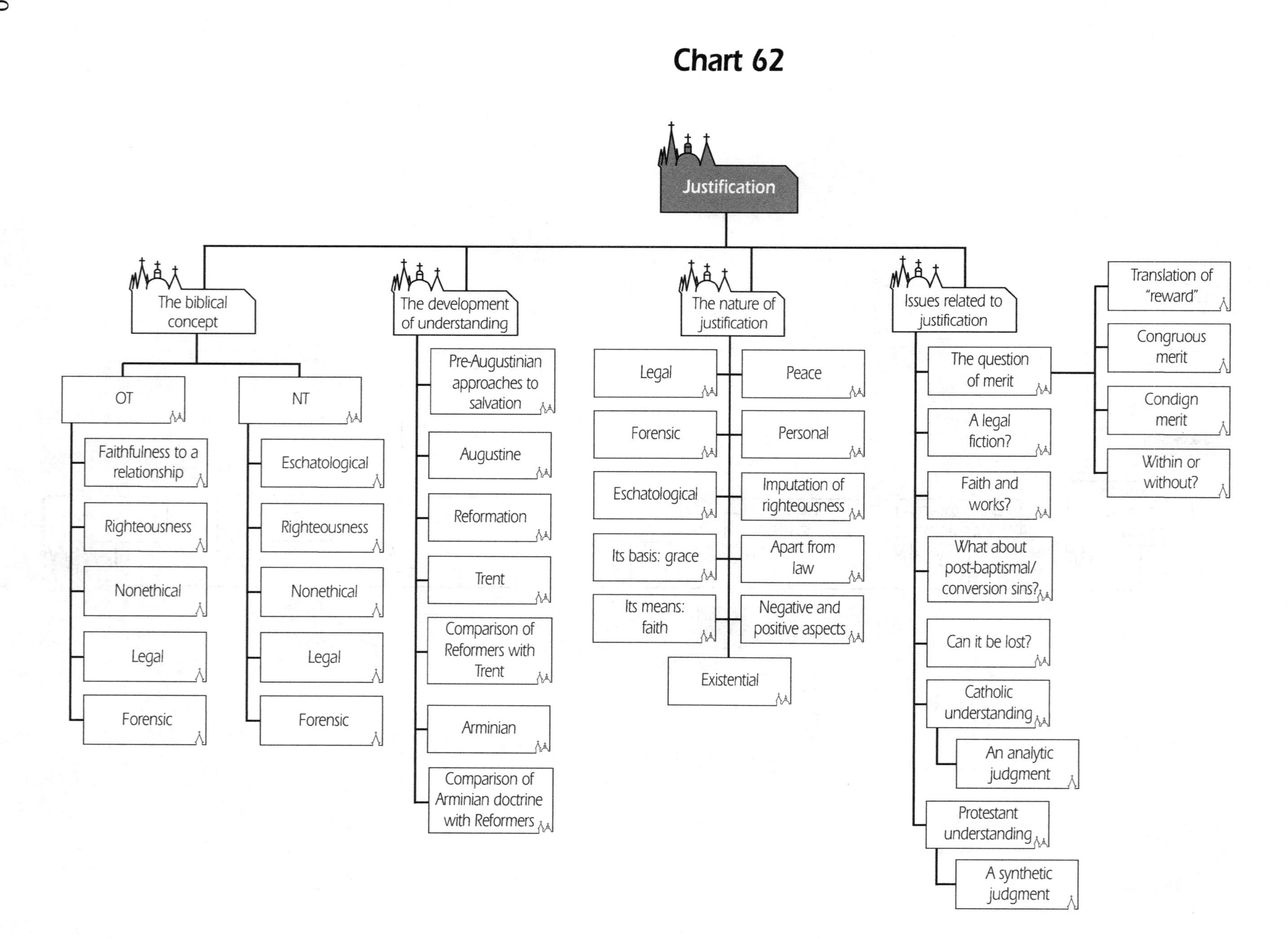

Justification
The biblical concept
OT
Faithfulness to a relationship
Righteousness
Nonethical
Legal
Forensic
NT
Eschatological
Righteousness
Nonethical
Legal
Forensic
The development of understanding
Pre-Augustinian approaches to salvation
Augustine
Reformation
Trent
Comparison of Reformers with Trent
Arminian
Comparison of Arminian doctrine with Reformers
The nature of justification
Legal
Forensic
Eschatological
Its basis: grace
Its means: faith
Peace
Personal
Imputation of righteousness
Apart from law
Negative and positive aspects
Existential
Issues related to justification
The question of merit
Translation of "reward"
Congruous merit
Condign merit
Within or without?
A legal fiction?
Faith and works?
What about post-baptismal/ conversion sins?
Can it be lost?
Catholic understanding
An analytic judgment
Protestant understanding
A synthetic judgment

Chart 63

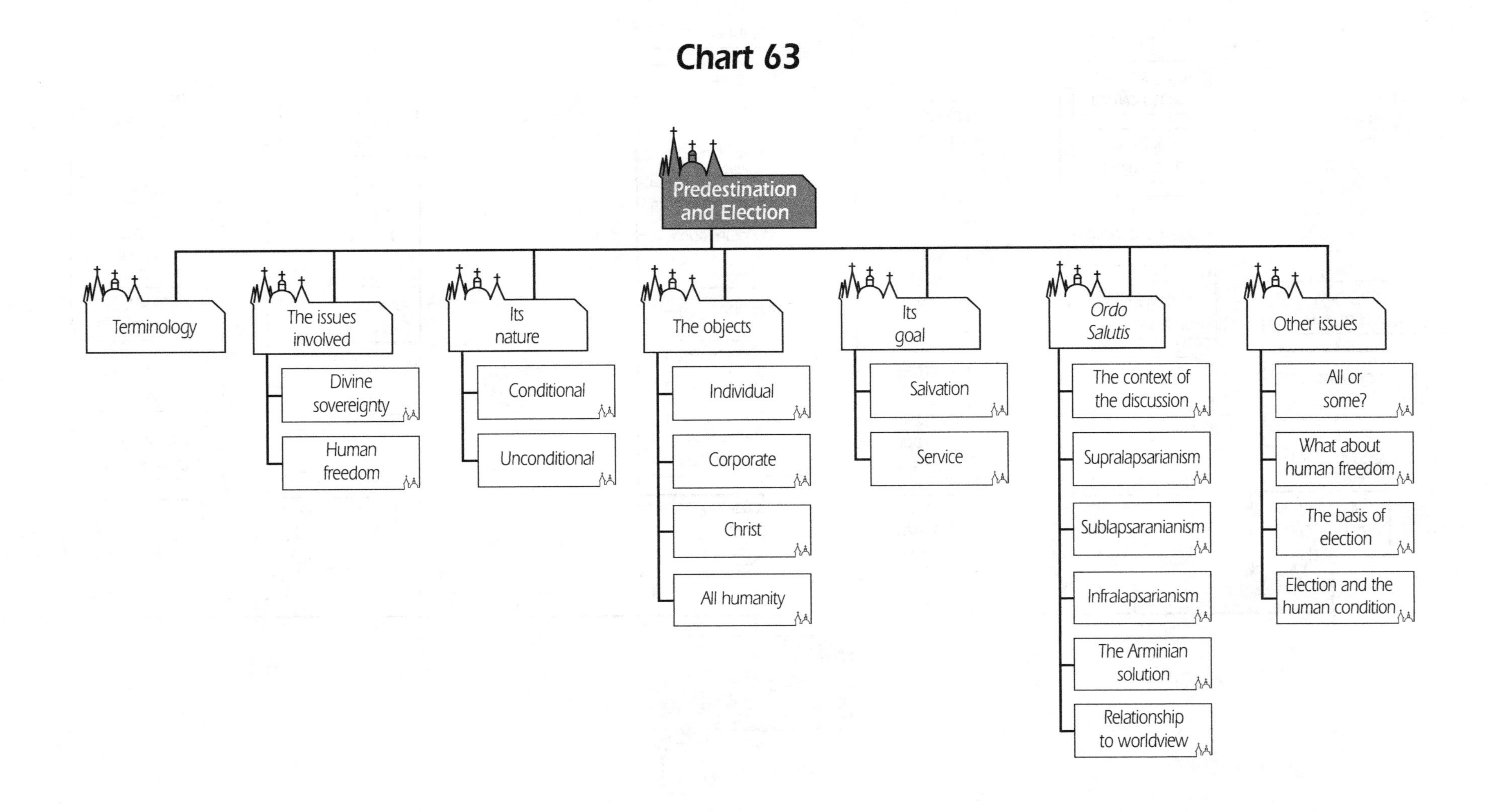

Predestination and Election
Terminology
The issues involved
Divine sovereignty
Human freedom
Its nature
Conditional
Unconditional
The objects
Individual
Corporate
Christ
All humanity
Its goal
Salvation
Service
Ordo Salutis
The context of the discussion
Supralapsarianism
Sublapsaranianism
Infralapsarianism
The Arminian solution
Relationship to worldview
Other issues
All or some?
What about human freedom
The basis of election
Election and the human condition

Chart 64

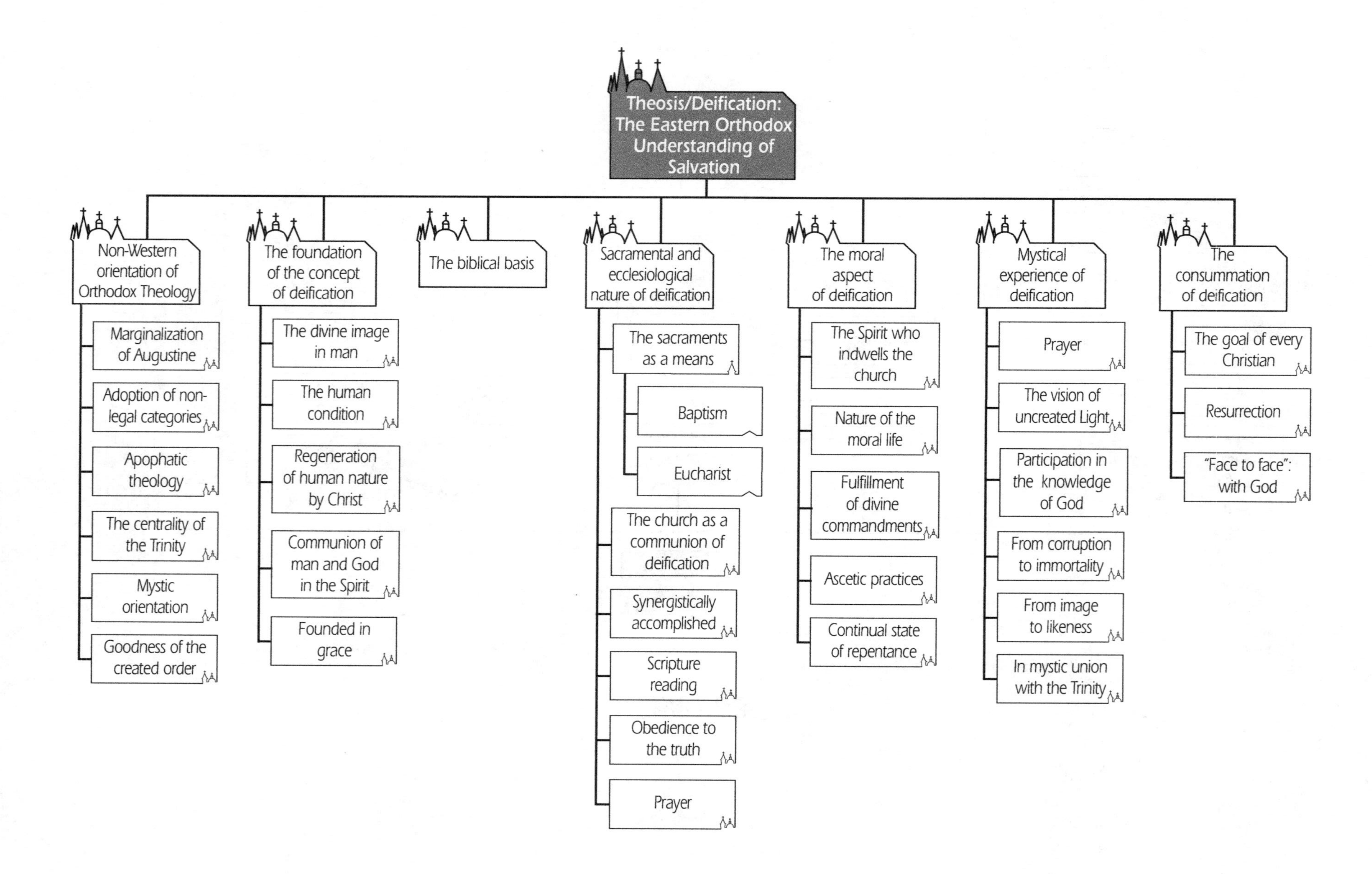

Theosis/Deification: The Eastern Orthodox Understanding of Salvation
Non-Western orientation of Orthodox Theology
Marginalization of Augustine
Adoption of non-legal categories
Apophatic theology
The centrality of the Trinity
Mystic orientation
Goodness of the created order
The foundation of the concept of deification
The divine image in man
The human condition
Regeneration of human nature by Christ
Communion of man and God in the Spirit
Founded in grace
The biblical basis
Sacramental and ecclesiological nature of deification
The sacraments as a means
Baptism
Eucharist
The church as a communion of deification
Synergistically accomplished
Scripture reading
Obedience to the truth
Prayer
The moral aspect of deification
The Spirit who indwells the church
Nature of the moral life
Fulfillment of divine commandments
Ascetic practices
Continual state of repentance
Mystical experience of deification
Prayer
The vision of uncreated Light
Participation in the knowledge of God
From corruption to immortality
From image to likeness
In mystic union with the Trinity
The consummation of deification
The goal of every Christian
Resurrection
"Face to face": with God

Chart 65

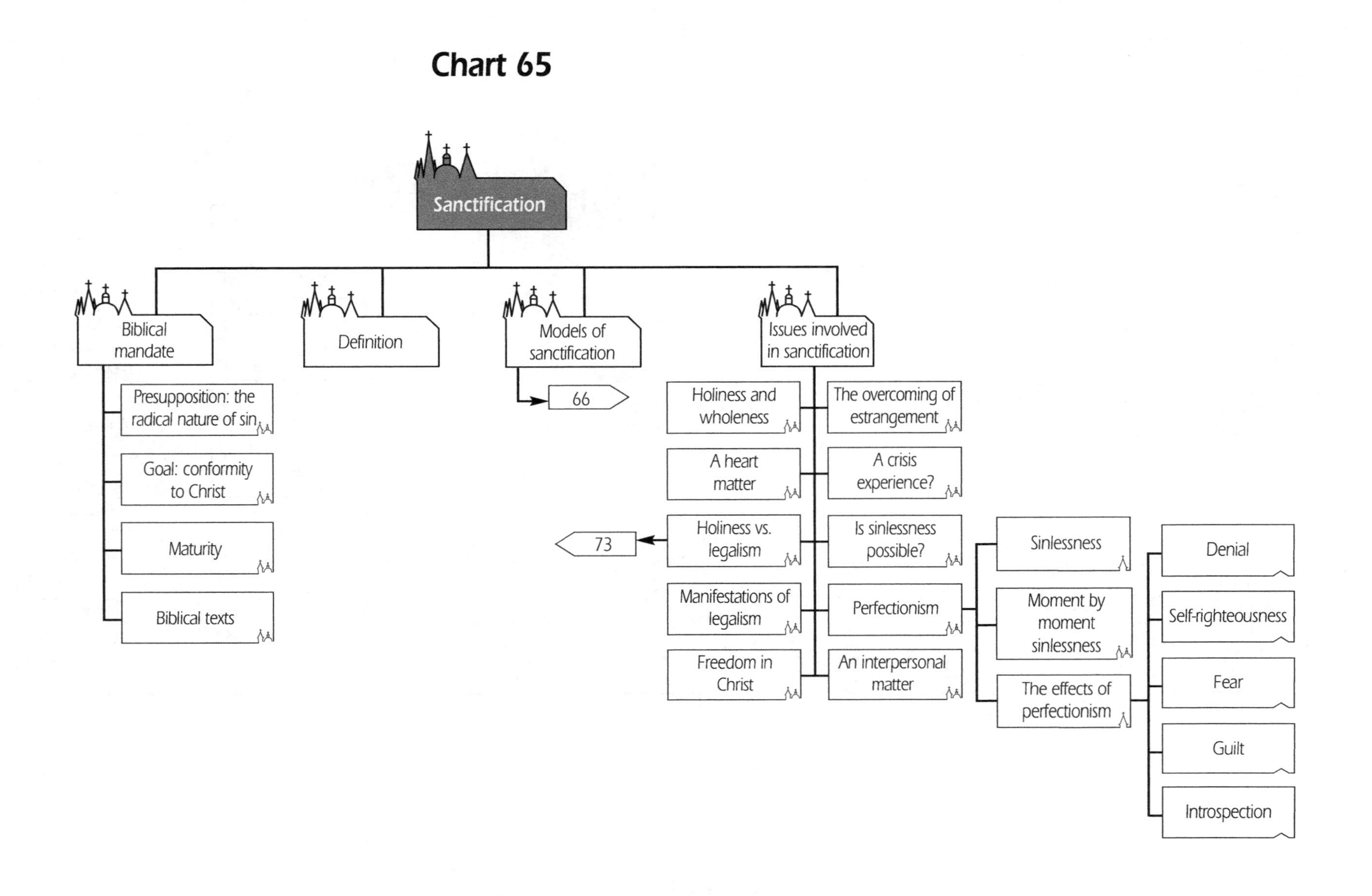

Sanctification
Biblical mandate
Presupposition: the radical nature of sin
Goal: conformity to Christ
Maturity
Biblical texts
Definition
Models of sanctification
66
Issues involved in sanctification
Holiness and wholeness
The overcoming of estrangement
A heart matter
A crisis experience?
Holiness vs. legalism
73
Is sinlessness possible?
Manifestations of legalism
Perfectionism
Sinlessness
Moment by moment sinlessness
The effects of perfectionism
Denial
Self-righteousness
Fear
Guilt
Introspection
Freedom in Christ
An interpersonal matter

Chart 66

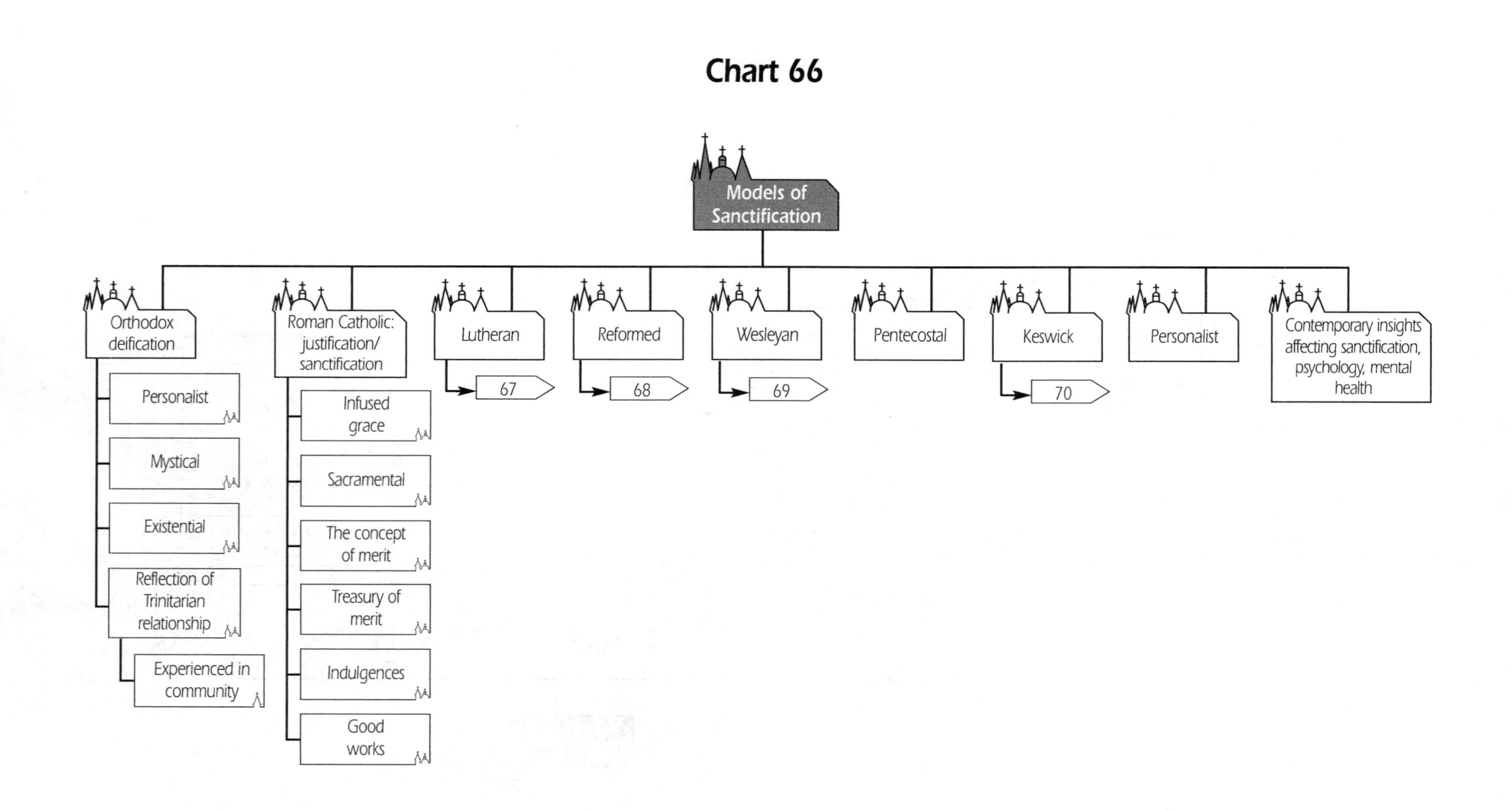
Models of Sanctification
Orthodox deification
Personalist
Mystical
Existential
Reflection of Trinitarian relationship
Experienced in community
Roman Catholic: justification/ sanctification
Infused grace
Sacramental
The concept of merit
Treasury of merit
Indulgences
Good works
Lutheran
67
Reformed
68
Wesleyan
69
Pentecostal
Keswick
70
Personalist
Contemporary insights affecting sanctification, psychology, mental health

Chart 67

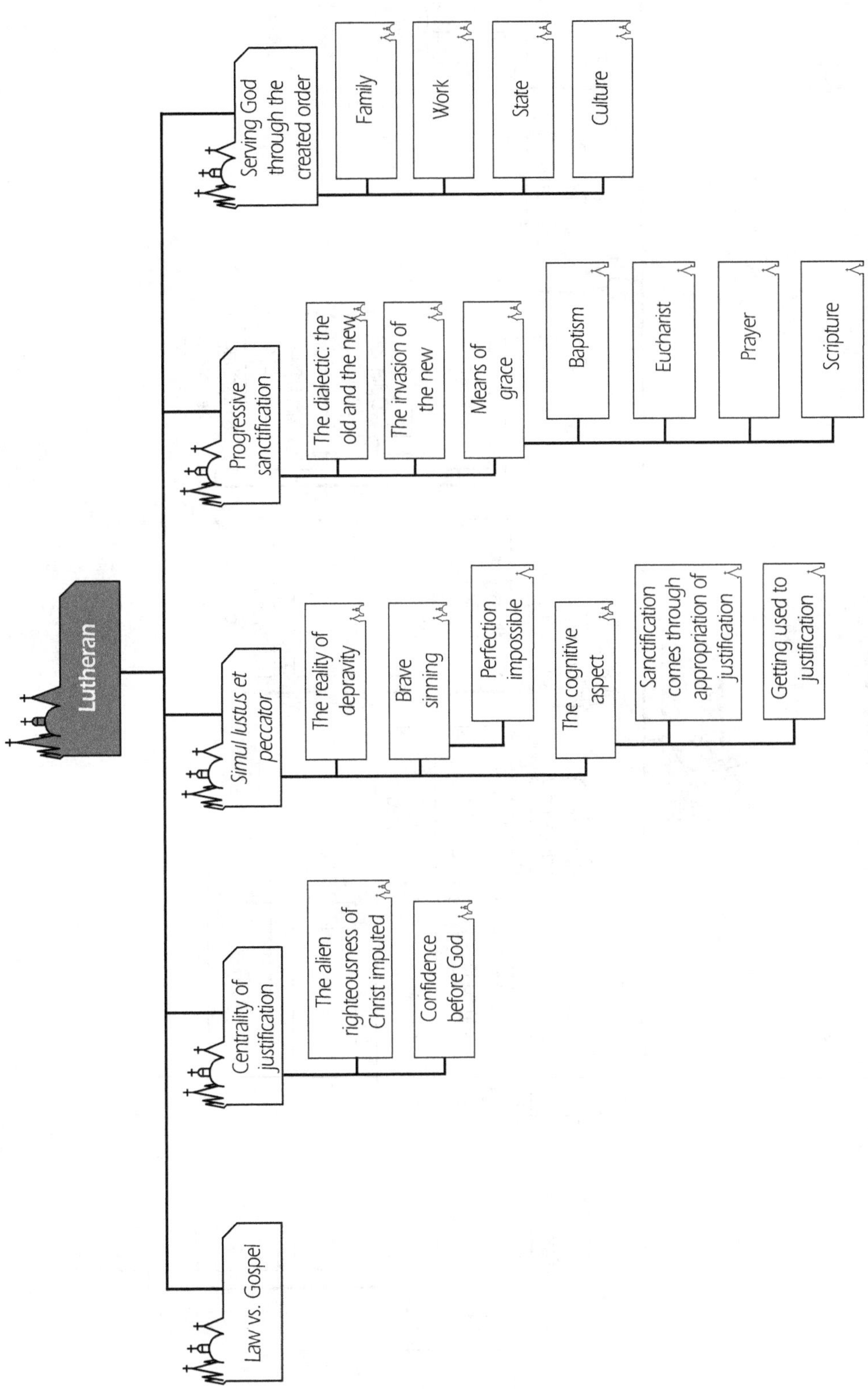

- **Lutheran**
  - Law vs. Gospel
  - Centrality of justification
    - The alien righteousness of Christ imputed
    - Confidence before God
  - *Simul Iustus et peccator*
    - The reality of depravity
    - Brave sinning
      - Perfection impossible
    - The cognitive aspect
      - Sanctification comes through appropriation of justification
      - Getting used to justification
  - Progressive sanctification
    - The dialectic: the old and the new
    - The invasion of the new
    - Means of grace
      - Baptism
      - Eucharist
      - Prayer
      - Scripture
  - Serving God through the created order
    - Family
    - Work
    - State
    - Culture

Chart 68

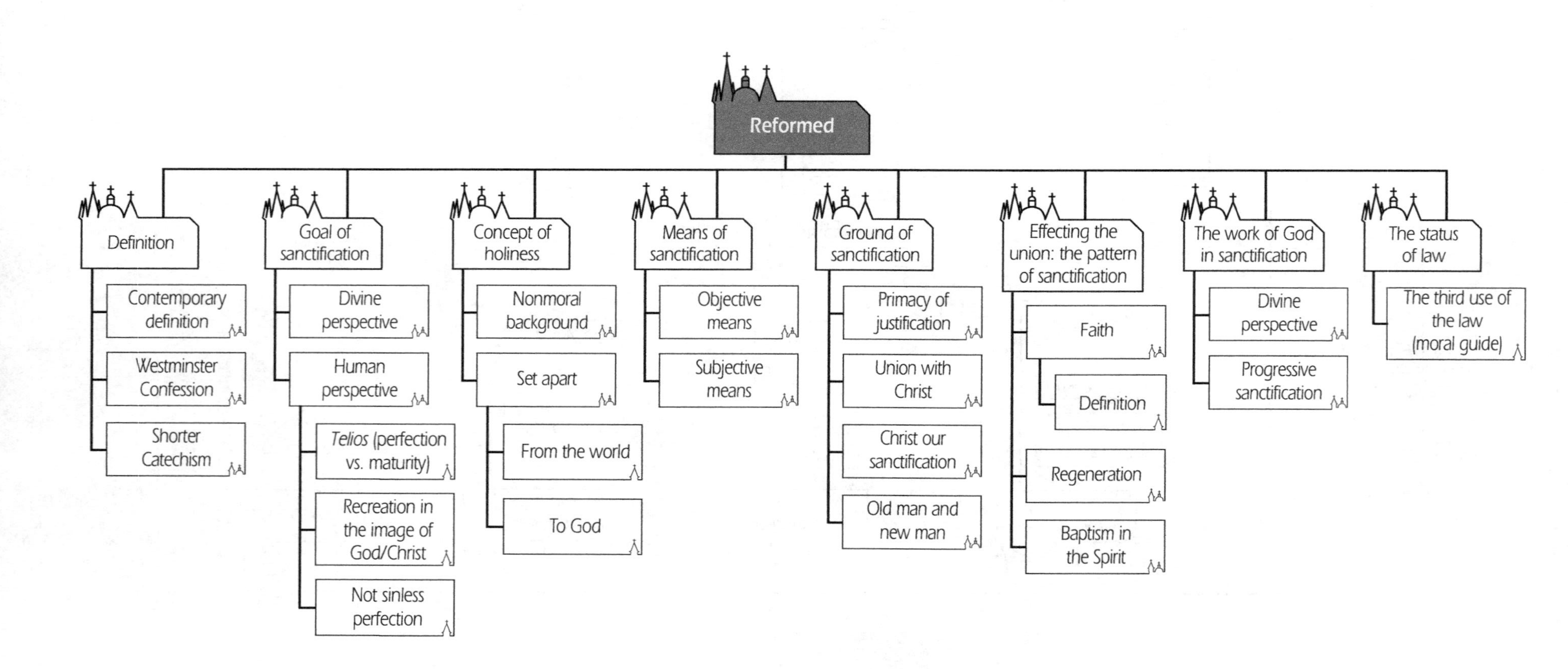
Reformed
Definition
Contemporary definition
Westminster Confession
Shorter Catechism
Goal of sanctification
Divine perspective
Human perspective
Telios (perfection vs. maturity)
Recreation in the image of God/Christ
Not sinless perfection
Concept of holiness
Nonmoral background
Set apart
From the world
To God
Means of sanctification
Objective means
Subjective means
Ground of sanctification
Primacy of justification
Union with Christ
Christ our sanctification
Old man and new man
Effecting the union: the pattern of sanctification
Faith
Definition
Regeneration
Baptism in the Spirit
The work of God in sanctification
Divine perspective
Progressive sanctification
The status of law
The third use of the law (moral guide)

Chart 69

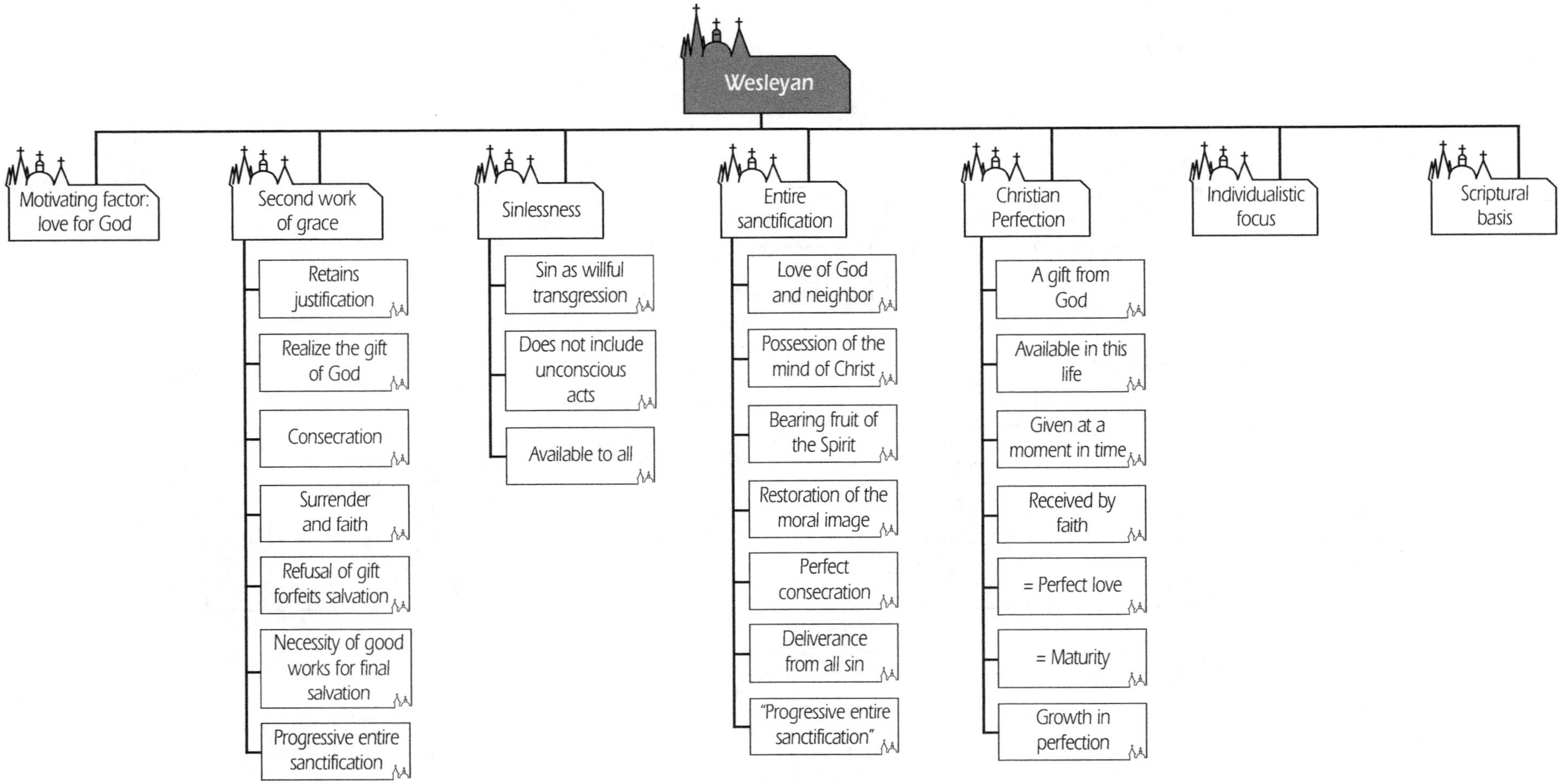

- **Wesleyan**
  - Motivating factor: love for God
  - Second work of grace
    - Retains justification
    - Realize the gift of God
    - Consecration
    - Surrender and faith
    - Refusal of gift forfeits salvation
    - Necessity of good works for final salvation
    - Progressive entire sanctification
  - Sinlessness
    - Sin as willful transgression
    - Does not include unconscious acts
    - Available to all
  - Entire sanctification
    - Love of God and neighbor
    - Possession of the mind of Christ
    - Bearing fruit of the Spirit
    - Restoration of the moral image
    - Perfect consecration
    - Deliverance from all sin
    - "Progressive entire sanctification"
  - Christian Perfection
    - A gift from God
    - Available in this life
    - Given at a moment in time
    - Received by faith
    - = Perfect love
    - = Maturity
    - Growth in perfection
  - Individualistic focus
  - Scriptural basis

Chart 70

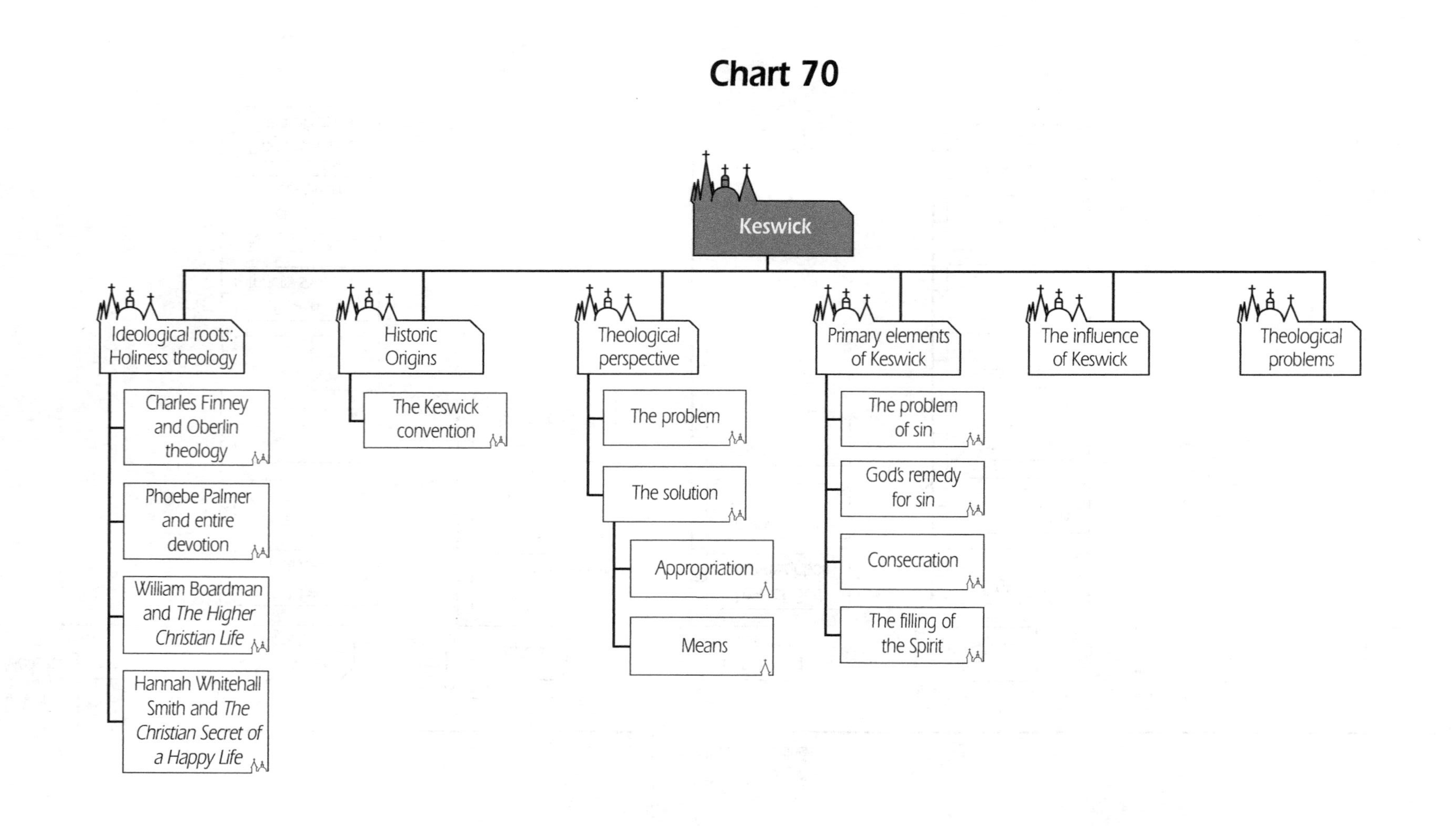

Keswick
Ideological roots: Holiness theology
Charles Finney and Oberlin theology
Phoebe Palmer and entire devotion
William Boardman and *The Higher Christian Life*
Hannah Whitehall Smith and *The Christian Secret of a Happy Life*
Historic Origins
The Keswick convention
Theological perspective
The problem
The solution
Appropriation
Means
Primary elements of Keswick
The problem of sin
God's remedy for sin
Consecration
The filling of the Spirit
The influence of Keswick
Theological problems

Chart 71

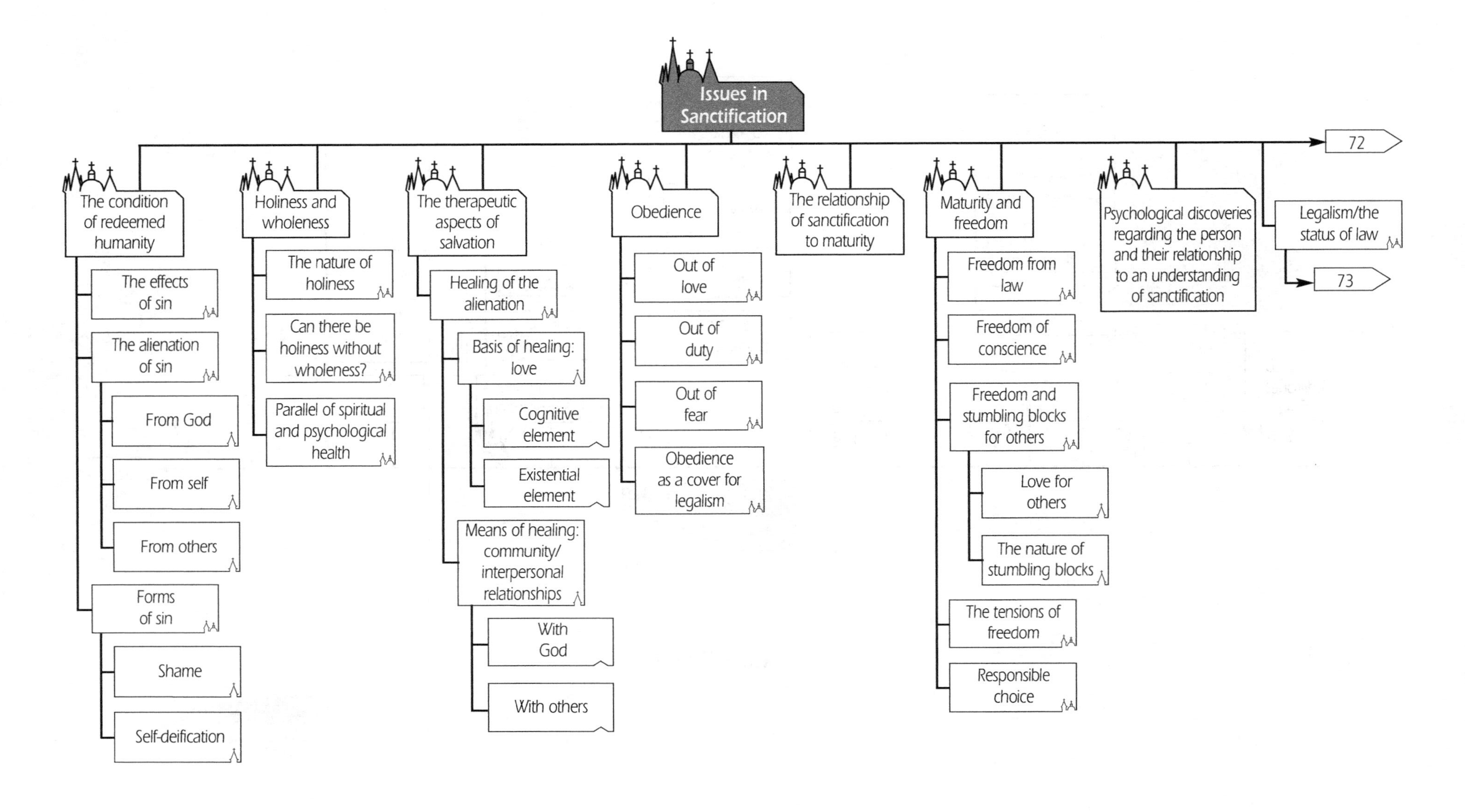

Issues in Sanctification
The condition of redeemed humanity
The effects of sin
The alienation of sin
From God
From self
From others
Forms of sin
Shame
Self-deification
Holiness and wholeness
The nature of holiness
Can there be holiness without wholeness?
Parallel of spiritual and psychological health
The therapeutic aspects of salvation
Healing of the alienation
Basis of healing: love
Cognitive element
Existential element
Means of healing: community/ interpersonal relationships
With God
With others
Obedience
Out of love
Out of duty
Out of fear
Obedience as a cover for legalism
The relationship of sanctification to maturity
Maturity and freedom
Freedom from law
Freedom of conscience
Freedom and stumbling blocks for others
Love for others
The nature of stumbling blocks
The tensions of freedom
Responsible choice
Psychological discoveries regarding the person and their relationship to an understanding of sanctification
Legalism/the status of law
72
73

Chart 72

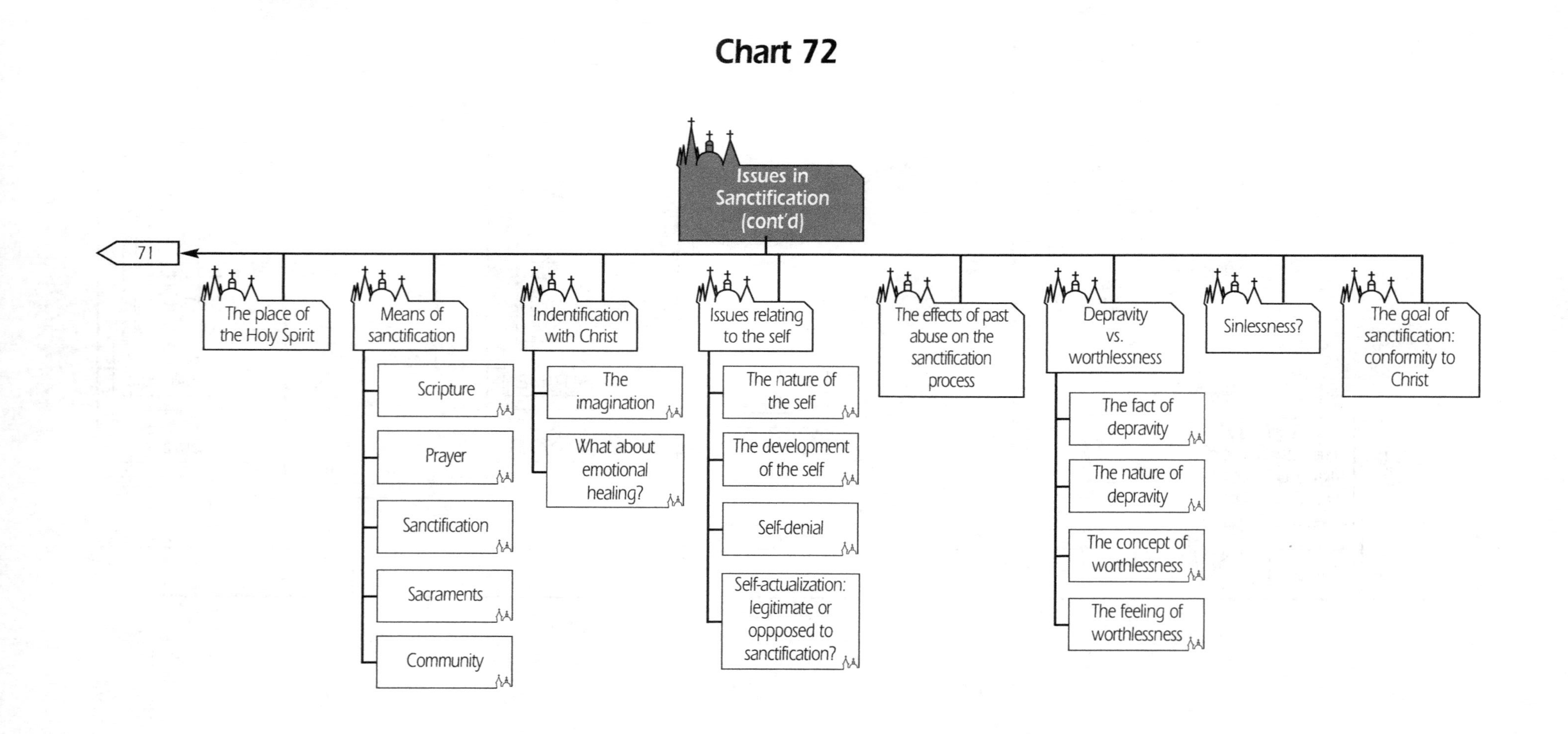

Issues in Sanctification (cont'd)
71
The place of the Holy Spirit
Means of sanctification
Scripture
Prayer
Sanctification
Sacraments
Community
Indentification with Christ
The imagination
What about emotional healing?
Issues relating to the self
The nature of the self
The development of the self
Self-denial
Self-actualization: legitimate or oppposed to sanctification?
The effects of past abuse on the sanctification process
Depravity vs. worthlessness
The fact of depravity
The nature of depravity
The concept of worthlessness
The feeling of worthlessness
Sinlessness?
The goal of sanctification: conformity to Christ

Chart 73

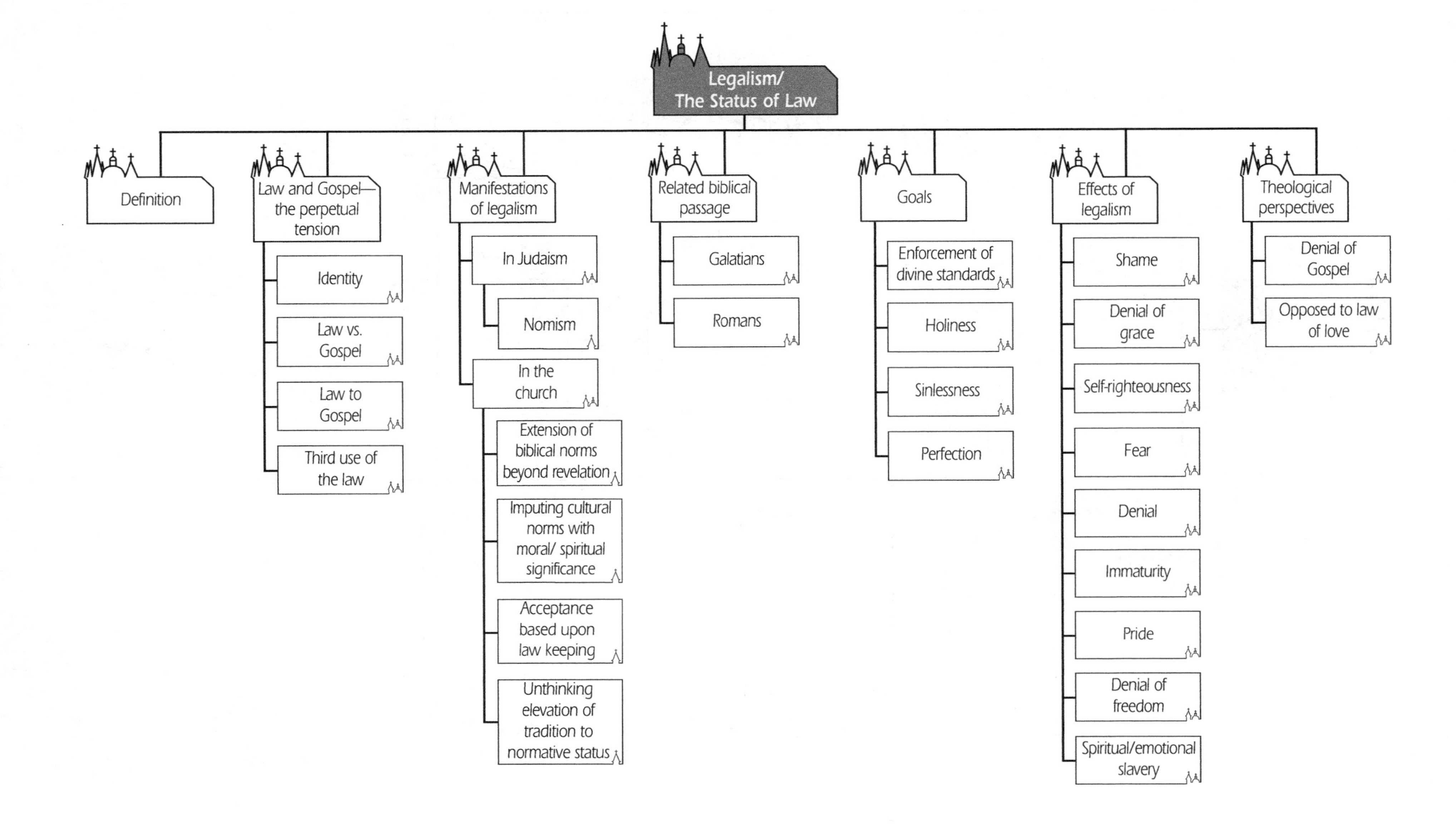
Legalism/
The Status of Law
Definition
Law and Gospel—the perpetual tension
Identity
Law vs. Gospel
Law to Gospel
Third use of the law
Manifestations of legalism
In Judaism
Nomism
In the church
Extension of biblical norms beyond revelation
Imputing cultural norms with moral/ spiritual significance
Acceptance based upon law keeping
Unthinking elevation of tradition to normative status
Related biblical passage
Galatians
Romans
Goals
Enforcement of divine standards
Holiness
Sinlessness
Perfection
Effects of legalism
Shame
Denial of grace
Self-righteousness
Fear
Denial
Immaturity
Pride
Denial of freedom
Spiritual/emotional slavery
Theological perspectives
Denial of Gospel
Opposed to law of love

Chart 74

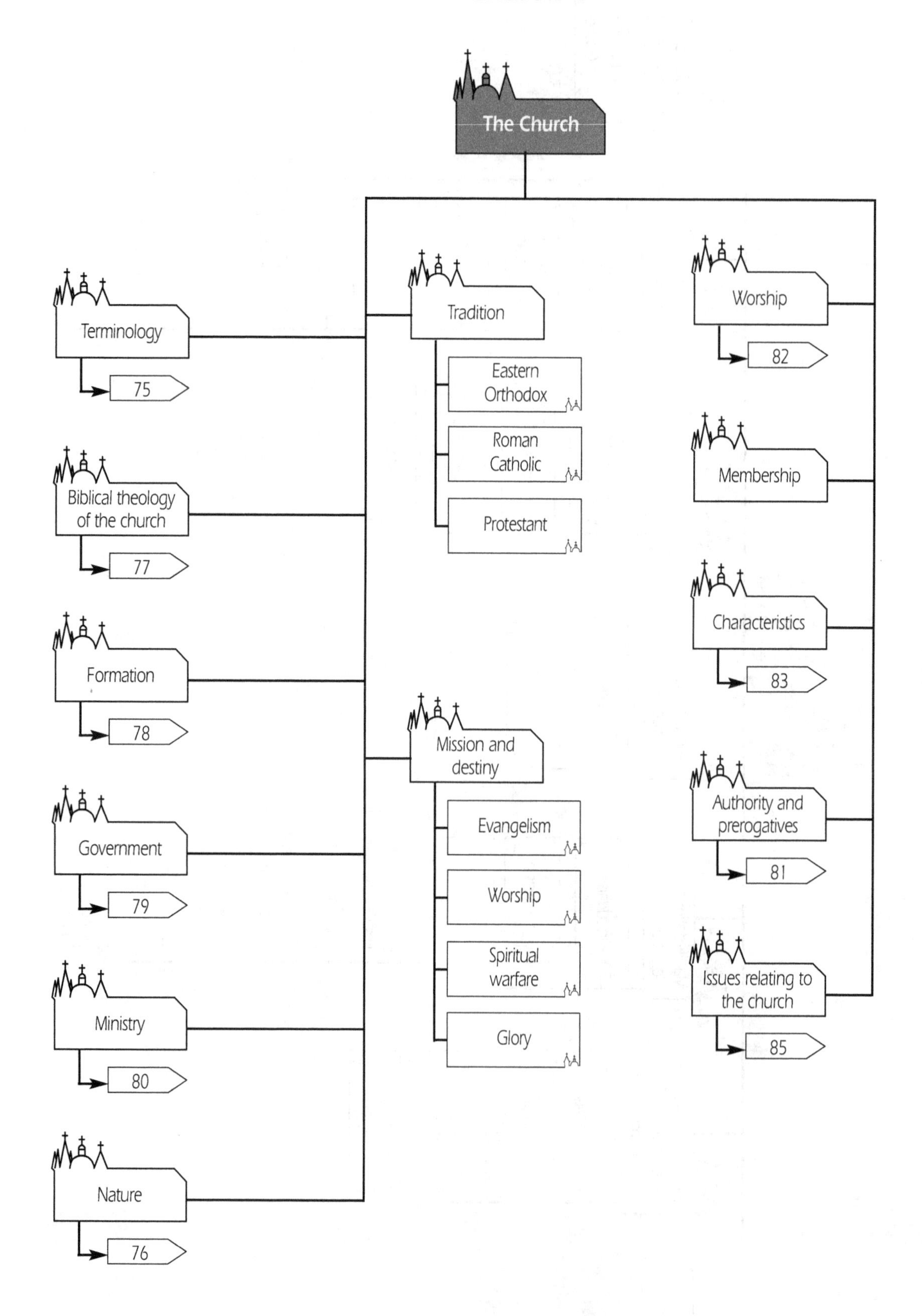
The Church
Terminology
75
Biblical theology of the church
77
Formation
78
Government
79
Ministry
80
Nature
76
Tradition
Eastern Orthodox
Roman Catholic
Protestant
Mission and destiny
Evangelism
Worship
Spiritual warfare
Glory
Worship
82
Membership
Characteristics
83
Authority and prerogatives
81
Issues relating to the church
85

Chart 75

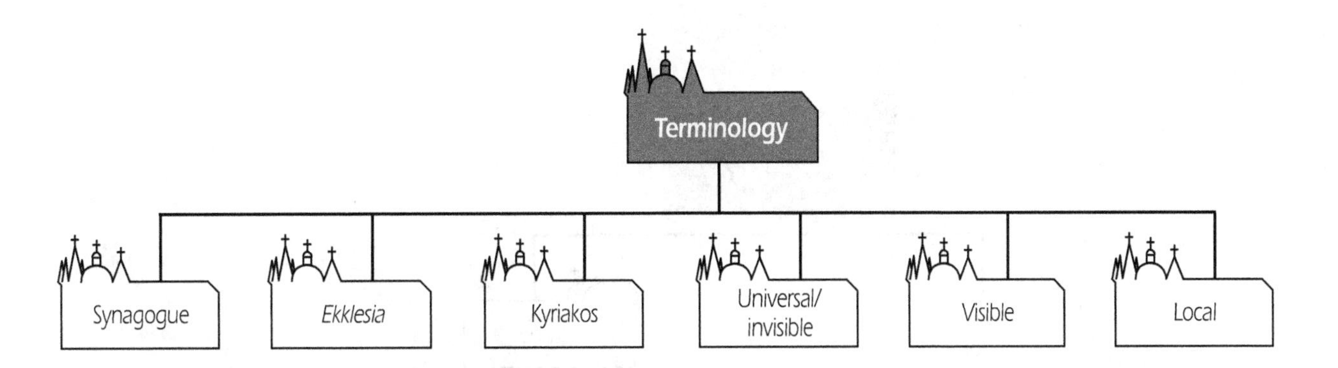

Chart 76

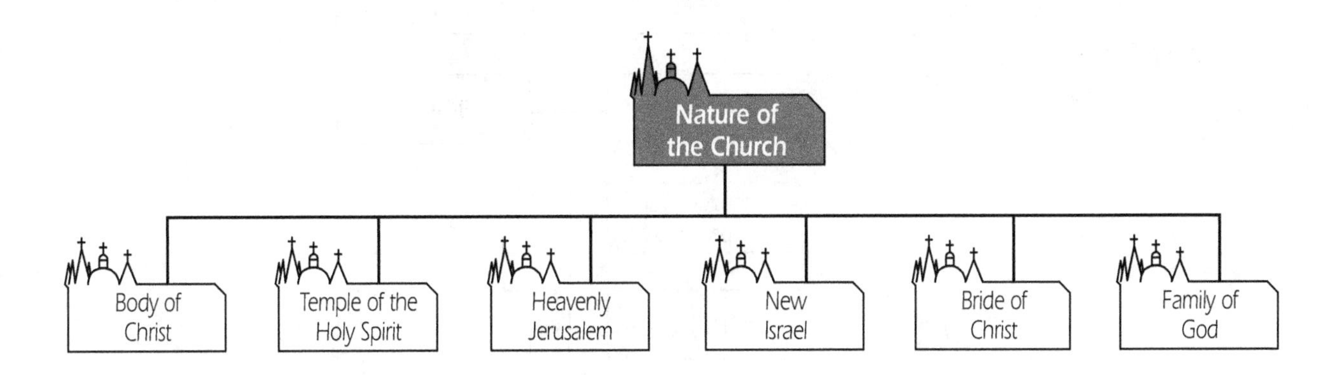

Chart 77

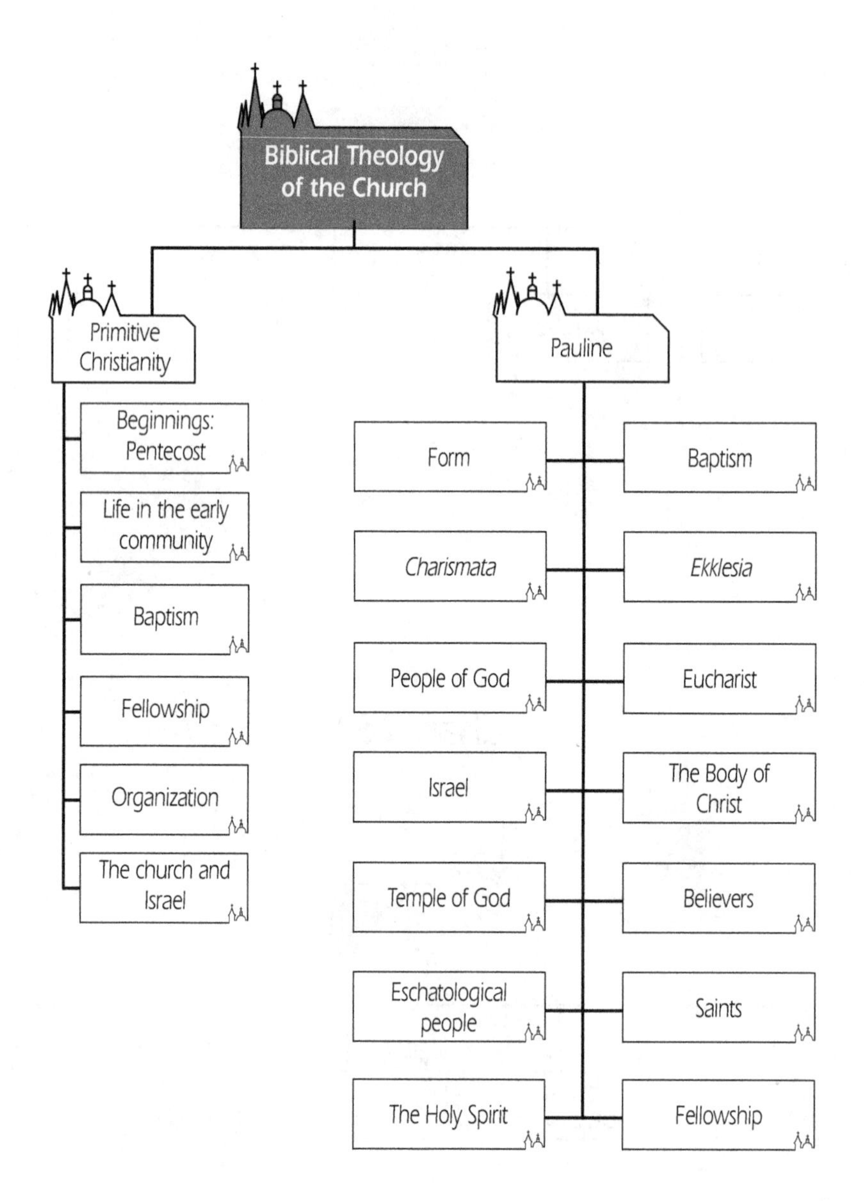

Biblical Theology of the Church
Primitive Christianity
Beginnings: Pentecost
Life in the early community
Baptism
Fellowship
Organization
The church and Israel
Pauline
Form
Baptism
Charismata
Ekklesia
People of God
Eucharist
Israel
The Body of Christ
Temple of God
Believers
Eschatological people
Saints
The Holy Spirit
Fellowship

Chart 78

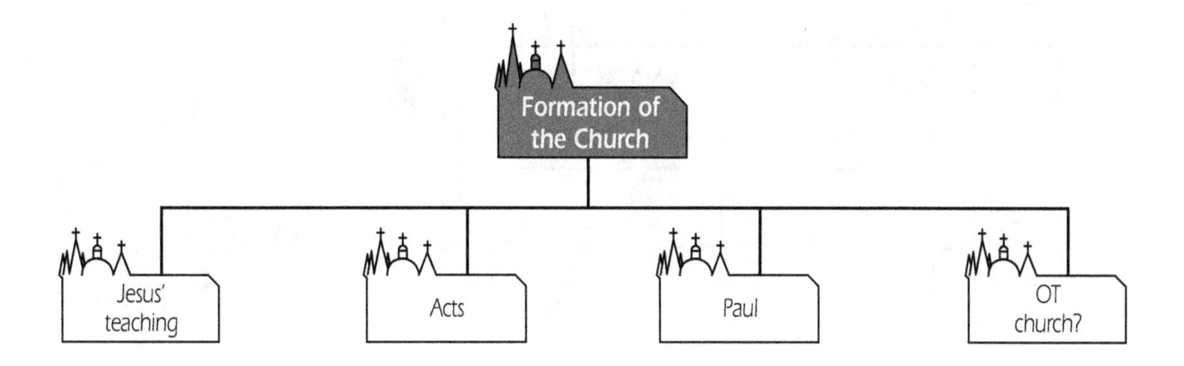

Chart 79

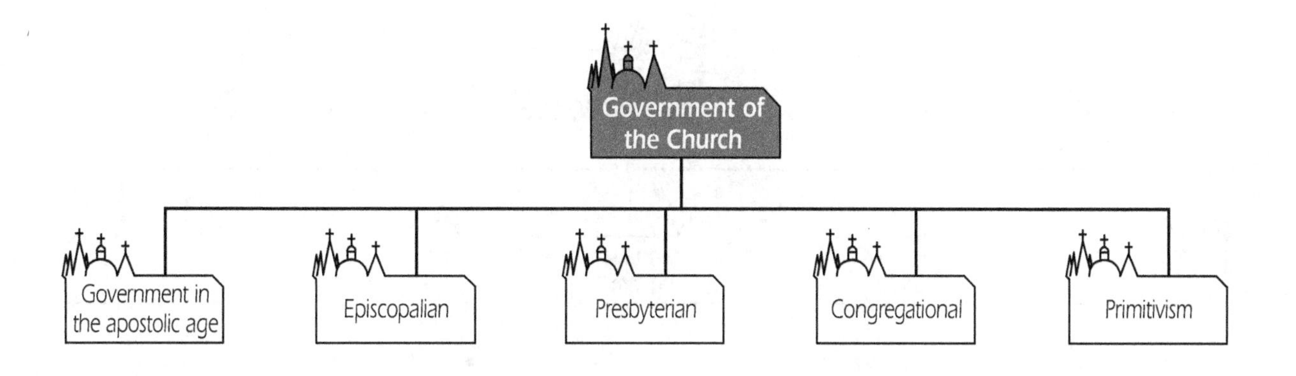

Chart 80

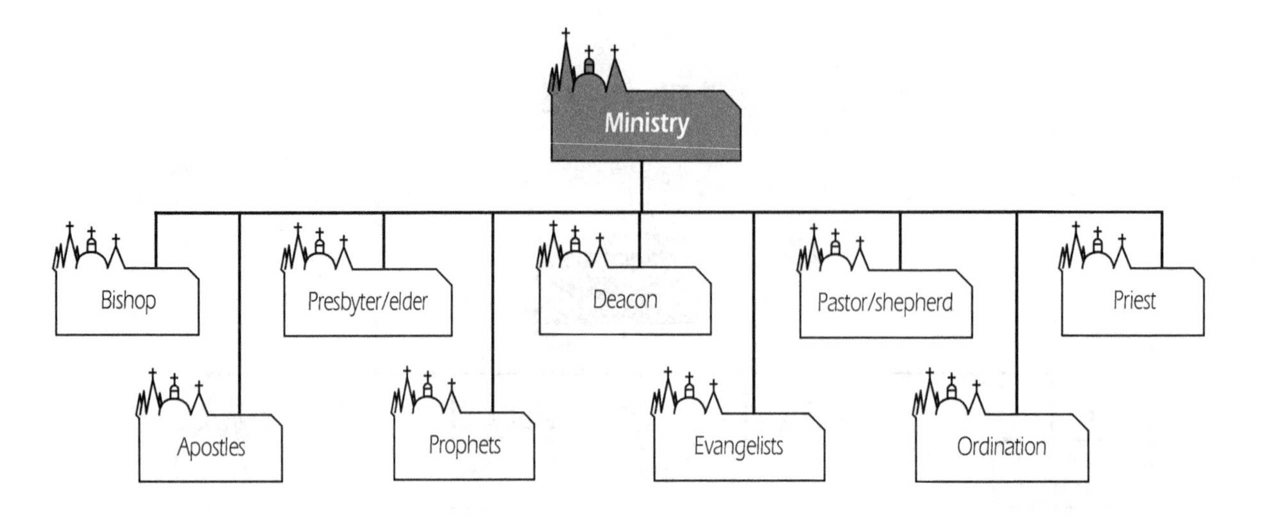

Chart 81

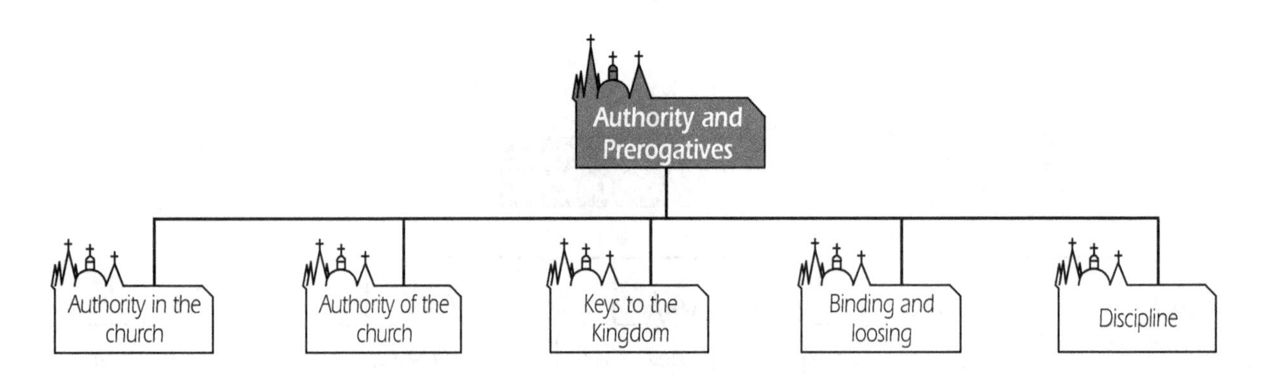

Chart 82

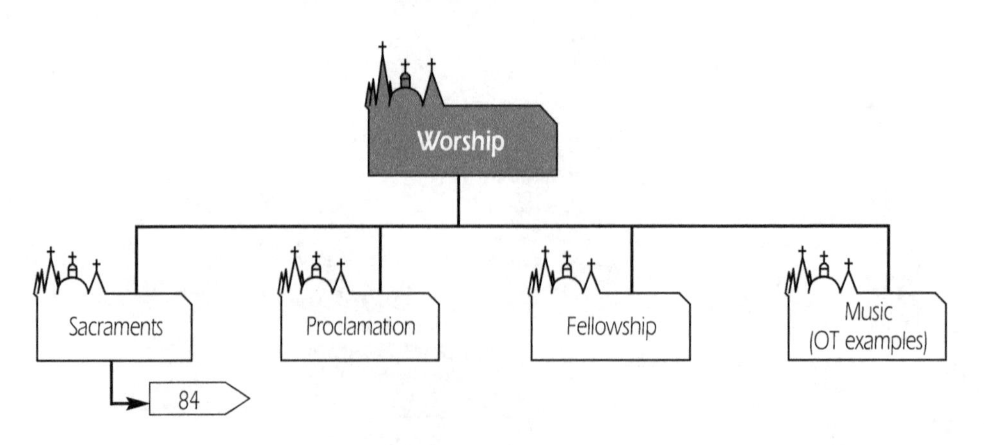

Chart 83

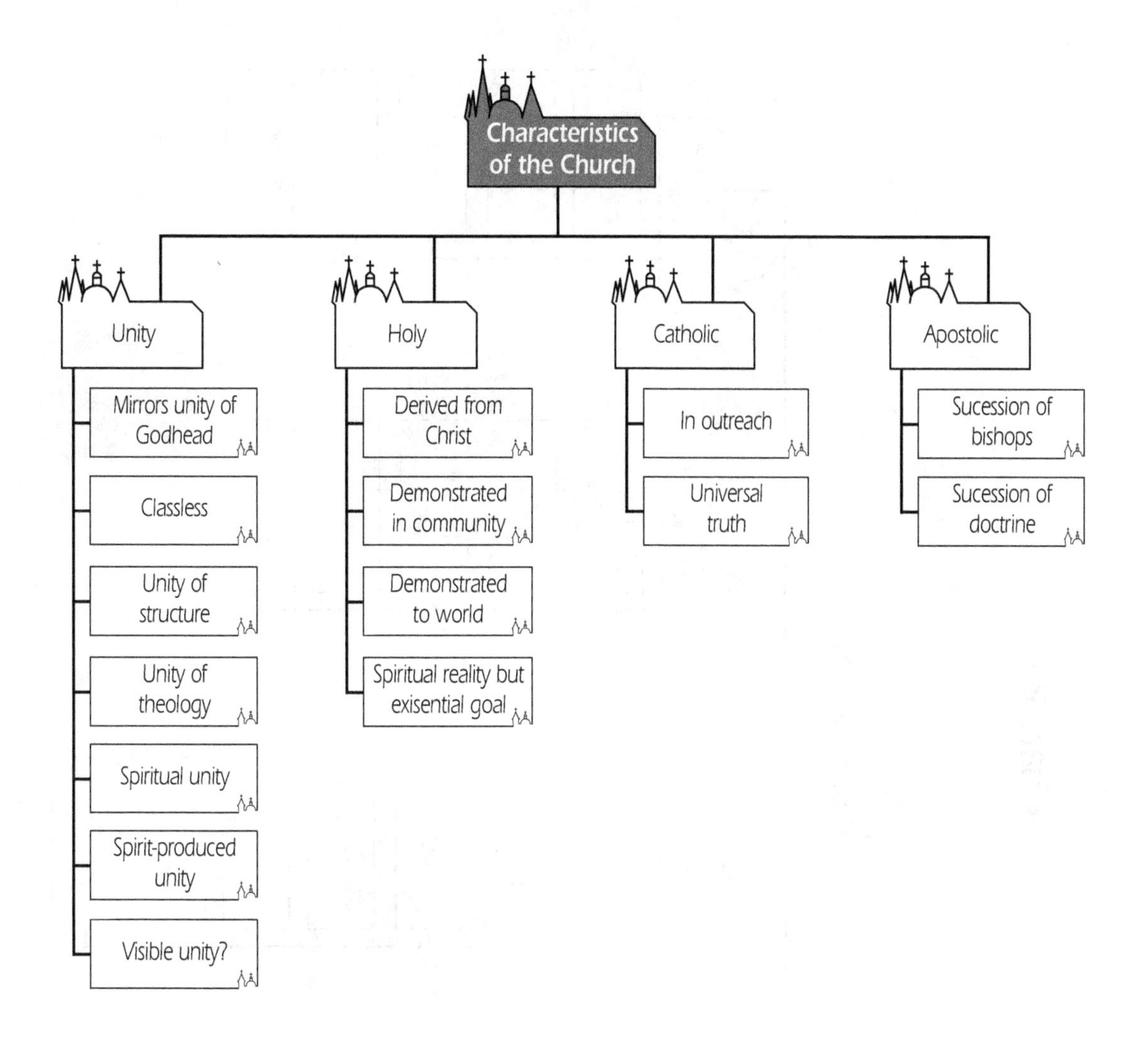

Characteristics of the Church
Unity
Mirrors unity of Godhead
Classless
Unity of structure
Unity of theology
Spiritual unity
Spirit-produced unity
Visible unity?
Holy
Derived from Christ
Demonstrated in community
Demonstrated to world
Spiritual reality but exisential goal
Catholic
In outreach
Universal truth
Apostolic
Sucession of bishops
Sucession of doctrine

Chart 84

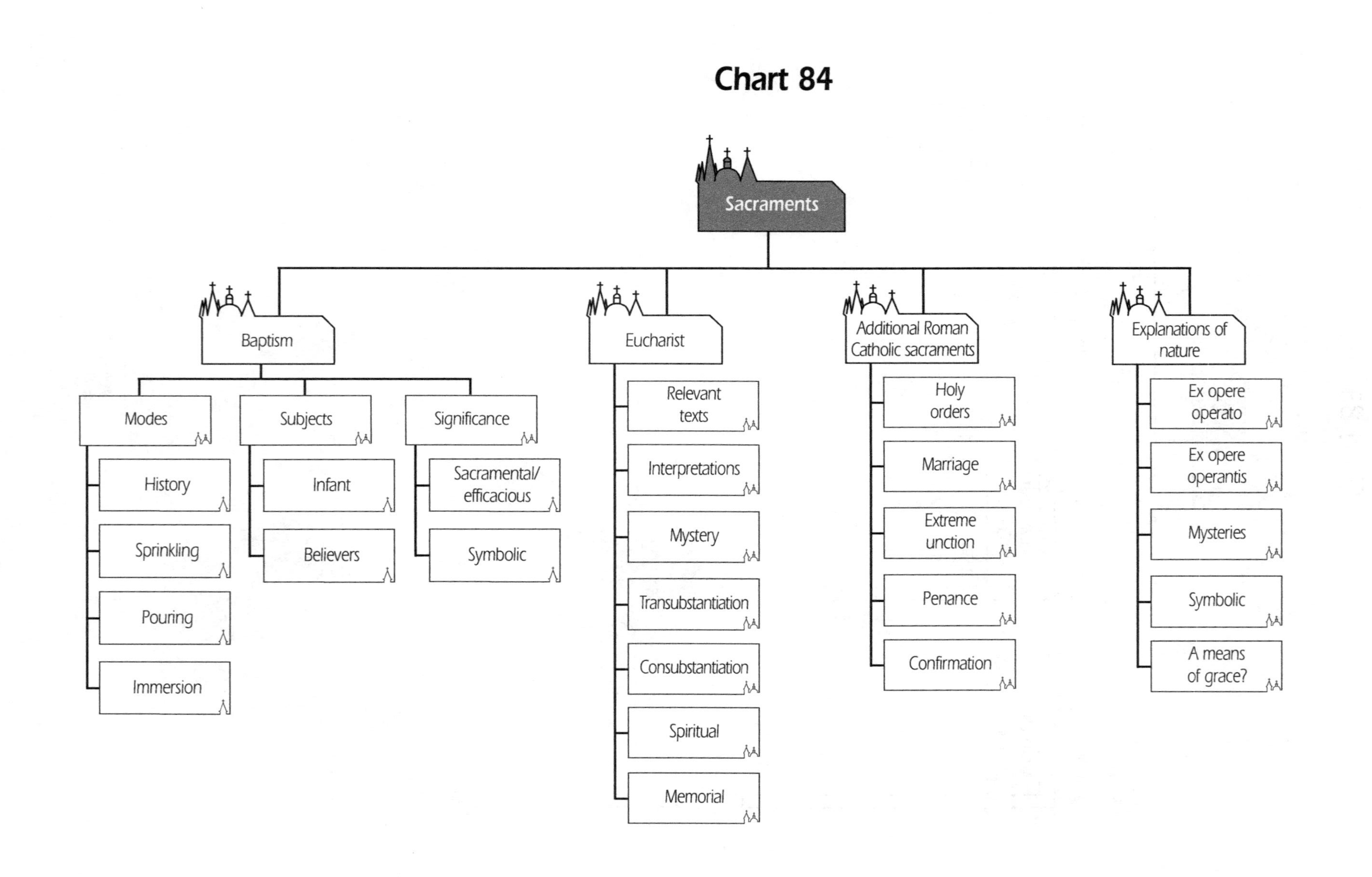

Sacraments
Baptism
Modes
History
Sprinkling
Pouring
Immersion
Subjects
Infant
Believers
Significance
Sacramental/ efficacious
Symbolic
Eucharist
Relevant texts
Interpretations
Mystery
Transubstantiation
Consubstantiation
Spiritual
Memorial
Additional Roman Catholic sacraments
Holy orders
Marriage
Extreme unction
Penance
Confirmation
Explanations of nature
Ex opere operato
Ex opere operantis
Mysteries
Symbolic
A means of grace?

Chart 85

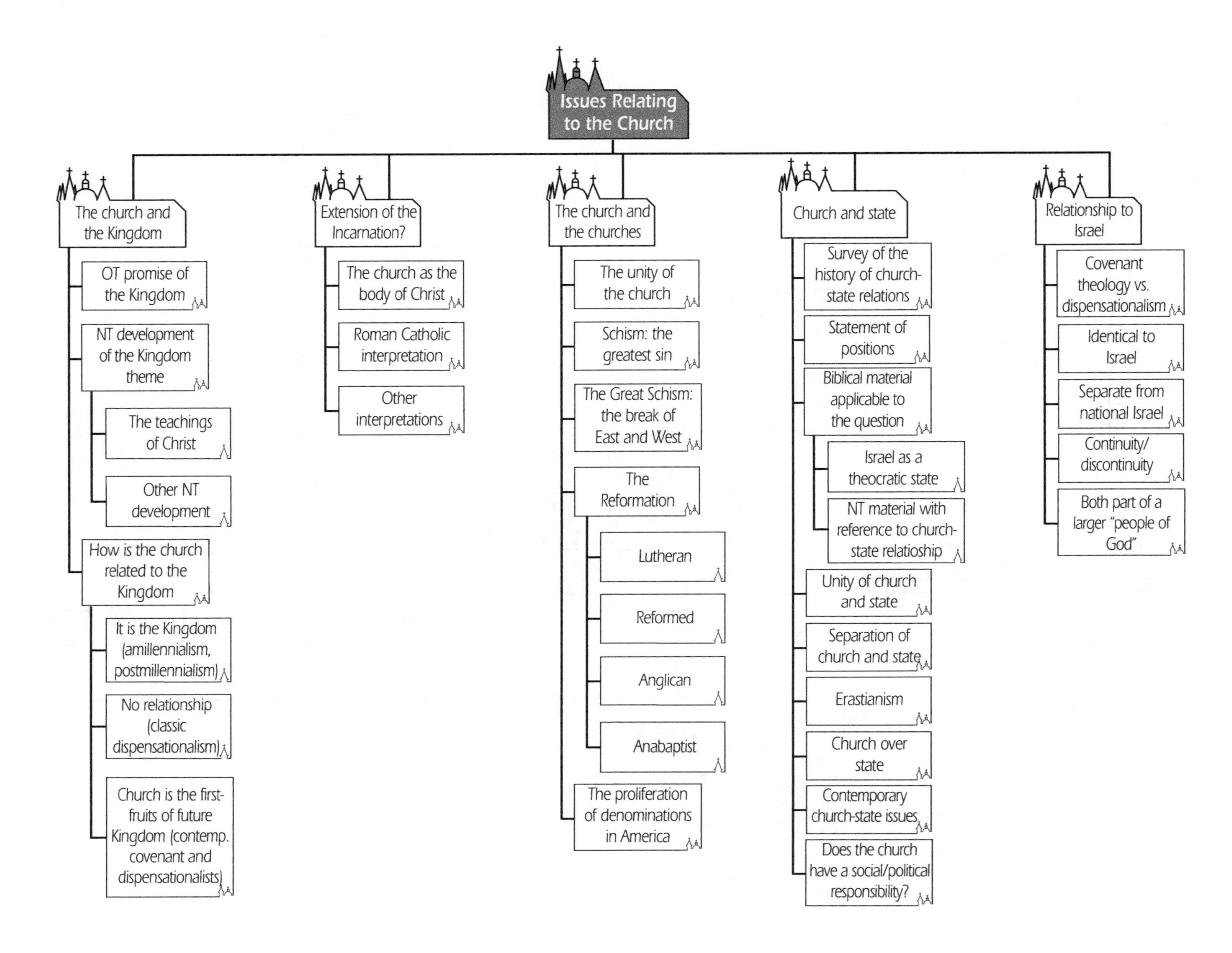
Issues Relating to the Church
The church and the Kingdom
OT promise of the Kingdom
NT development of the Kingdom theme
The teachings of Christ
Other NT development
How is the church related to the Kingdom
It is the Kingdom (amillennialism, postmillennialism)
No relationship (classic dispensationalism)
Church is the first-fruits of future Kingdom (contemp. covenant and dispensationalists)
Extension of the Incarnation?
The church as the body of Christ
Roman Catholic interpretation
Other interpretations
The church and the churches
The unity of the church
Schism: the greatest sin
The Great Schism: the break of East and West
The Reformation
Lutheran
Reformed
Anglican
Anabaptist
The proliferation of denominations in America
Church and state
Survey of the history of church-state relations
Statement of positions
Biblical material applicable to the question
Israel as a theocratic state
NT material with reference to church-state relatioship
Unity of church and state
Separation of church and state
Erastianism
Church over state
Contemporary church-state issues
Does the church have a social/political responsibility?
Relationship to Israel
Covenant theology vs. dispensationalism
Identical to Israel
Separate from national Israel
Continuity/ discontinuity
Both part of a larger "people of God"

Chart 86

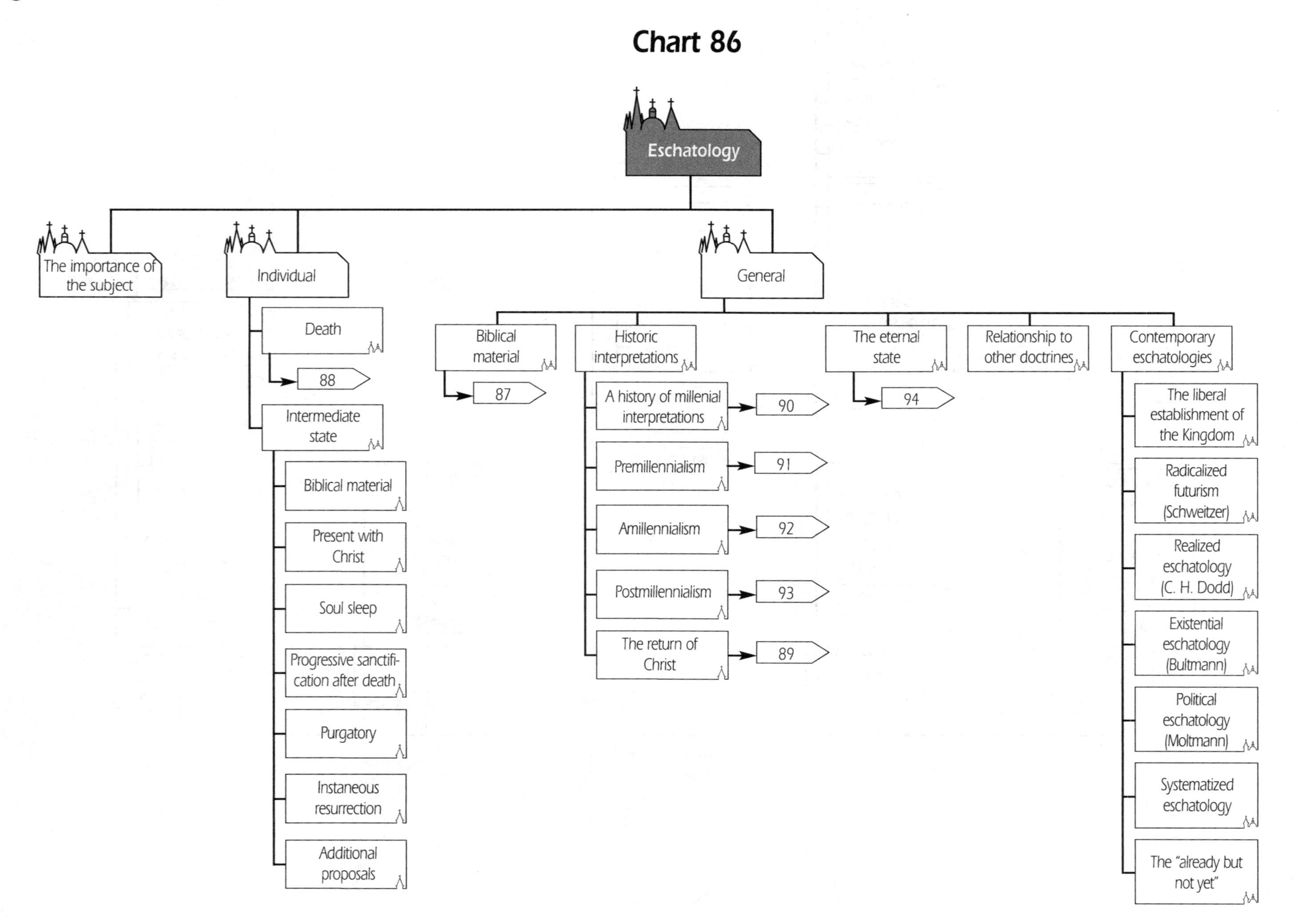

Eschatology
The importance of the subject
Individual
Death
88
Intermediate state
Biblical material
Present with Christ
Soul sleep
Progressive sanctification after death
Purgatory
Instaneous resurrection
Additional proposals
General
Biblical material
87
Historic interpretations
A history of millenial interpretations
90
Premillennialism
91
Amillennialism
92
Postmillennialism
93
The return of Christ
89
The eternal state
94
Relationship to other doctrines
Contemporary eschatologies
The liberal establishment of the Kingdom
Radicalized futurism (Schweitzer)
Realized eschatology (C. H. Dodd)
Existential eschatology (Bultmann)
Political eschatology (Moltmann)
Systematized eschatology
The "already but not yet"

Chart 87

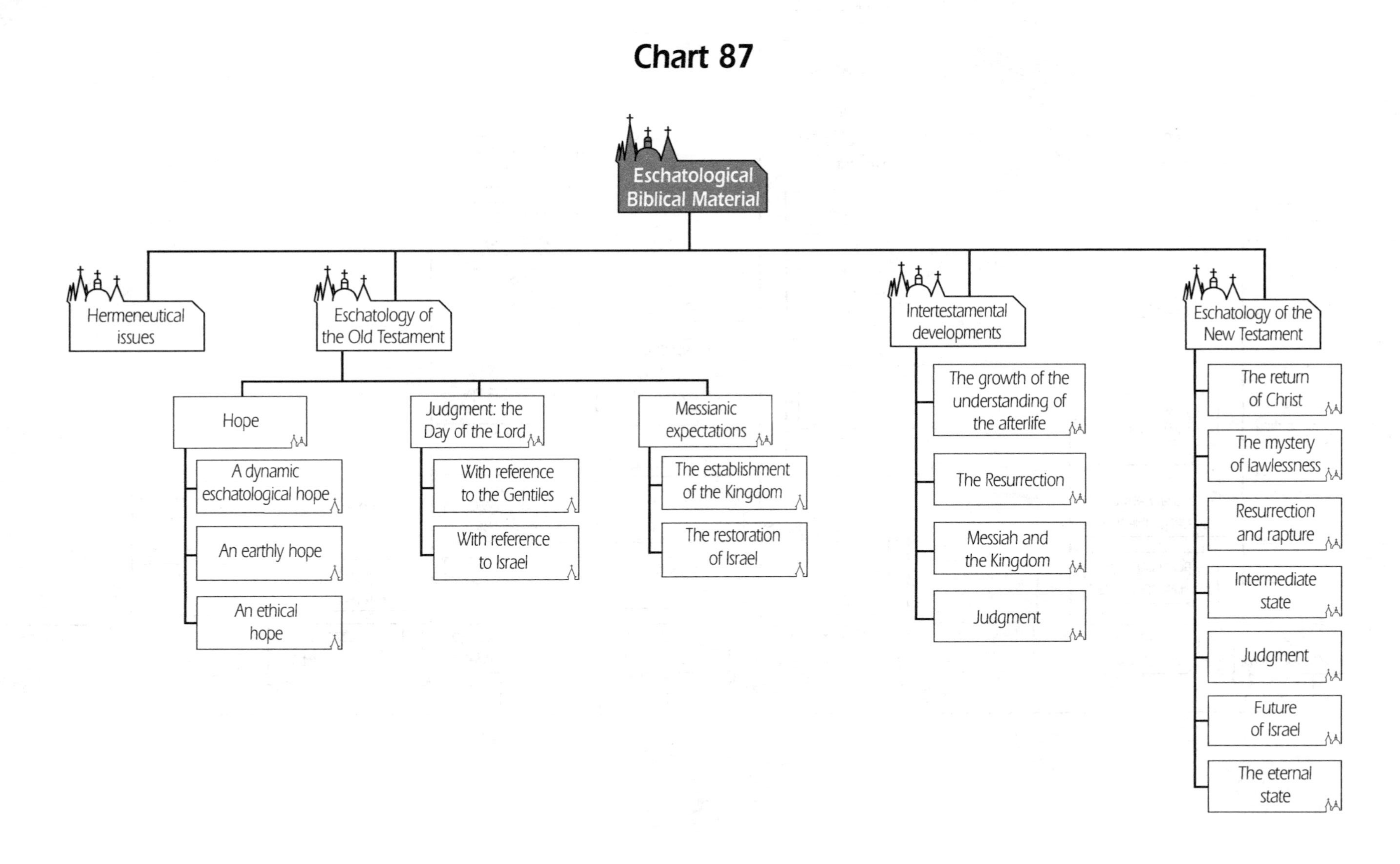

Eschatological Biblical Material
Hermeneutical issues
Eschatology of the Old Testament
Hope
A dynamic eschatological hope
An earthly hope
An ethical hope
Judgment: the Day of the Lord
With reference to the Gentiles
With reference to Israel
Messianic expectations
The establishment of the Kingdom
The restoration of Israel
Intertestamental developments
The growth of the understanding of the afterlife
The Resurrection
Messiah and the Kingdom
Judgment
Eschatology of the New Testament
The return of Christ
The mystery of lawlessness
Resurrection and rapture
Intermediate state
Judgment
Future of Israel
The eternal state

Chart 88

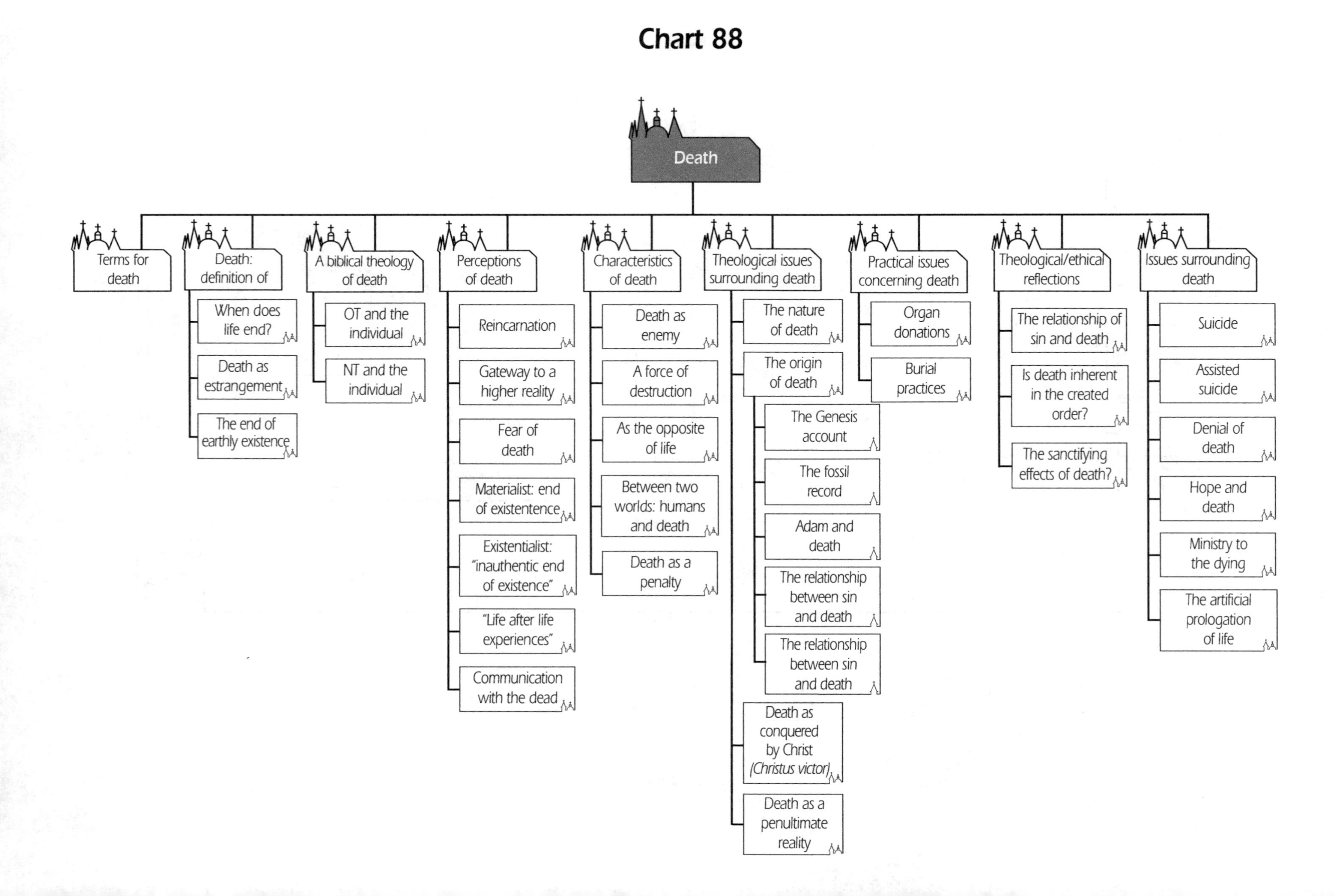
Death
Terms for death
Death: definition of
When does life end?
Death as estrangement
The end of earthly existence
A biblical theology of death
OT and the individual
NT and the individual
Perceptions of death
Reincarnation
Gateway to a higher reality
Fear of death
Materialist: end of existentence
Existentialist: "inauthentic end of existence"
"Life after life experiences"
Communication with the dead
Characteristics of death
Death as enemy
A force of destruction
As the opposite of life
Between two worlds: humans and death
Death as a penalty
Theological issues surrounding death
The nature of death
The origin of death
The Genesis account
The fossil record
Adam and death
The relationship between sin and death
The relationship between sin and death
Death as conquered by Christ (Christus victor)
Death as a penultimate reality
Practical issues concerning death
Organ donations
Burial practices
Theological/ethical reflections
The relationship of sin and death
Is death inherent in the created order?
The sanctifying effects of death?
Issues surrounding death
Suicide
Assisted suicide
Denial of death
Hope and death
Ministry to the dying
The artificial prologation of life

Chart 89

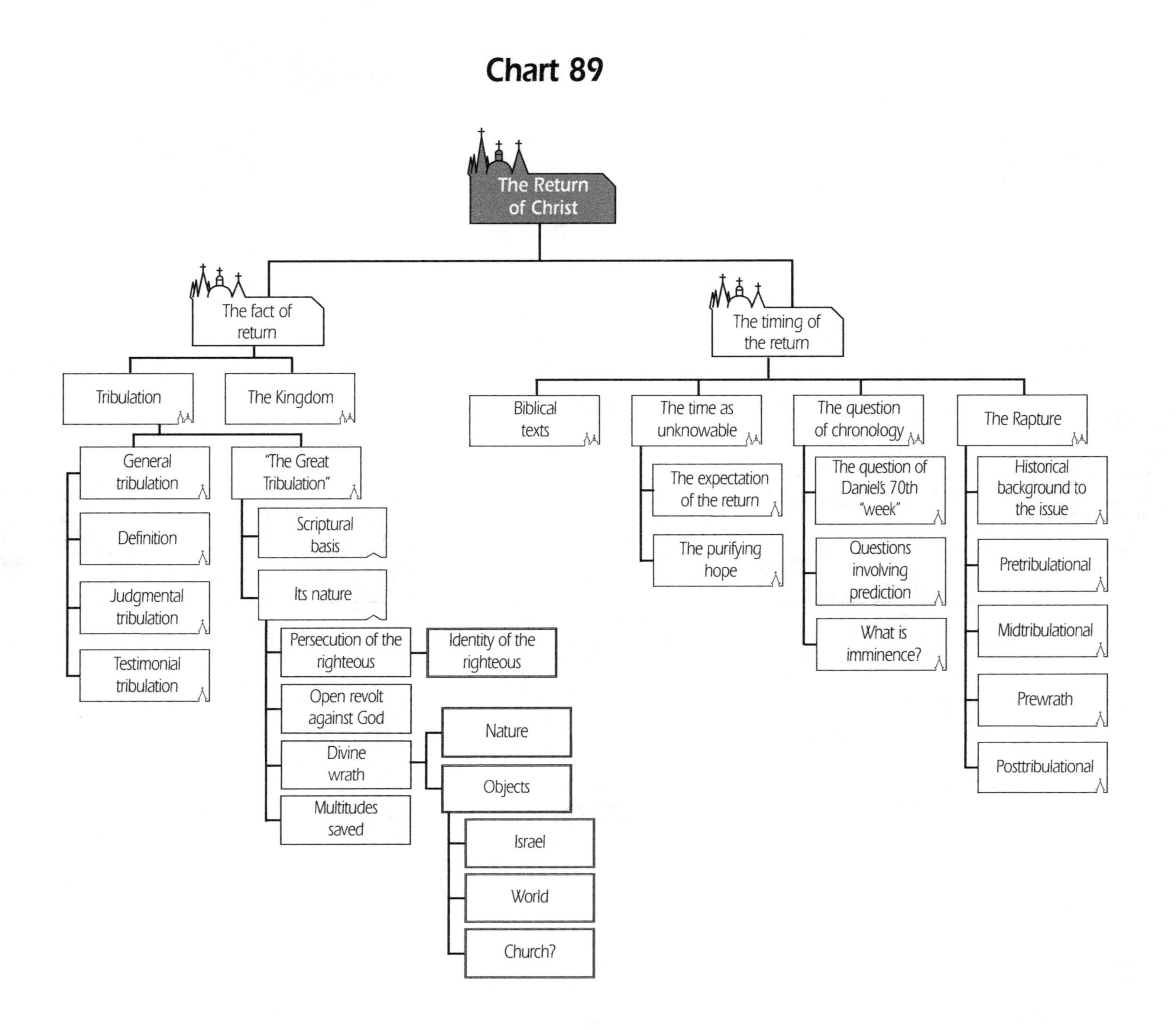
The Return of Christ
The fact of return
Tribulation
General tribulation
Definition
Judgmental tribulation
Testimonial tribulation
The Kingdom
"The Great Tribulation"
Scriptural basis
Its nature
Persecution of the righteous
Identity of the righteous
Open revolt against God
Divine wrath
Nature
Objects
Israel
World
Church?
Multitudes saved
The timing of the return
Biblical texts
The time as unknowable
The expectation of the return
The purifying hope
The question of chronology
The question of Daniel's 70th "week"
Questions involving prediction
What is imminence?
The Rapture
Historical background to the issue
Pretribulational
Midtribulational
Prewrath
Posttribulational

Chart 90

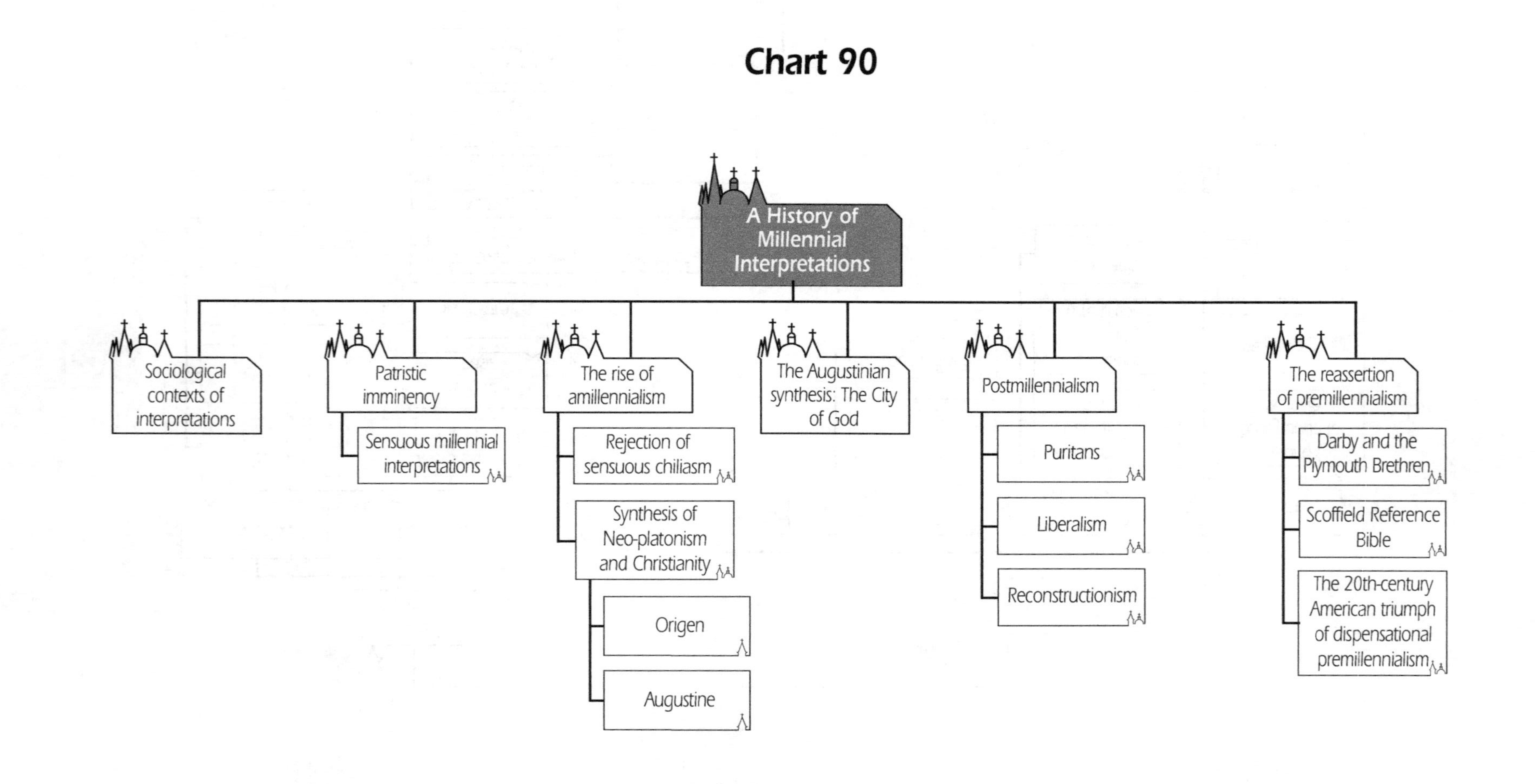

A History of Millennial Interpretations
Sociological contexts of interpretations
Patristic imminency
Sensuous millennial interpretations
The rise of amillennialism
Rejection of sensuous chiliasm
Synthesis of Neo-platonism and Christianity
Origen
Augustine
The Augustinian synthesis: The City of God
Postmillennialism
Puritans
Liberalism
Reconstructionism
The reassertion of premillennialism
Darby and the Plymouth Brethren
Scoffield Reference Bible
The 20th-century American triumph of dispensational premillennialism

Chart 91

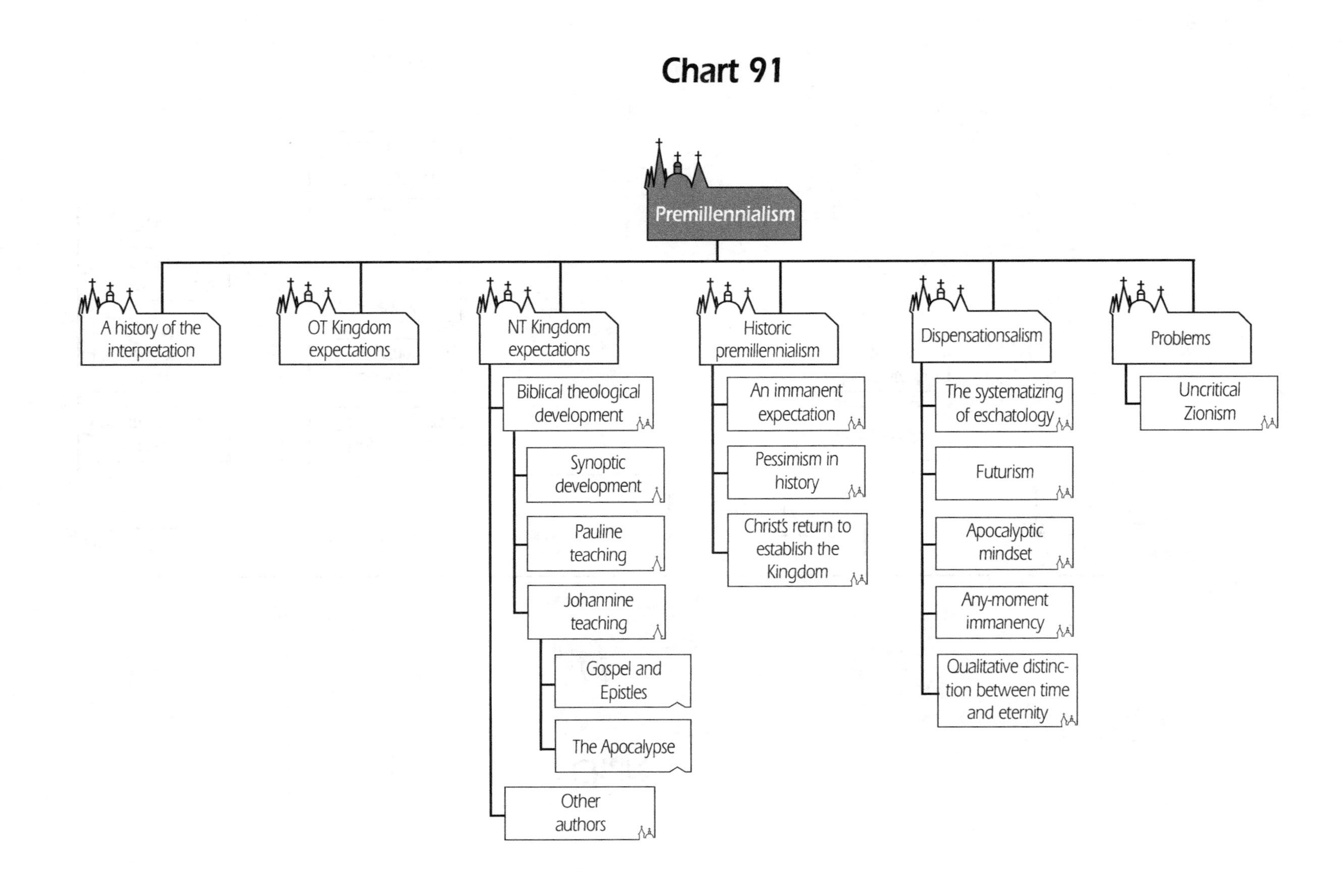
Premillennialism
A history of the interpretation
OT Kingdom expectations
NT Kingdom expectations
Biblical theological development
Synoptic development
Pauline teaching
Johannine teaching
Gospel and Epistles
The Apocalypse
Other authors
Historic premillennialism
An immanent expectation
Pessimism in history
Christ's return to establish the Kingdom
Dispensationsalism
The systematizing of eschatology
Futurism
Apocalyptic mindset
Any-moment immanency
Qualitative distinction between time and eternity
Problems
Uncritical Zionism

Chart 92

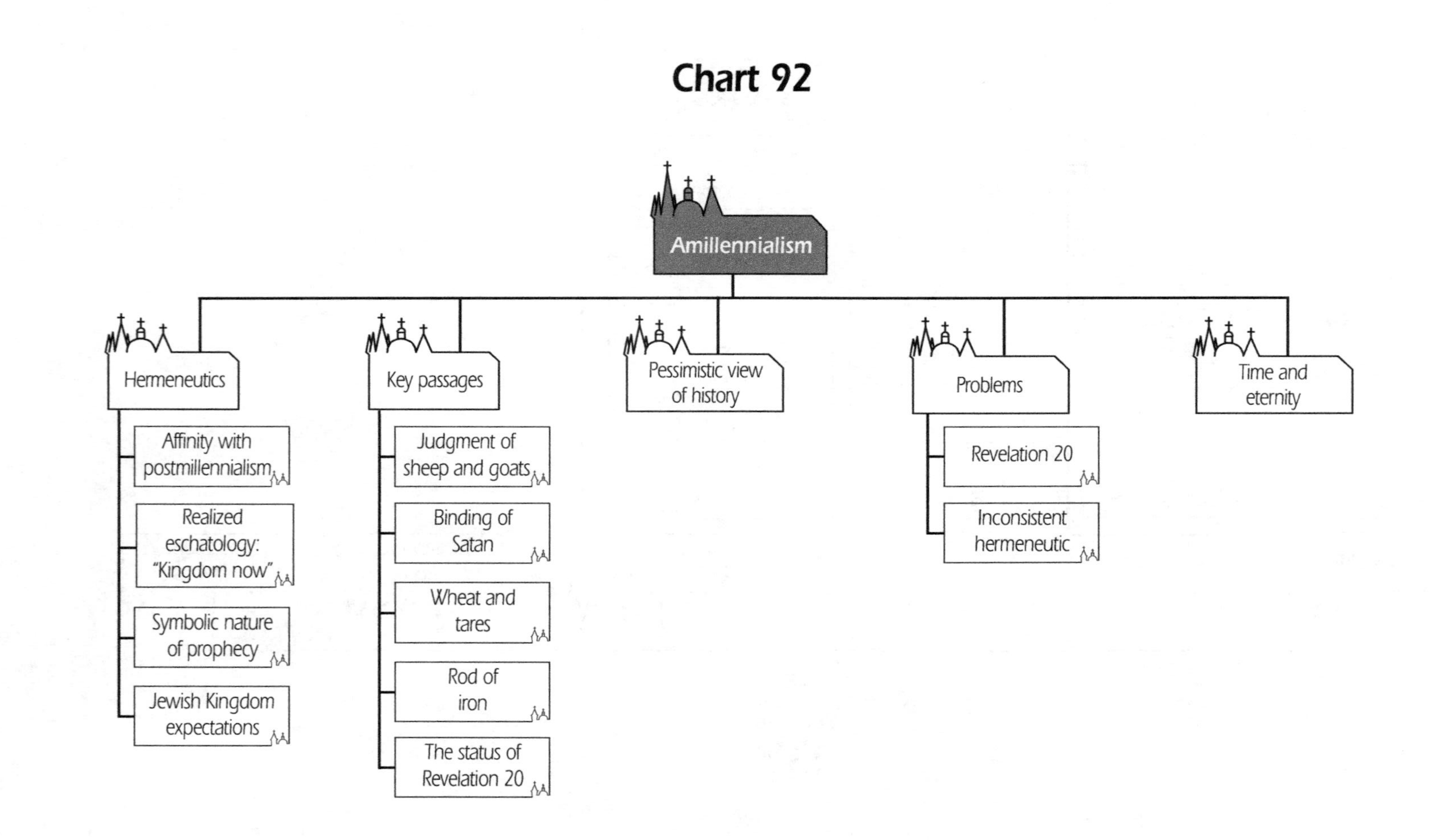

Amillennialism
Hermeneutics
Affinity with postmillennialism
Realized eschatology: "Kingdom now"
Symbolic nature of prophecy
Jewish Kingdom expectations
Key passages
Judgment of sheep and goats
Binding of Satan
Wheat and tares
Rod of iron
The status of Revelation 20
Pessimistic view of history
Problems
Revelation 20
Inconsistent hermeneutic
Time and eternity

Chart 93

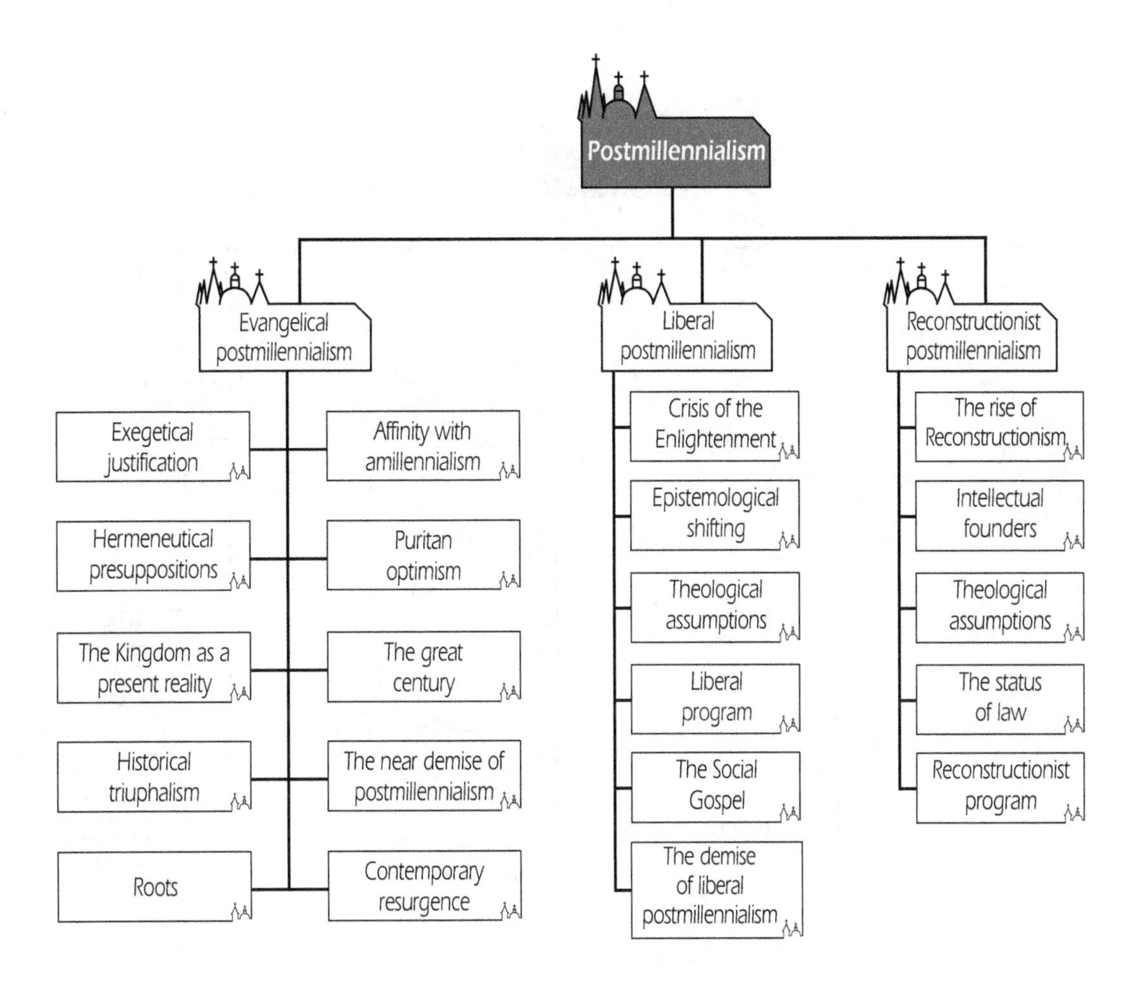

Postmillennialism
Evangelical postmillennialism
Exegetical justification
Hermeneutical presuppositions
The Kingdom as a present reality
Historical triuphalism
Roots
Affinity with amillennialism
Puritan optimism
The great century
The near demise of postmillennialism
Contemporary resurgence
Liberal postmillennialism
Crisis of the Enlightenment
Epistemological shifting
Theological assumptions
Liberal program
The Social Gospel
The demise of liberal postmillennialism
Reconstructionist postmillennialism
The rise of Reconstructionism
Intellectual founders
Theological assumptions
The status of law
Reconstructionist program

Chart 94

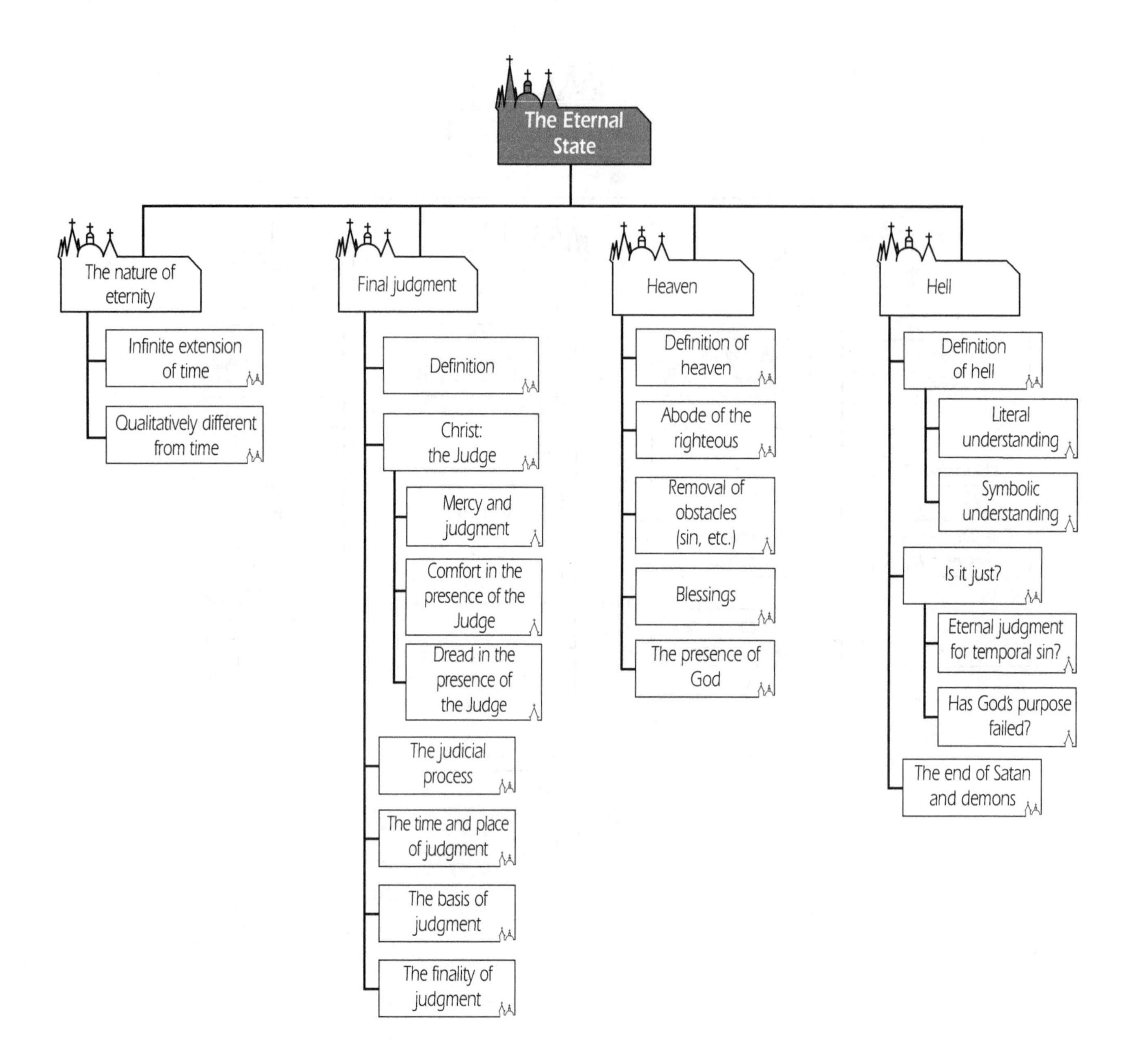

The Eternal State
The nature of eternity
Infinite extension of time
Qualitatively different from time
Final judgment
Definition
Christ: the Judge
Mercy and judgment
Comfort in the presence of the Judge
Dread in the presence of the Judge
The judicial process
The time and place of judgment
The basis of judgment
The finality of judgment
Heaven
Definition of heaven
Abode of the righteous
Removal of obstacles (sin, etc.)
Blessings
The presence of God
Hell
Definition of hell
Literal understanding
Symbolic understanding
Is it just?
Eternal judgment for temporal sin?
Has God's purpose failed?
The end of Satan and demons

Chart 95

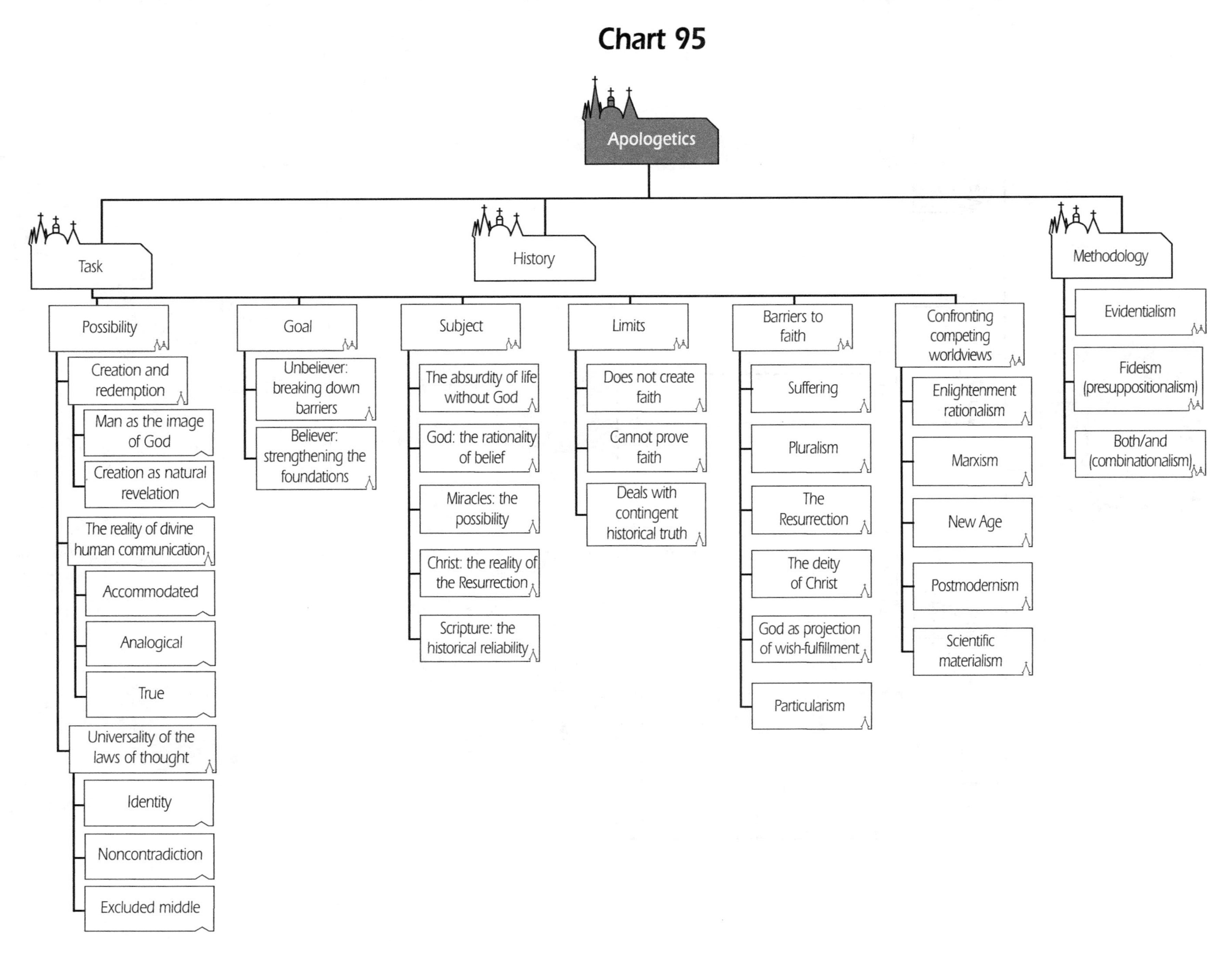

Apologetics
Task
History
Methodology
Possibility
Creation and redemption
Man as the image of God
Creation as natural revelation
The reality of divine human communication
Accommodated
Analogical
True
Universality of the laws of thought
Identity
Noncontradiction
Excluded middle
Goal
Unbeliever: breaking down barriers
Believer: strengthening the foundations
Subject
The absurdity of life without God
God: the rationality of belief
Miracles: the possibility
Christ: the reality of the Resurrection
Scripture: the historical reliability
Limits
Does not create faith
Cannot prove faith
Deals with contingent historical truth
Barriers to faith
Suffering
Pluralism
The Resurrection
The deity of Christ
God as projection of wish-fulfillment
Particularism
Confronting competing worldviews
Enlightenment rationalism
Marxism
New Age
Postmodernism
Scientific materialism
Evidentialism
Fideism (presuppositionalism)
Both/and (combinationalism)

Chart 96

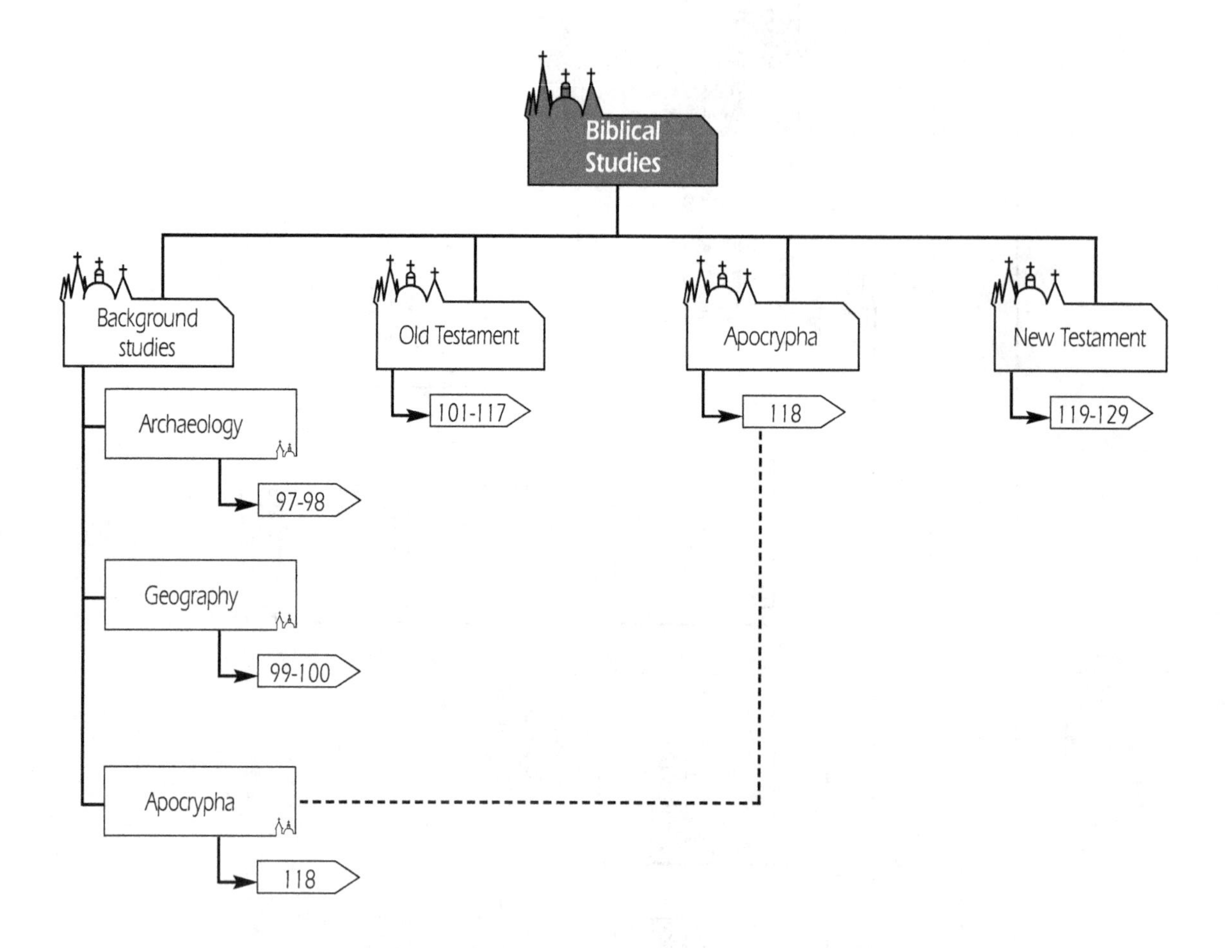

Biblical Studies
Background studies
Old Testament
Apocrypha
New Testament
Archaeology
101-117
118
119-129
97-98
Geography
99-100
Apocrypha
118

Chart 97

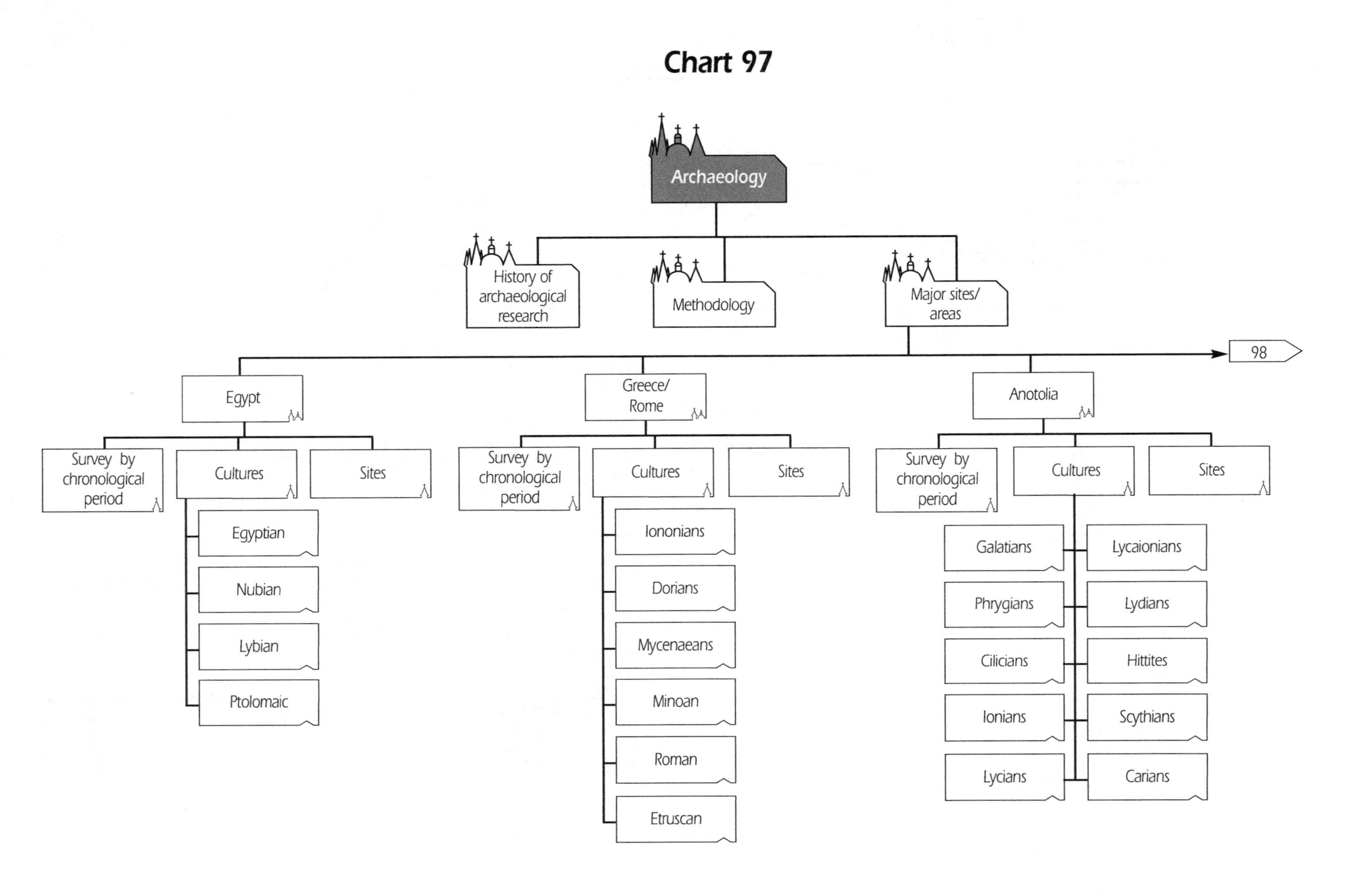
Archaeology
History of archaeological research
Methodology
Major sites/ areas
98
Egypt
Survey by chronological period
Cultures
Sites
Egyptian
Nubian
Lybian
Ptolomaic
Greece/ Rome
Survey by chronological period
Cultures
Sites
Iononians
Dorians
Mycenaeans
Minoan
Roman
Etruscan
Anotolia
Survey by chronological period
Cultures
Sites
Galatians
Phrygians
Cilicians
Ionians
Lycians
Lycaionians
Lydians
Hittites
Scythians
Carians

Chart 98

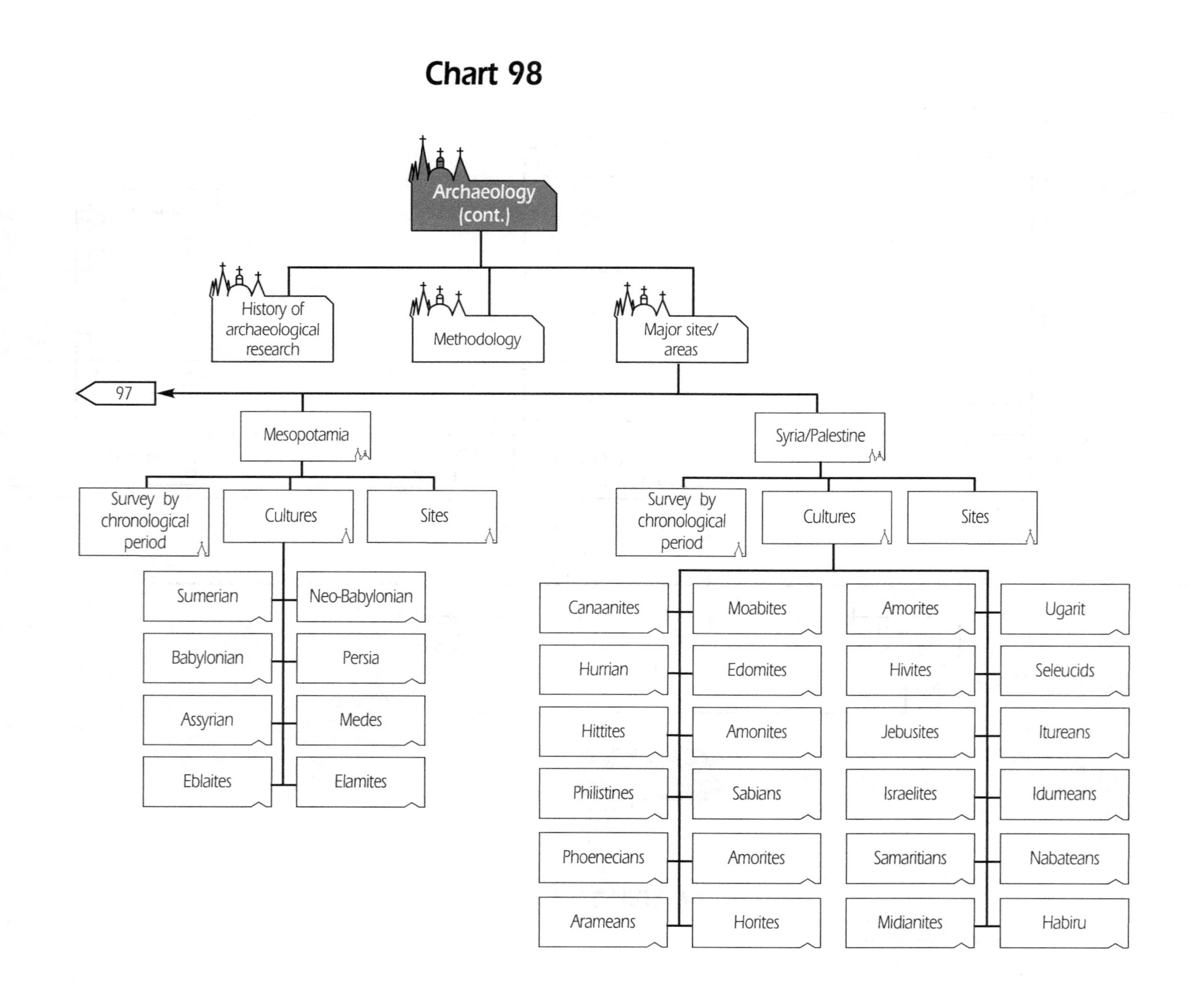

Archaeology (cont.)
History of archaeological research
Methodology
Major sites/ areas
97
Mesopotamia
Survey by chronological period
Cultures
Sites
Sumerian
Neo-Babylonian
Babylonian
Persia
Assyrian
Medes
Eblaites
Elamites
Syria/Palestine
Survey by chronological period
Cultures
Sites
Canaanites
Moabites
Amorites
Ugarit
Hurrian
Edomites
Hivites
Seleucids
Hittites
Amonites
Jebusites
Itureans
Philistines
Sabians
Israelites
Idumeans
Phoenecians
Amorites
Samaritians
Nabateans
Arameans
Horites
Midianites
Habiru

Chart 99

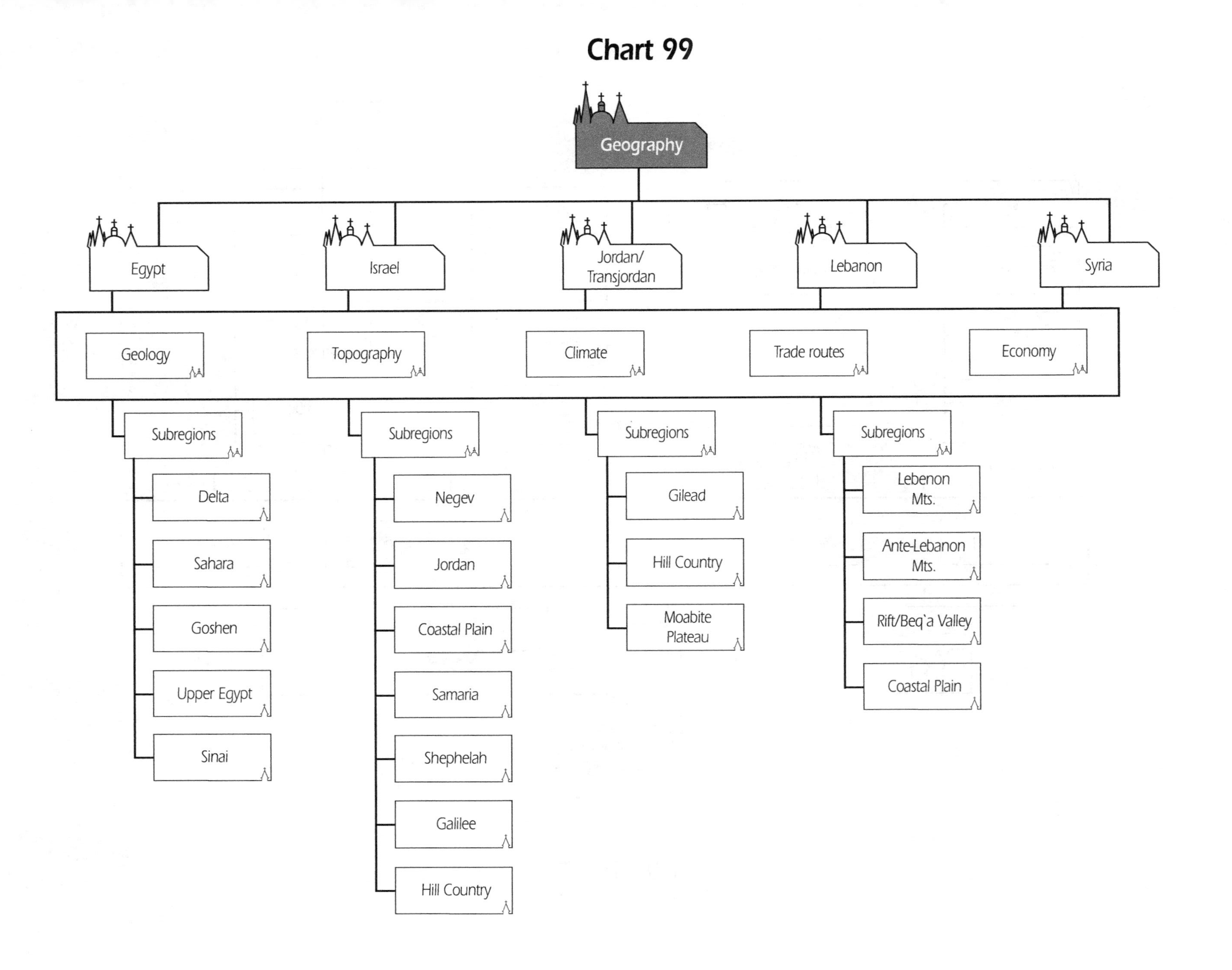

Geography
Egypt
Israel
Jordan/
Transjordan
Lebanon
Syria
Geology
Topography
Climate
Trade routes
Economy
Subregions
Delta
Sahara
Goshen
Upper Egypt
Sinai
Subregions
Negev
Jordan
Coastal Plain
Samaria
Shephelah
Galilee
Hill Country
Subregions
Gilead
Hill Country
Moabite
Plateau
Subregions
Lebenon
Mts.
Ante-Lebanon
Mts.
Rift/Beq`a Valley
Coastal Plain

Chart 100

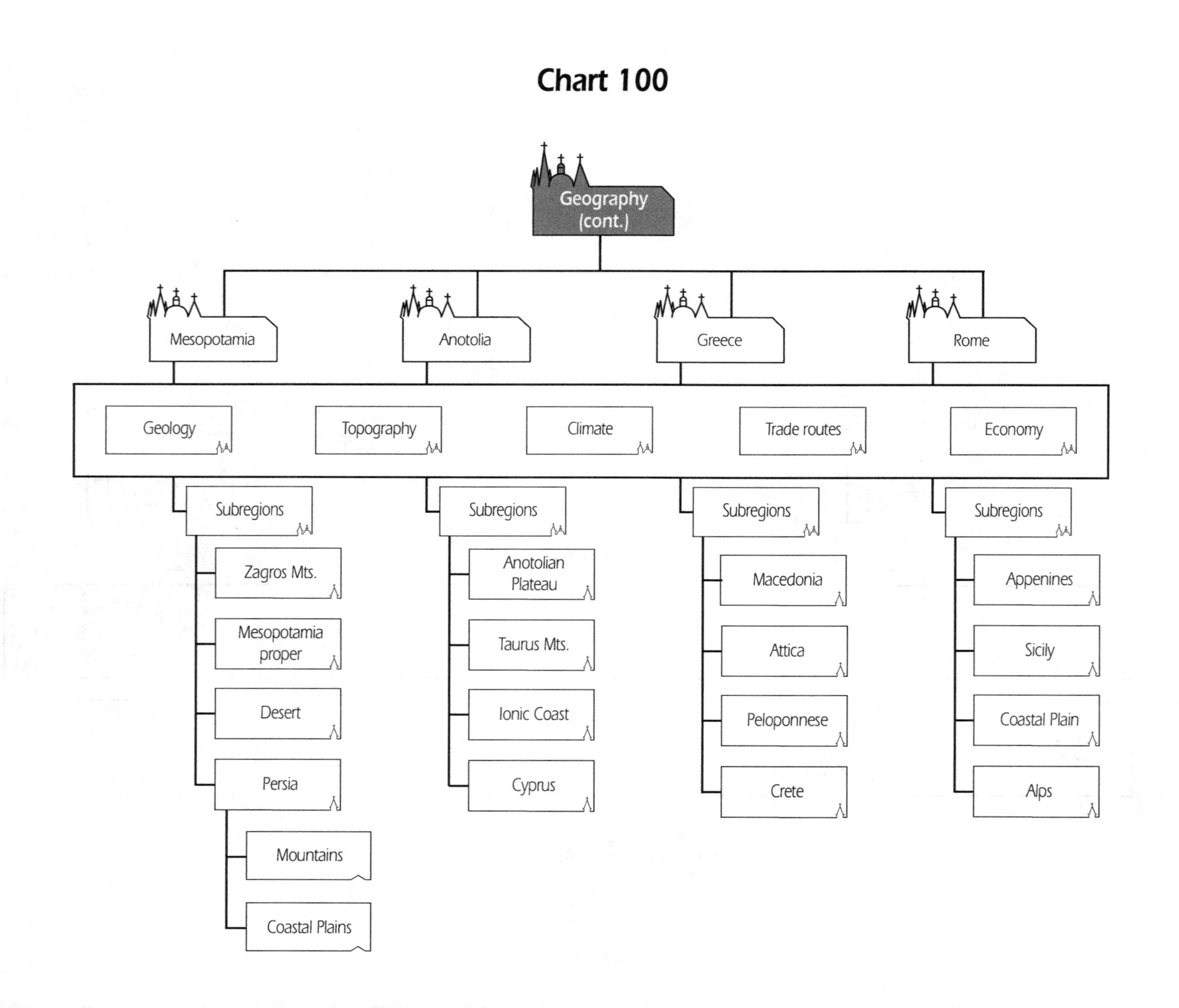

Geography (cont.)
Mesopotamia
Anotolia
Greece
Rome
Geology
Topography
Climate
Trade routes
Economy
Subregions
Zagros Mts.
Mesopotamia proper
Desert
Persia
Mountains
Coastal Plains
Subregions
Anotolian Plateau
Taurus Mts.
Ionic Coast
Cyprus
Subregions
Macedonia
Attica
Peloponnese
Crete
Subregions
Appenines
Sicily
Coastal Plain
Alps

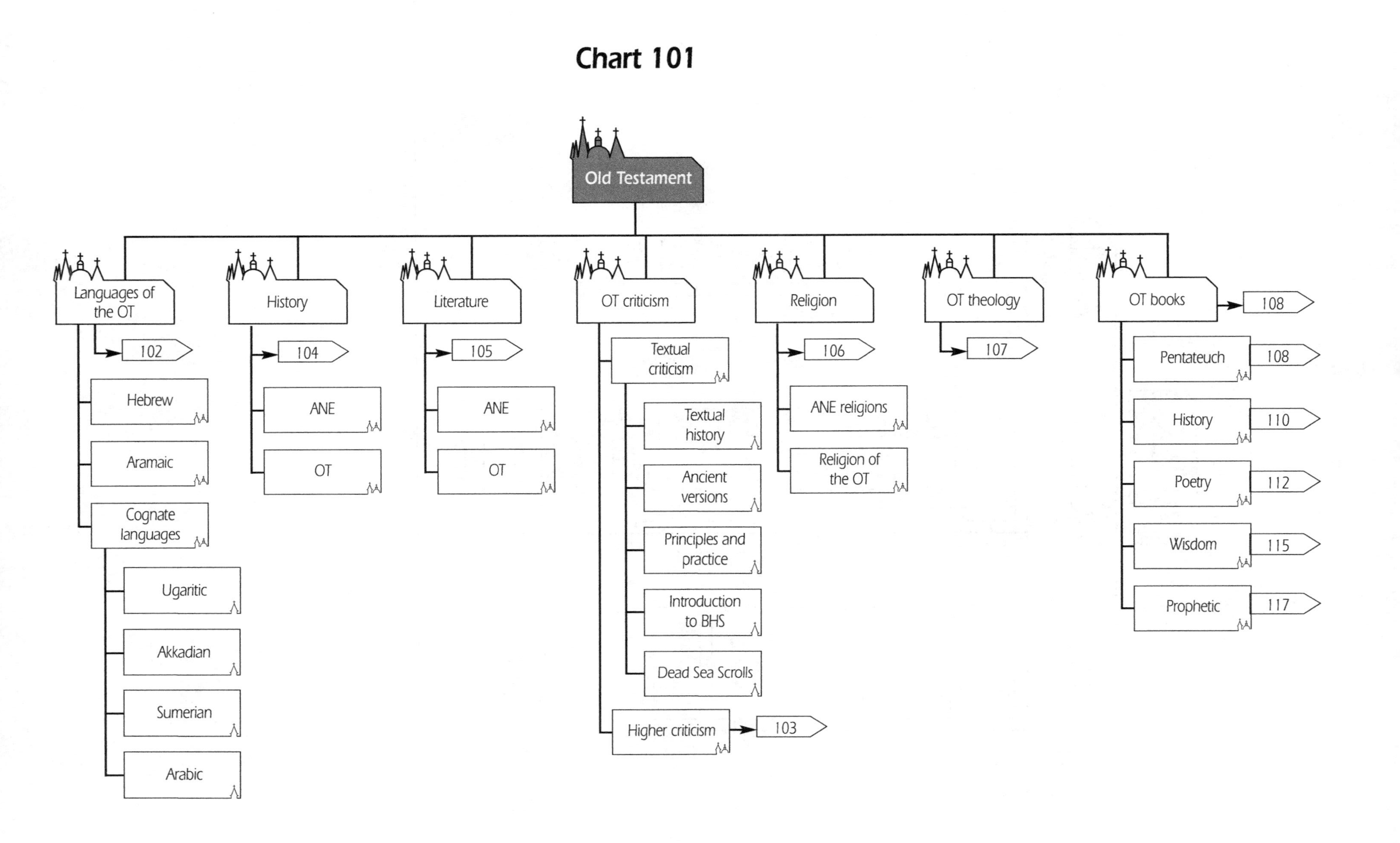
Chart 101
Old Testament
Languages of the OT
102
Hebrew
Aramaic
Cognate languages
Ugaritic
Akkadian
Sumerian
Arabic
History
104
ANE
OT
Literature
105
ANE
OT
OT criticism
Textual criticism
Textual history
Ancient versions
Principles and practice
Introduction to BHS
Dead Sea Scrolls
Higher criticism
103
Religion
106
ANE religions
Religion of the OT
OT theology
107
OT books
108
Pentateuch
108
History
110
Poetry
112
Wisdom
115
Prophetic
117

Chart 102

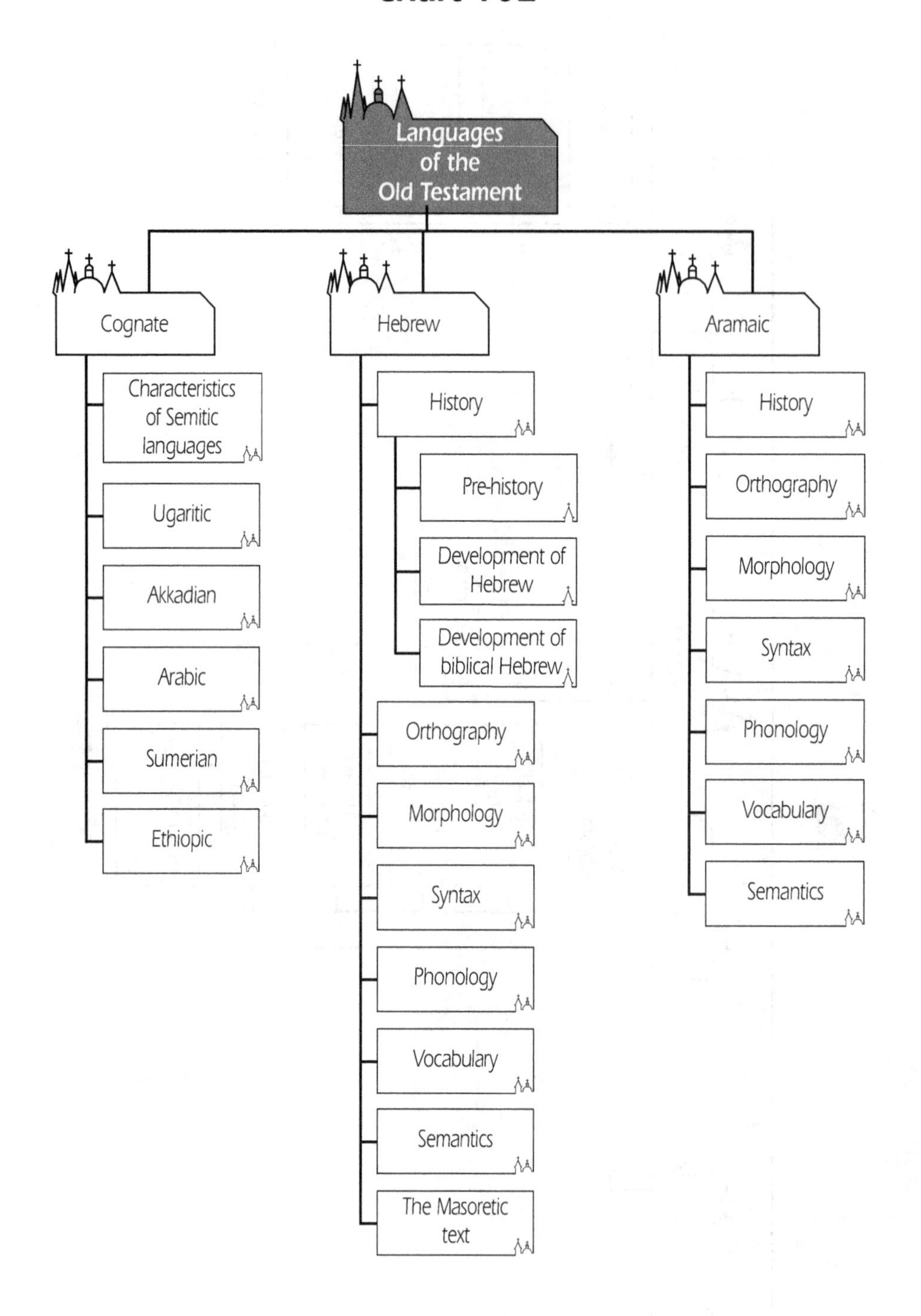

Languages of the Old Testament
Cognate
Characteristics of Semitic languages
Ugaritic
Akkadian
Arabic
Sumerian
Ethiopic
Hebrew
History
Pre-history
Development of Hebrew
Development of biblical Hebrew
Orthography
Morphology
Syntax
Phonology
Vocabulary
Semantics
The Masoretic text
Aramaic
History
Orthography
Morphology
Syntax
Phonology
Vocabulary
Semantics

Chart 103

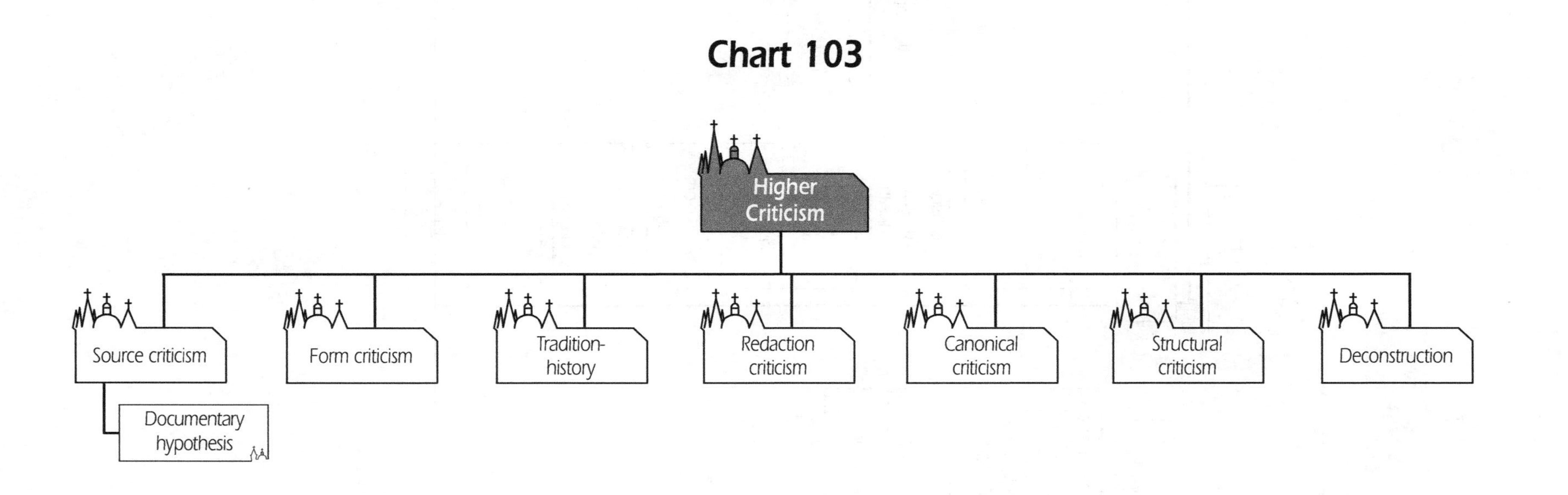
Higher Criticism
Source criticism
Documentary hypothesis
Form criticism
Tradition-history
Redaction criticism
Canonical criticism
Structural criticism
Deconstruction

Chart 104

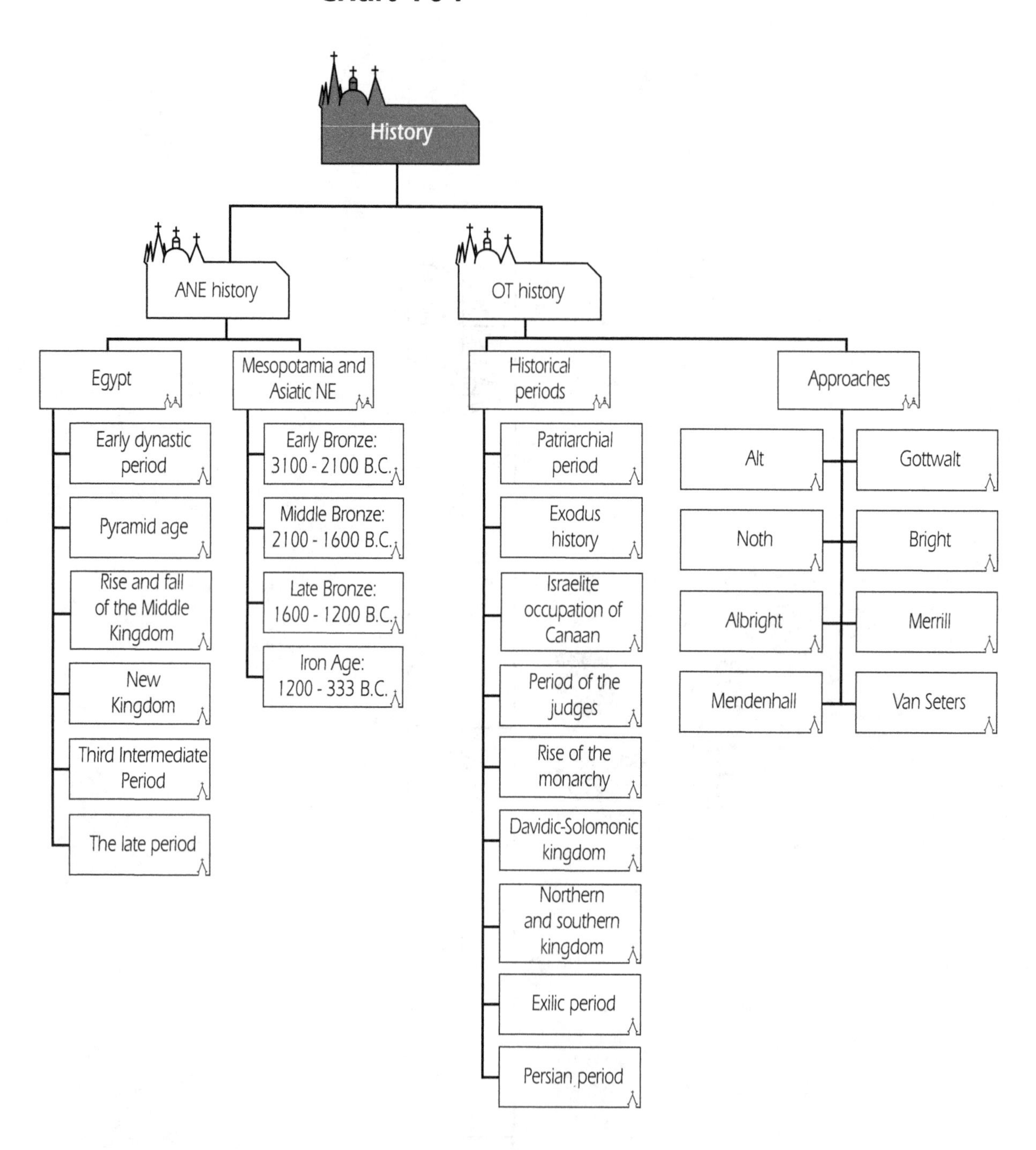

History
ANE history
OT history
Egypt
Mesopotamia and Asiatic NE
Historical periods
Approaches
Early dynastic period
Pyramid age
Rise and fall of the Middle Kingdom
New Kingdom
Third Intermediate Period
The late period
Early Bronze: 3100 - 2100 B.C.
Middle Bronze: 2100 - 1600 B.C.
Late Bronze: 1600 - 1200 B.C.
Iron Age: 1200 - 333 B.C.
Patriarchial period
Exodus history
Israelite occupation of Canaan
Period of the judges
Rise of the monarchy
Davidic-Solomonic kingdom
Northern and southern kingdom
Exilic period
Persian period
Alt
Gottwalt
Noth
Bright
Albright
Merrill
Mendenhall
Van Seters

Chart 105

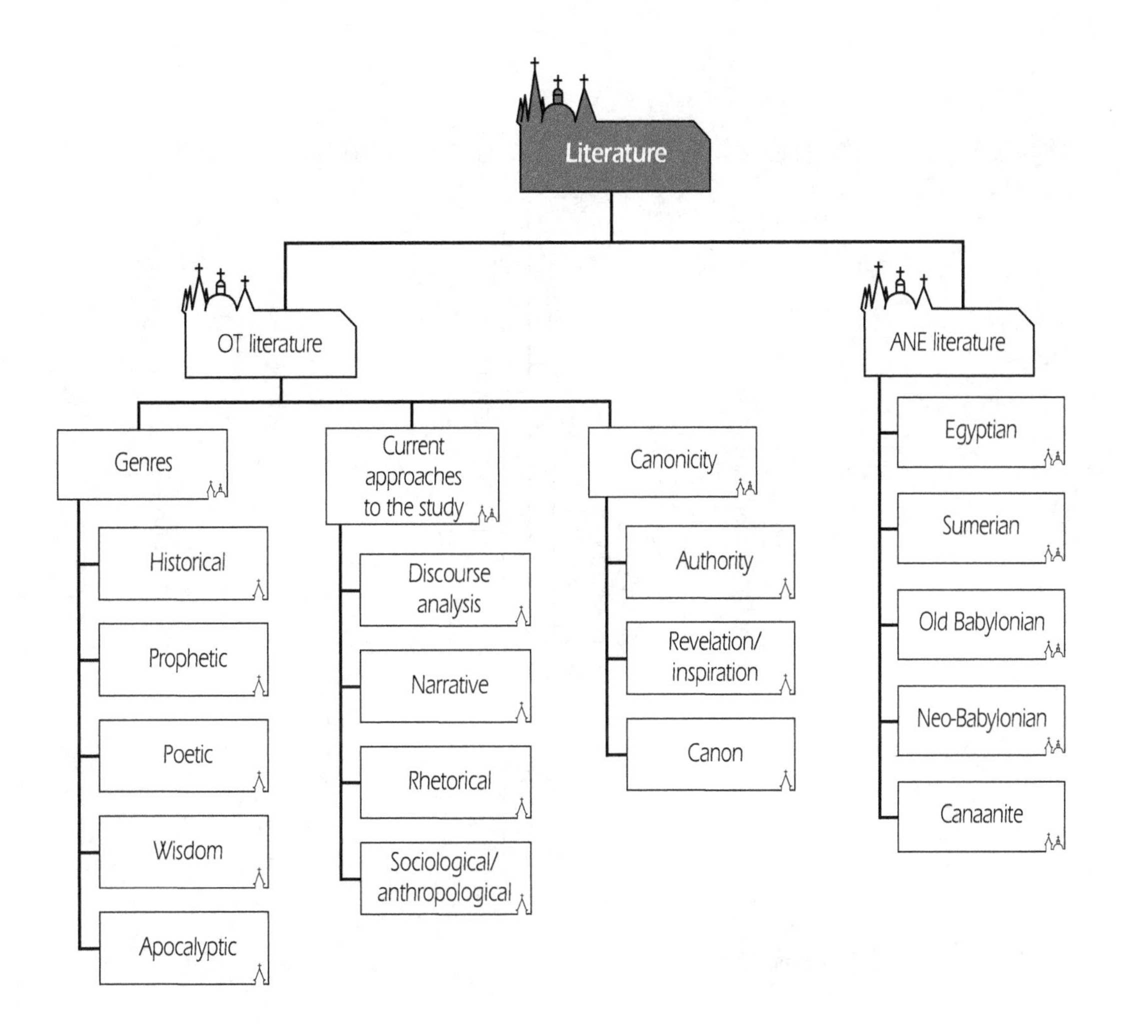

Literature
OT literature
ANE literature
Genres
Historical
Prophetic
Poetic
Wisdom
Apocalyptic
Current approaches to the study
Discourse analysis
Narrative
Rhetorical
Sociological/ anthropological
Canonicity
Authority
Revelation/ inspiration
Canon
Egyptian
Sumerian
Old Babylonian
Neo-Babylonian
Canaanite

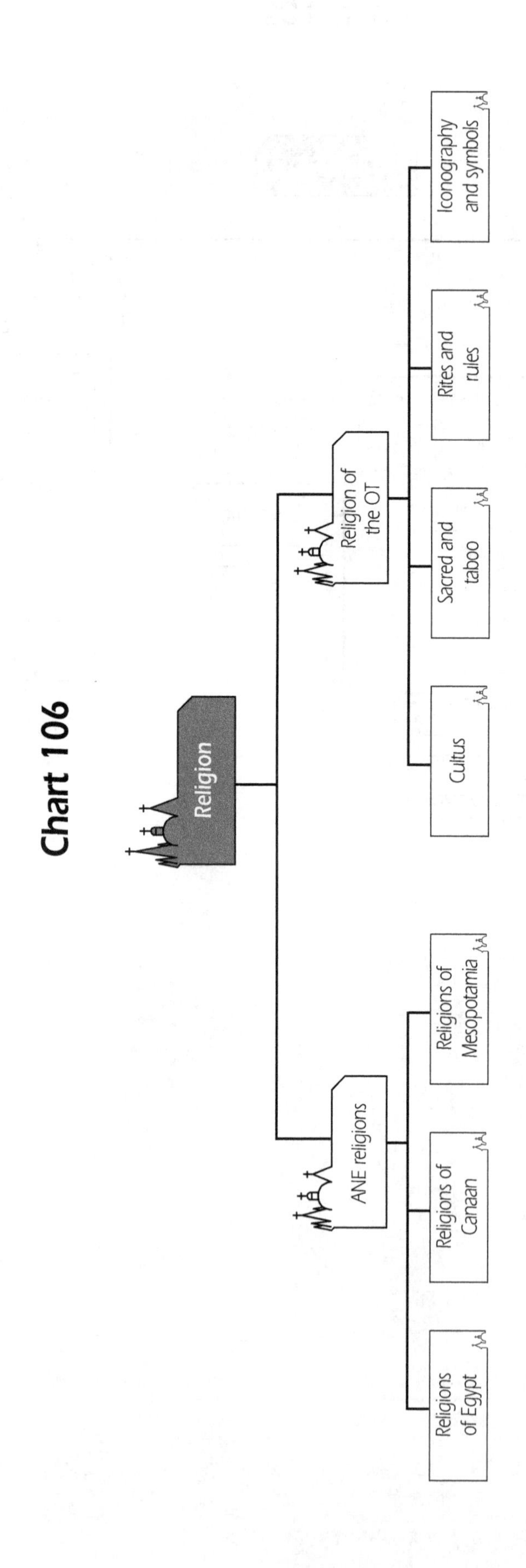
Chart 106
Religion
ANE religions
Religion of the OT
Religions of Egypt
Religions of Canaan
Religions of Mesopotamia
Cultus
Sacred and taboo
Rites and rules
Iconography and symbols

Chart 107

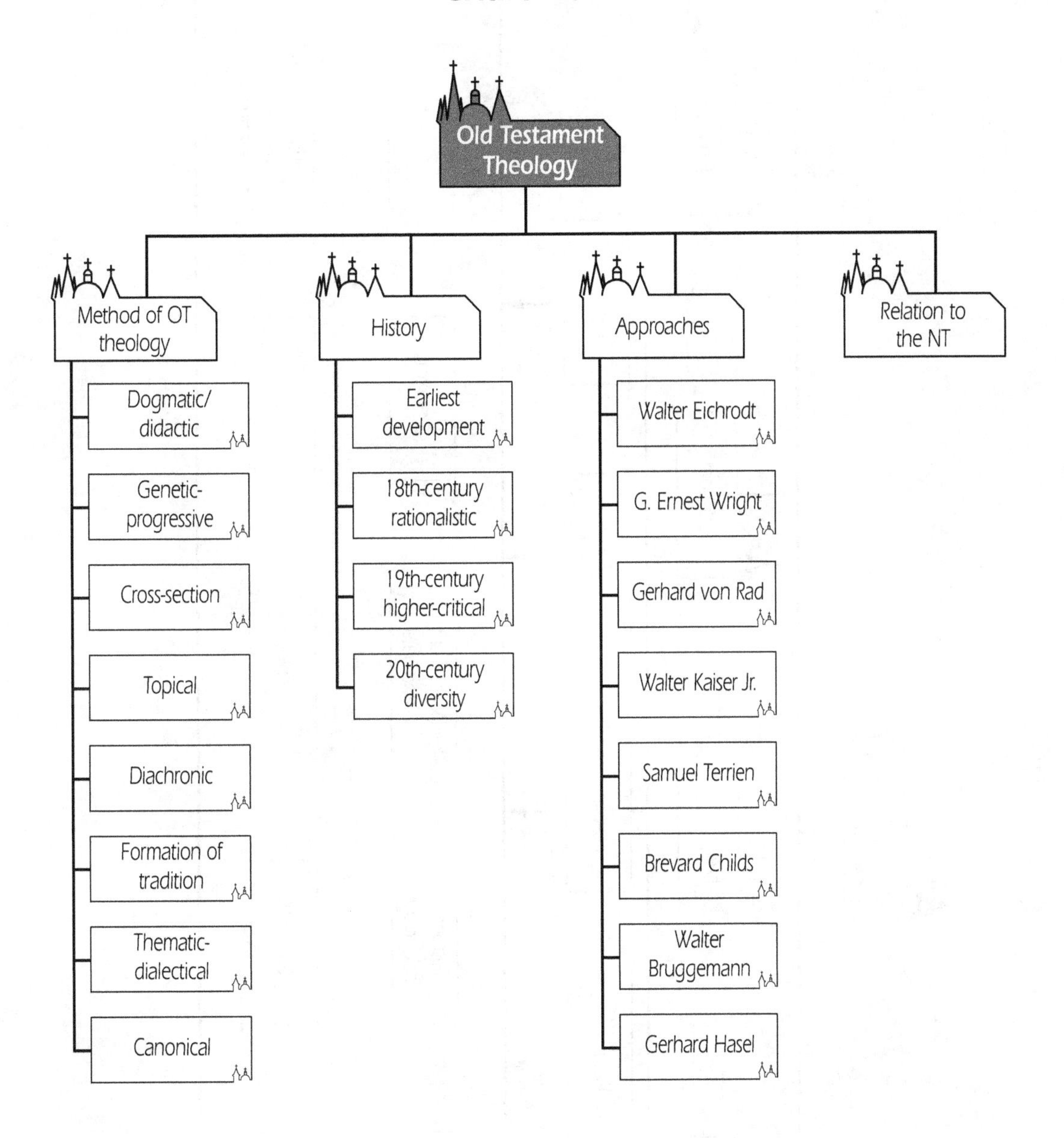
Old Testament Theology
Method of OT theology
Dogmatic/ didactic
Genetic-progressive
Cross-section
Topical
Diachronic
Formation of tradition
Thematic-dialectical
Canonical
History
Earliest development
18th-century rationalistic
19th-century higher-critical
20th-century diversity
Approaches
Walter Eichrodt
G. Ernest Wright
Gerhard von Rad
Walter Kaiser Jr.
Samuel Terrien
Brevard Childs
Walter Bruggemann
Gerhard Hasel
Relation to the NT

Chart 108

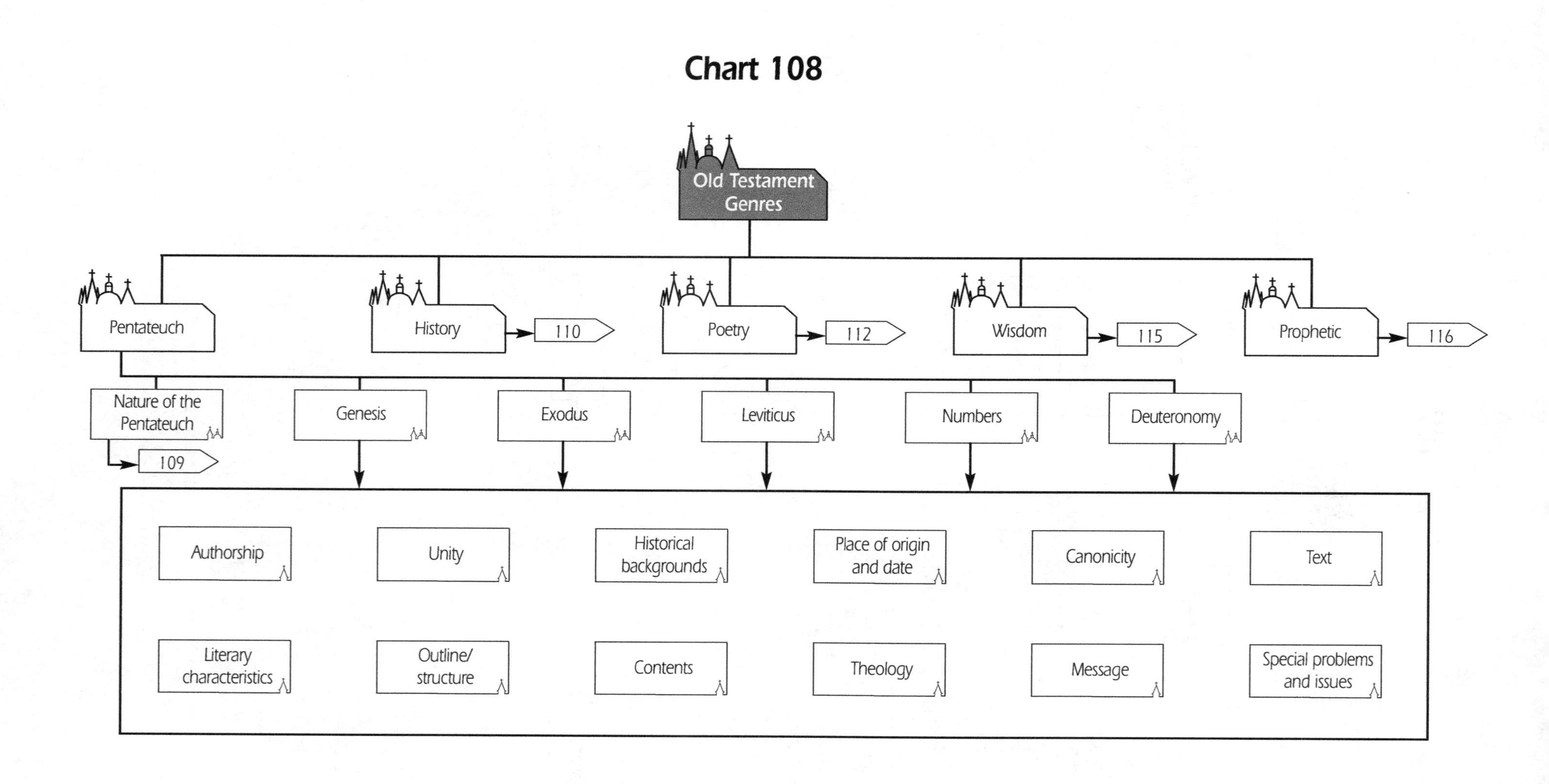
Old Testament Genres
Pentateuch
History
110
Poetry
112
Wisdom
115
Prophetic
116
Nature of the Pentateuch
109
Genesis
Exodus
Leviticus
Numbers
Deuteronomy
Authorship
Unity
Historical backgrounds
Place of origin and date
Canonicity
Text
Literary characteristics
Outline/ structure
Contents
Theology
Message
Special problems and issues

Chart 109

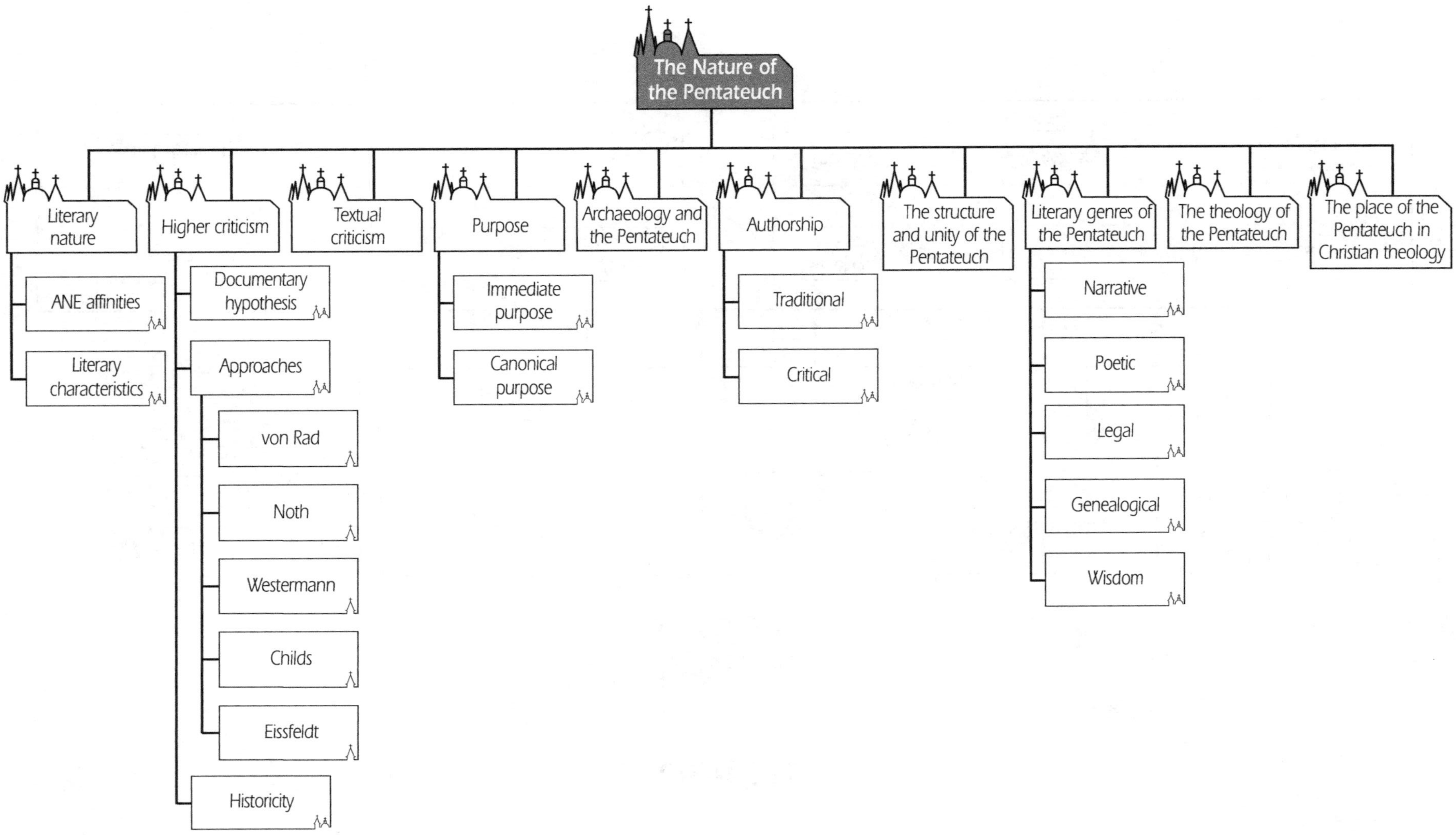

The Nature of the Pentateuch

- Literary nature
  - ANE affinities
  - Literary characteristics
- Higher criticism
  - Documentary hypothesis
  - Approaches
    - von Rad
    - Noth
    - Westermann
    - Childs
    - Eissfeldt
  - Historicity
- Textual criticism
- Purpose
  - Immediate purpose
  - Canonical purpose
- Archaeology and the Pentateuch
- Authorship
  - Traditional
  - Critical
- The structure and unity of the Pentateuch
- Literary genres of the Pentateuch
  - Narrative
  - Poetic
  - Legal
  - Genealogical
  - Wisdom
- The theology of the Pentateuch
- The place of the Pentateuch in Christian theology

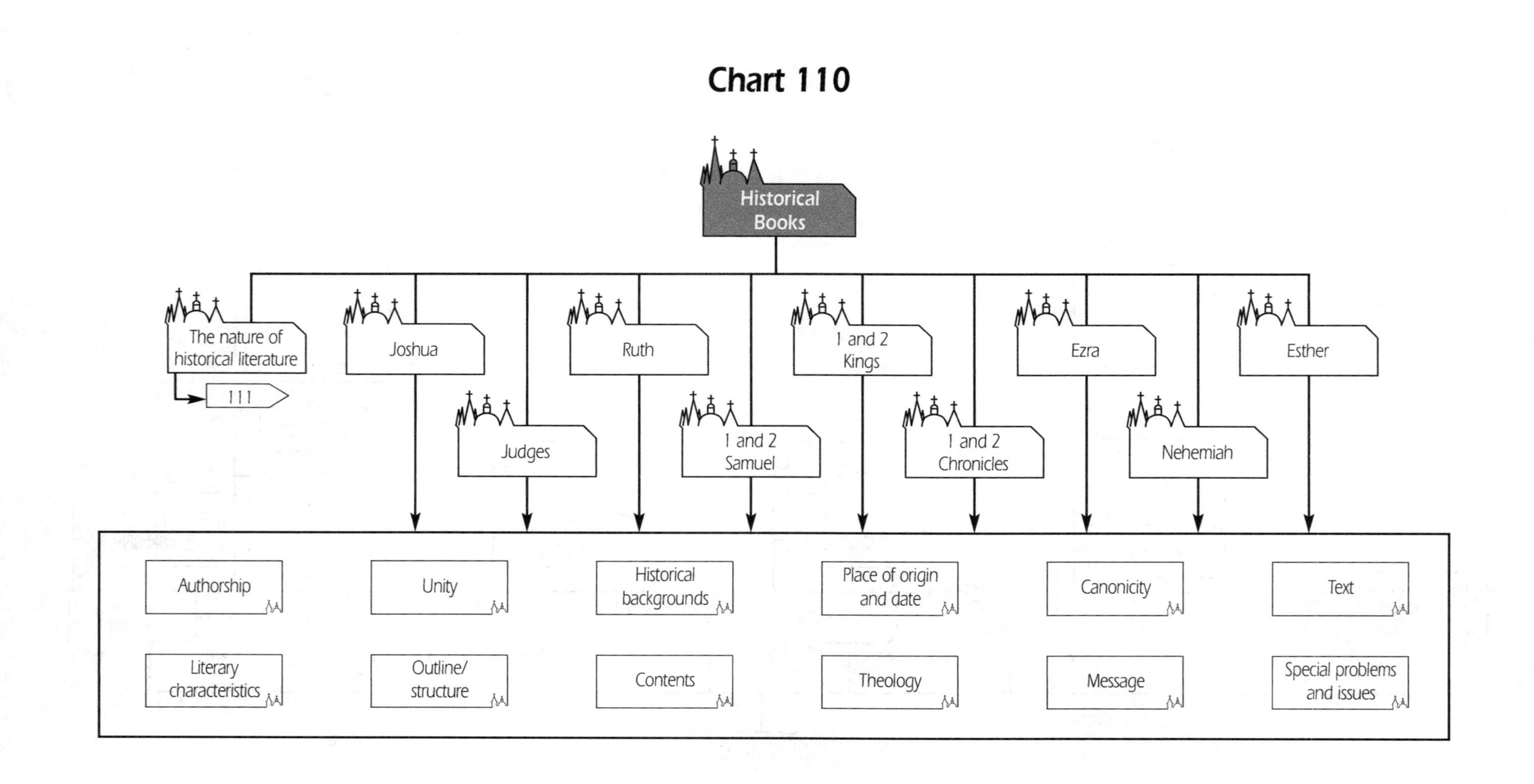
Chart 110
Historical Books
The nature of historical literature
111
Joshua
Judges
Ruth
1 and 2 Samuel
1 and 2 Kings
1 and 2 Chronicles
Ezra
Nehemiah
Esther
Authorship
Unity
Historical backgrounds
Place of origin and date
Canonicity
Text
Literary characteristics
Outline/structure
Contents
Theology
Message
Special problems and issues

Chart 111

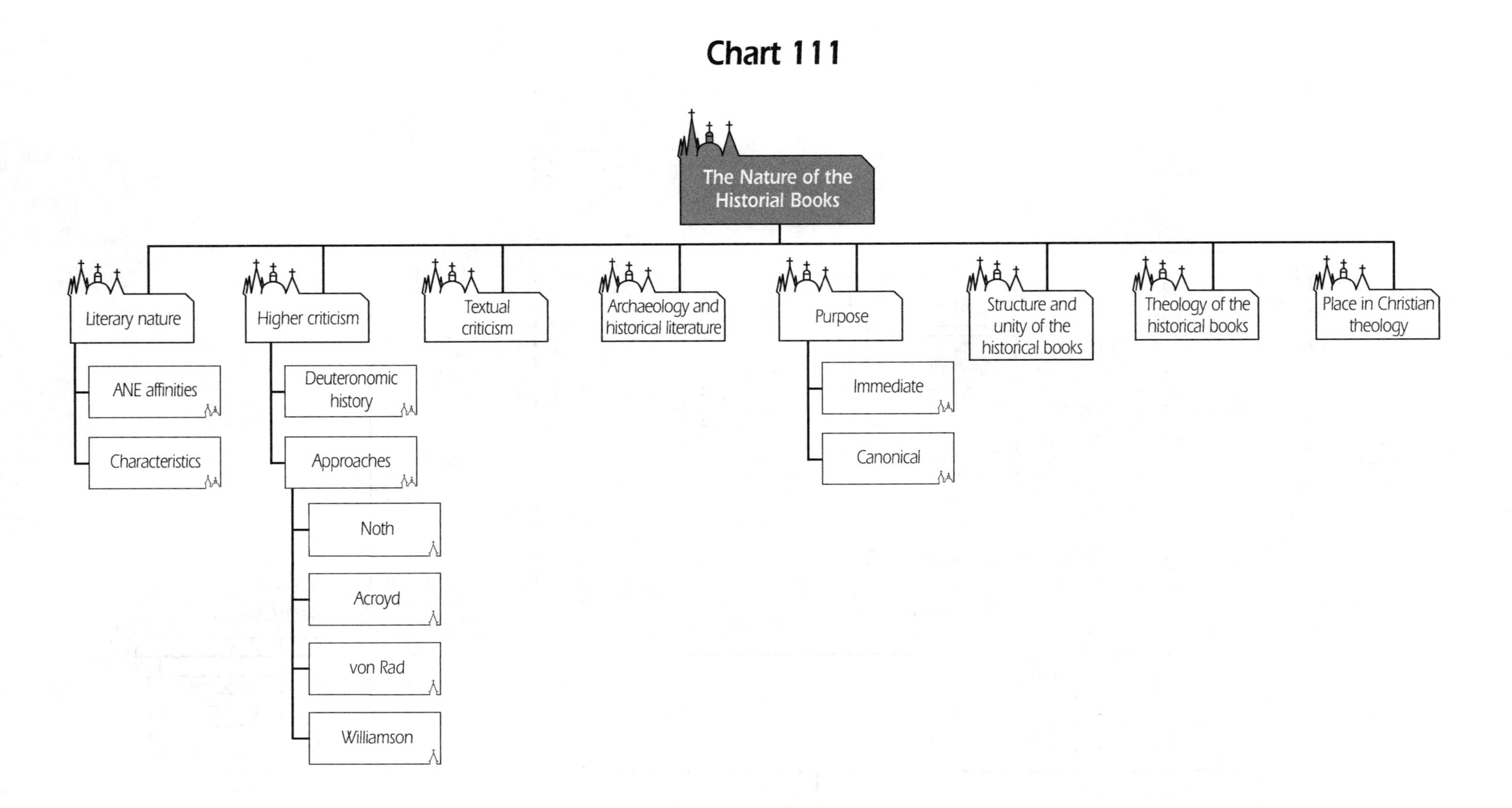

The Nature of the Historial Books
Literary nature
ANE affinities
Characteristics
Higher criticism
Deuteronomic history
Approaches
Noth
Acroyd
von Rad
Williamson
Textual criticism
Archaeology and historical literature
Purpose
Immediate
Canonical
Structure and unity of the historical books
Theology of the historical books
Place in Christian theology

Chart 112

- Poetry
  - The nature of biblical poetry
    - Definition of poetry
    - ANE parallels
    - Characteristics of Hebrew poetry
      - Parallelism
      - Accentuation
      - Meter
      - Figures of speech
    - Types of Hebrew poetry
      - Work songs
      - Wedding songs
      - Dirges
      - Laments
      - Thanksgiving songs
      - Praises
      - Royal songs
      - Wisdom songs
      - Pilgrim songs
      - Enthronement songs
    - Effects of Hebrew poetry
      - Intellectual connotations
      - Emotional connotations
      - Spiritual connotations
      - Allusion effects
      - Sound effects
    - Approaches
      - Dogmatic and liturgical
      - Literary-analytical
      - Traditional and historical
      - Form critical
      - Cultic
  - Psalms
    - 113
  - Song of Songs
    - Authorship
    - Unity
    - Historical background
    - Place of origin and date
    - Canonicity
    - Text
    - Literary characteristics
    - Outline/structure
    - Contents
    - Theology
    - Message
    - Special problems and issues

Chart 113

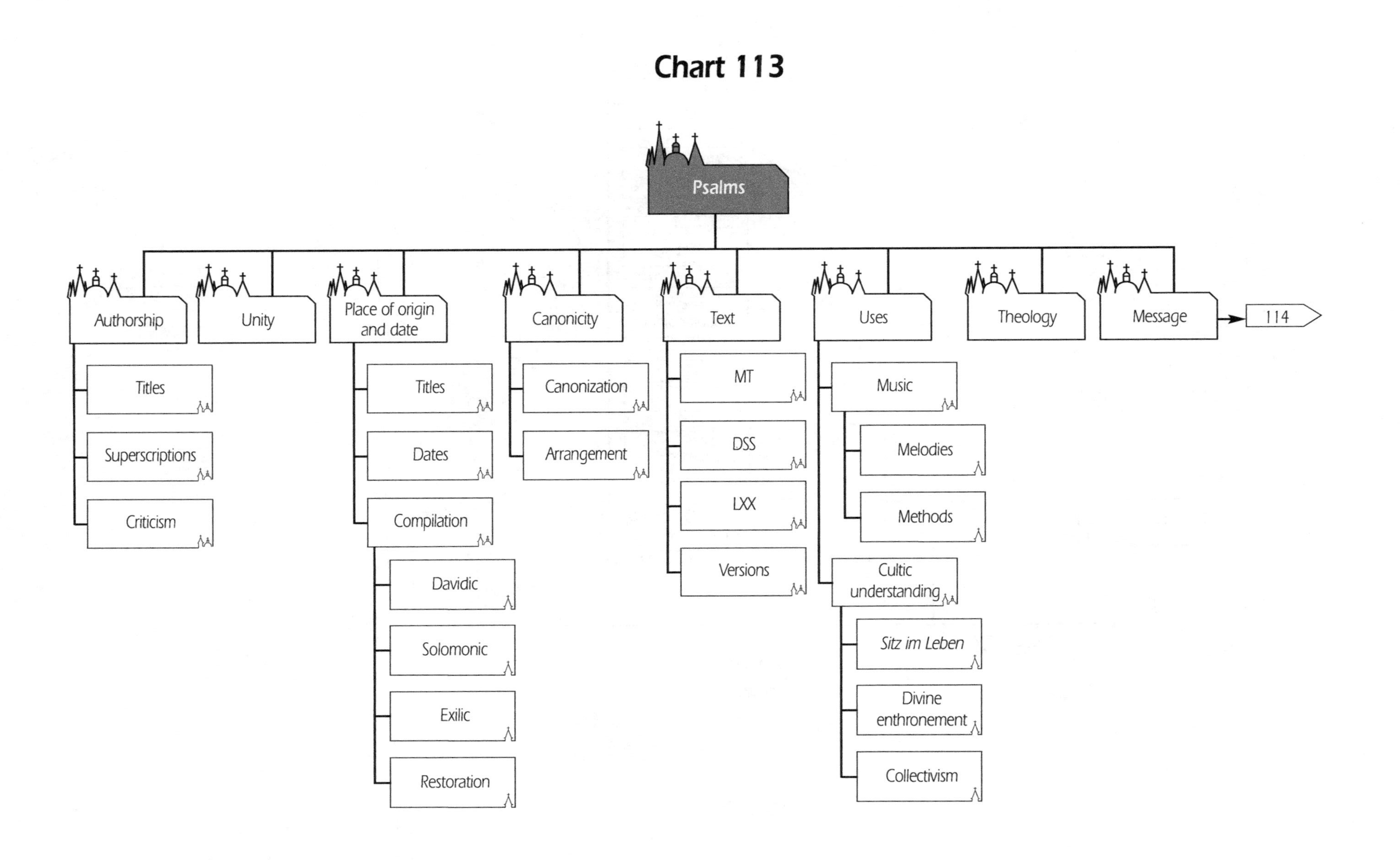
Psalms
Authorship
Titles
Superscriptions
Criticism
Unity
Place of origin and date
Titles
Dates
Compilation
Davidic
Solomonic
Exilic
Restoration
Canonicity
Canonization
Arrangement
Text
MT
DSS
LXX
Versions
Uses
Music
Melodies
Methods
Cultic understanding
Sitz im Leben
Divine enthronement
Collectivism
Theology
Message
114

Chart 114

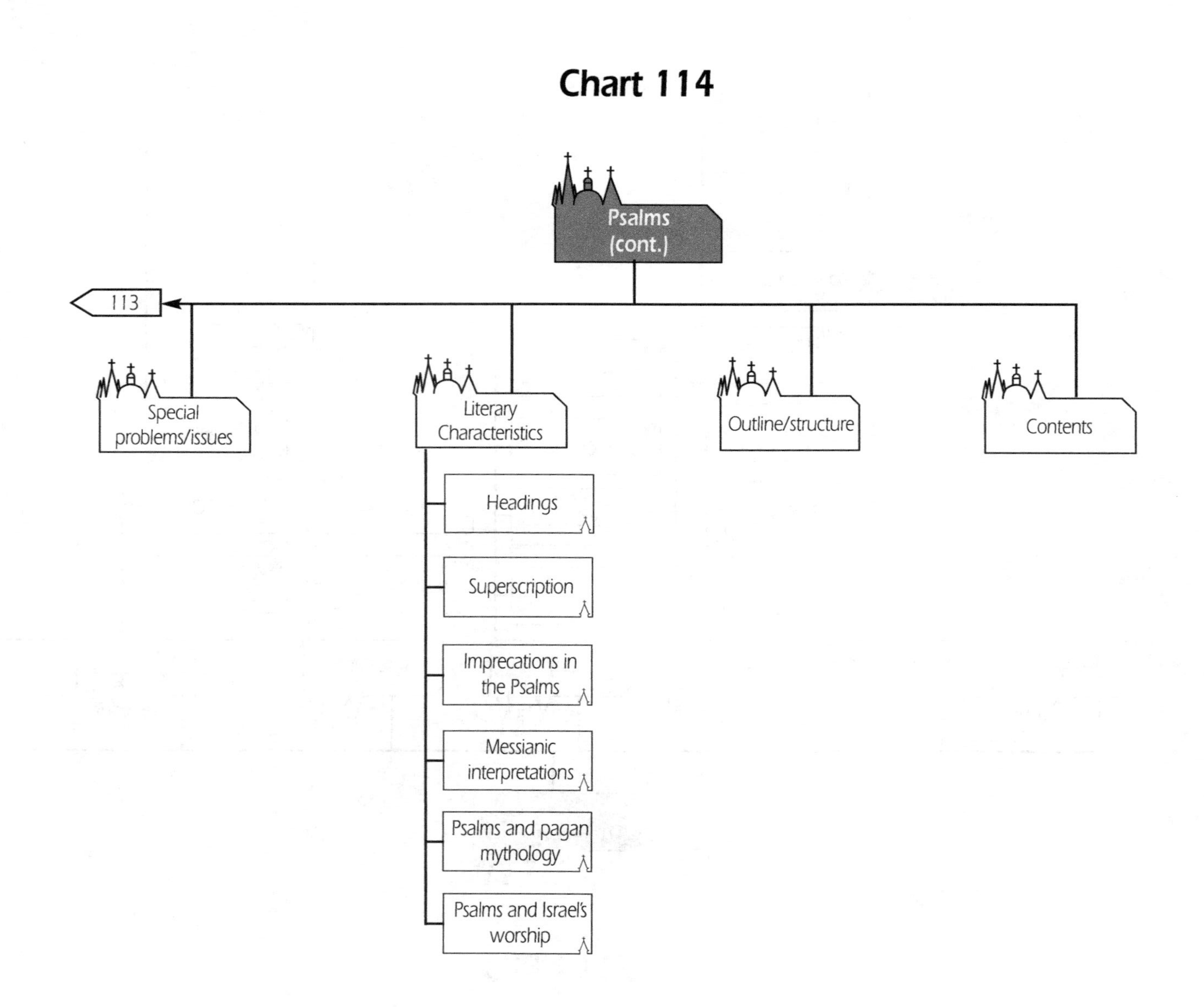
Psalms (cont.)
113
Special problems/issues
Literary Characteristics
Headings
Superscription
Imprecations in the Psalms
Messianic interpretations
Psalms and pagan mythology
Psalms and Israel's worship
Outline/structure
Contents

Chart 115

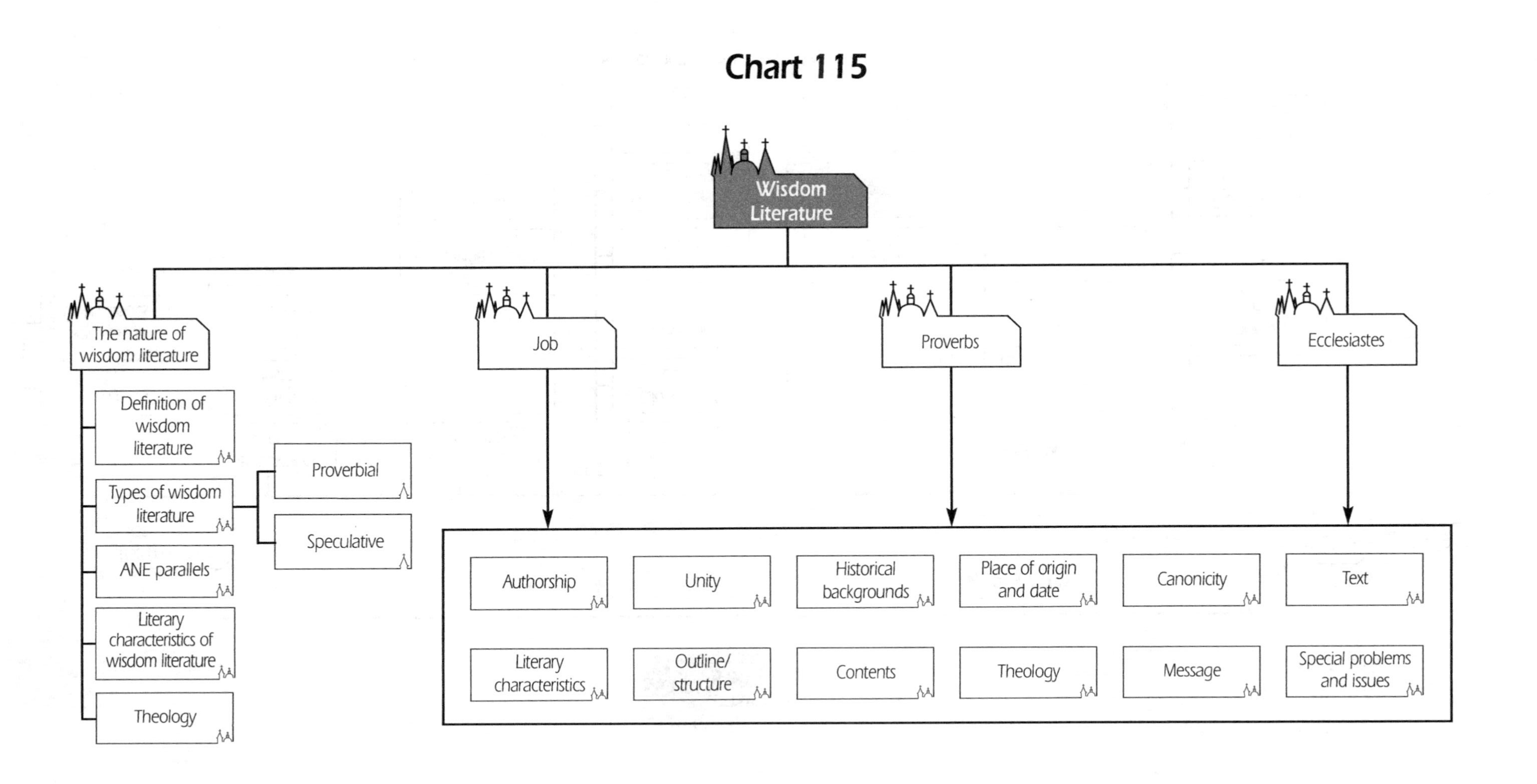

Wisdom Literature
The nature of wisdom literature
Definition of wisdom literature
Types of wisdom literature
Proverbial
Speculative
ANE parallels
Literary characteristics of wisdom literature
Theology
Job
Proverbs
Ecclesiastes
Authorship
Unity
Historical backgrounds
Place of origin and date
Canonicity
Text
Literary characteristics
Outline/ structure
Contents
Theology
Message
Special problems and issues

Chart 116

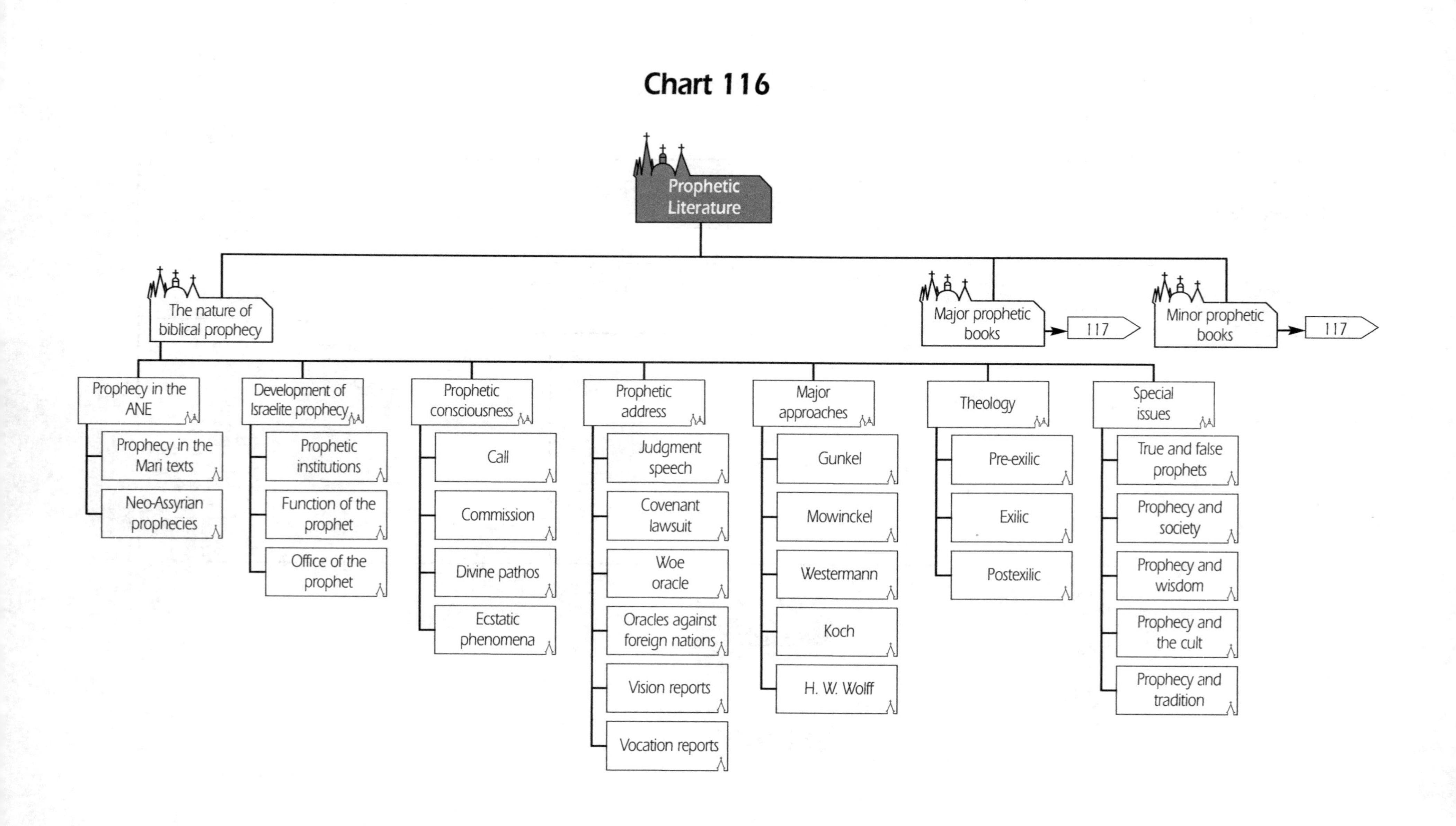
Prophetic Literature
The nature of biblical prophecy
Major prophetic books
117
Minor prophetic books
117
Prophecy in the ANE
Prophecy in the Mari texts
Neo-Assyrian prophecies
Development of Israelite prophecy
Prophetic institutions
Function of the prophet
Office of the prophet
Prophetic consciousness
Call
Commission
Divine pathos
Ecstatic phenomena
Prophetic address
Judgment speech
Covenant lawsuit
Woe oracle
Oracles against foreign nations
Vision reports
Vocation reports
Major approaches
Gunkel
Mowinckel
Westermann
Koch
H. W. Wolff
Theology
Pre-exilic
Exilic
Postexilic
Special issues
True and false prophets
Prophecy and society
Prophecy and wisdom
Prophecy and the cult
Prophecy and tradition

Chart 117

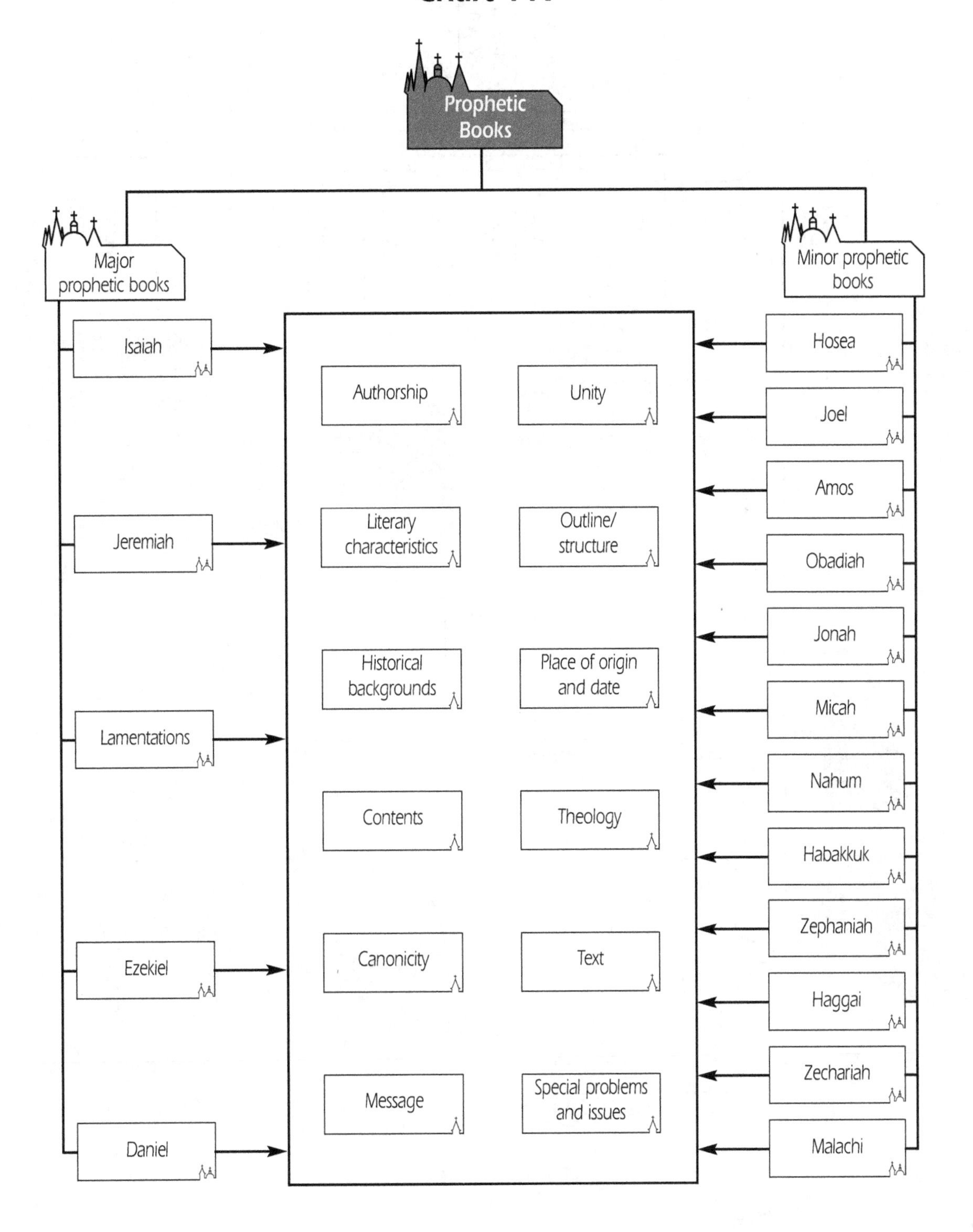

Prophetic Books
Major prophetic books
Minor prophetic books
Isaiah
Jeremiah
Lamentations
Ezekiel
Daniel
Authorship
Unity
Literary characteristics
Outline/ structure
Historical backgrounds
Place of origin and date
Contents
Theology
Canonicity
Text
Message
Special problems and issues
Hosea
Joel
Amos
Obadiah
Jonah
Micah
Nahum
Habakkuk
Zephaniah
Haggai
Zechariah
Malachi

Chart 118

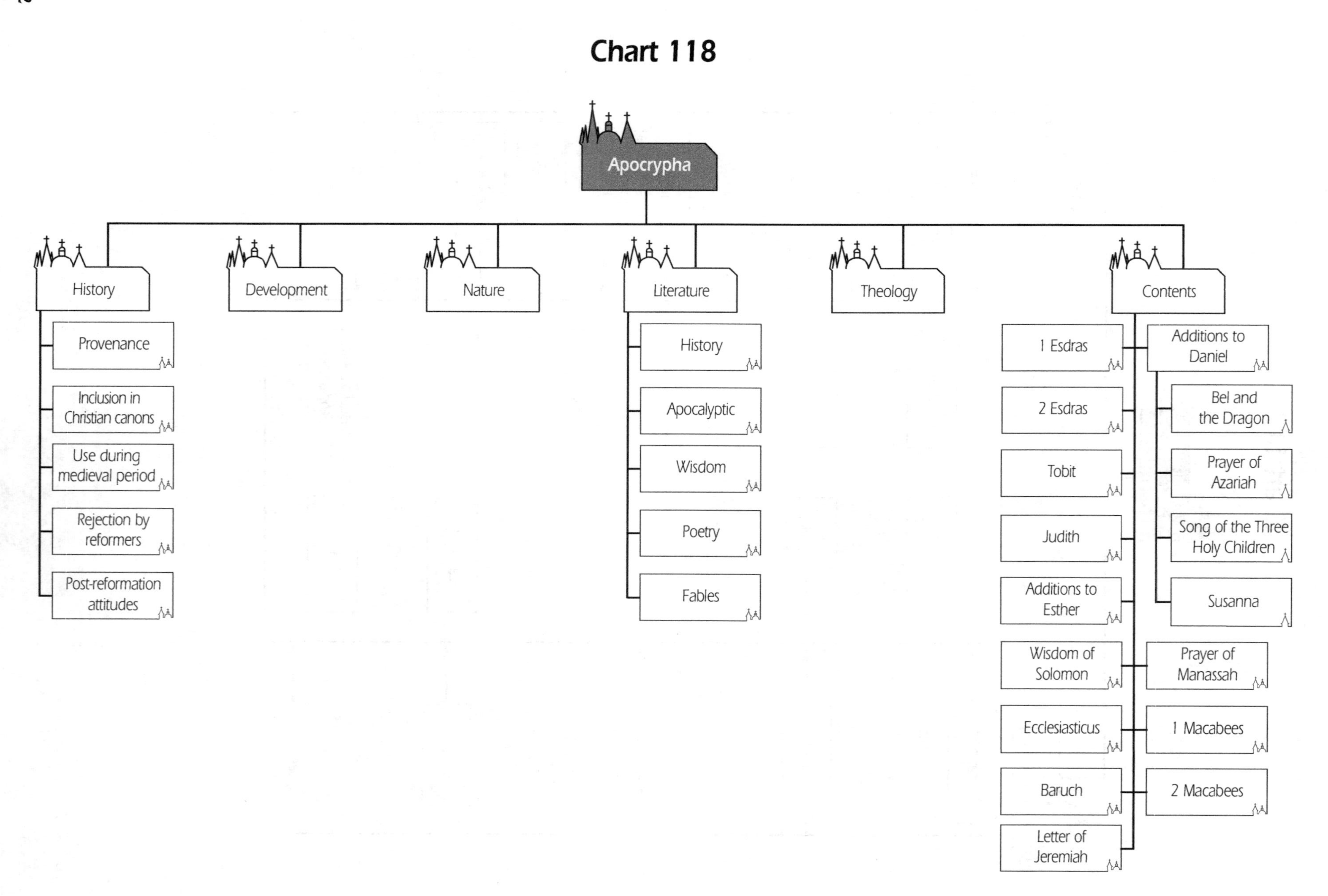
Apocrypha
History
Provenance
Inclusion in Christian canons
Use during medieval period
Rejection by reformers
Post-reformation attitudes
Development
Nature
Literature
History
Apocalyptic
Wisdom
Poetry
Fables
Theology
Contents
1 Esdras
2 Esdras
Tobit
Judith
Additions to Esther
Wisdom of Solomon
Ecclesiasticus
Baruch
Letter of Jeremiah
Additions to Daniel
Bel and the Dragon
Prayer of Azariah
Song of the Three Holy Children
Susanna
Prayer of Manassah
1 Macabees
2 Macabees

Chart 119

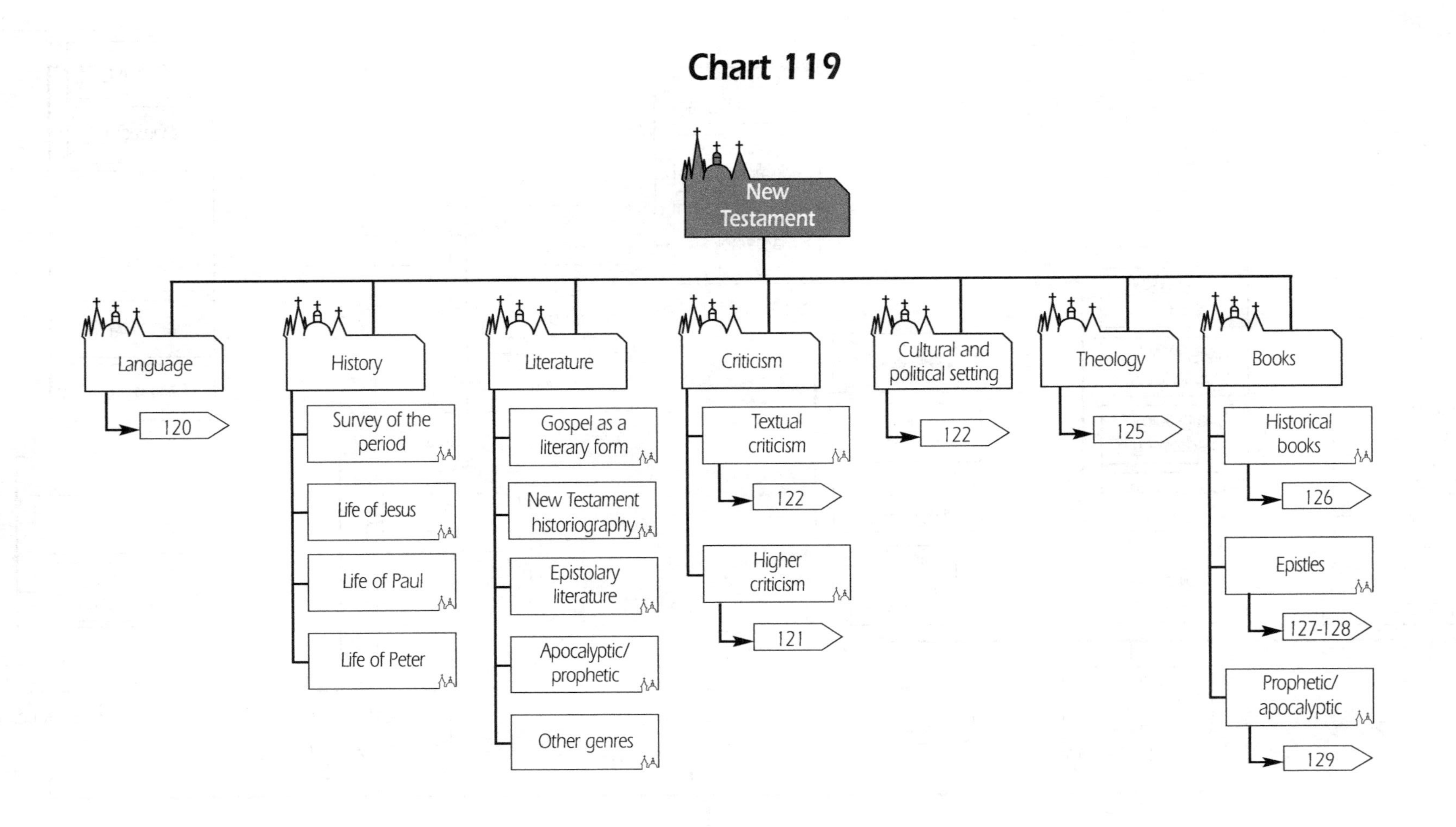
New Testament
Language
120
History
Survey of the period
Life of Jesus
Life of Paul
Life of Peter
Literature
Gospel as a literary form
New Testament historiography
Epistolary literature
Apocalyptic/ prophetic
Other genres
Criticism
Textual criticism
122
Higher criticism
121
Cultural and political setting
122
Theology
125
Books
Historical books
126
Epistles
127-128
Prophetic/ apocalyptic
129

Chart 120

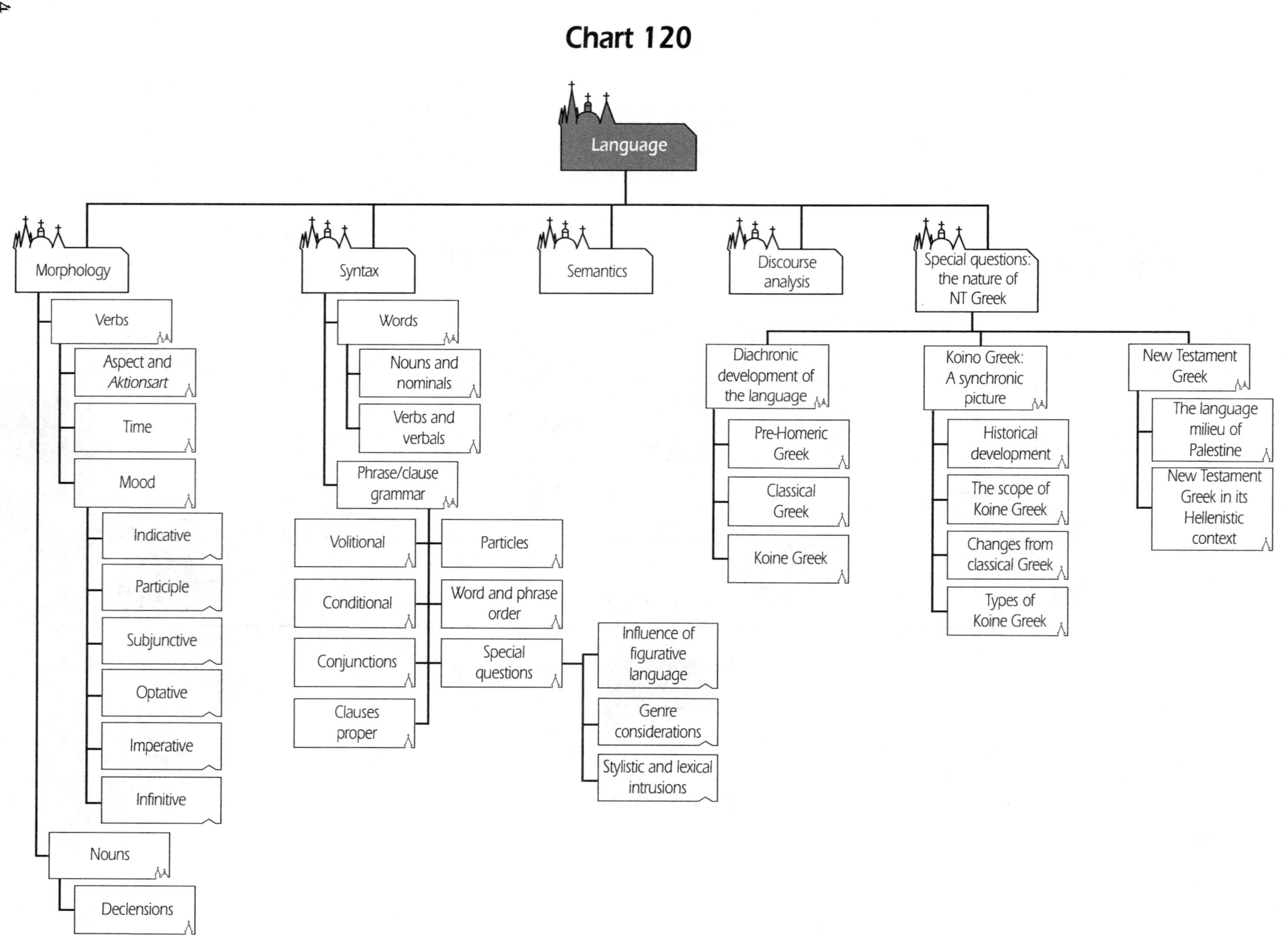

Language
Morphology
Verbs
Aspect and Aktionsart
Time
Mood
Indicative
Participle
Subjunctive
Optative
Imperative
Infinitive
Nouns
Declensions
Syntax
Words
Nouns and nominals
Verbs and verbals
Phrase/clause grammar
Volitional
Conditional
Conjunctions
Clauses proper
Particles
Word and phrase order
Special questions
Influence of figurative language
Genre considerations
Stylistic and lexical intrusions
Semantics
Discourse analysis
Special questions: the nature of NT Greek
Diachronic development of the language
Pre-Homeric Greek
Classical Greek
Koine Greek
Koino Greek: A synchronic picture
Historical development
The scope of Koine Greek
Changes from classical Greek
Types of Koine Greek
New Testament Greek
The language milieu of Palestine
New Testament Greek in its Hellenistic context

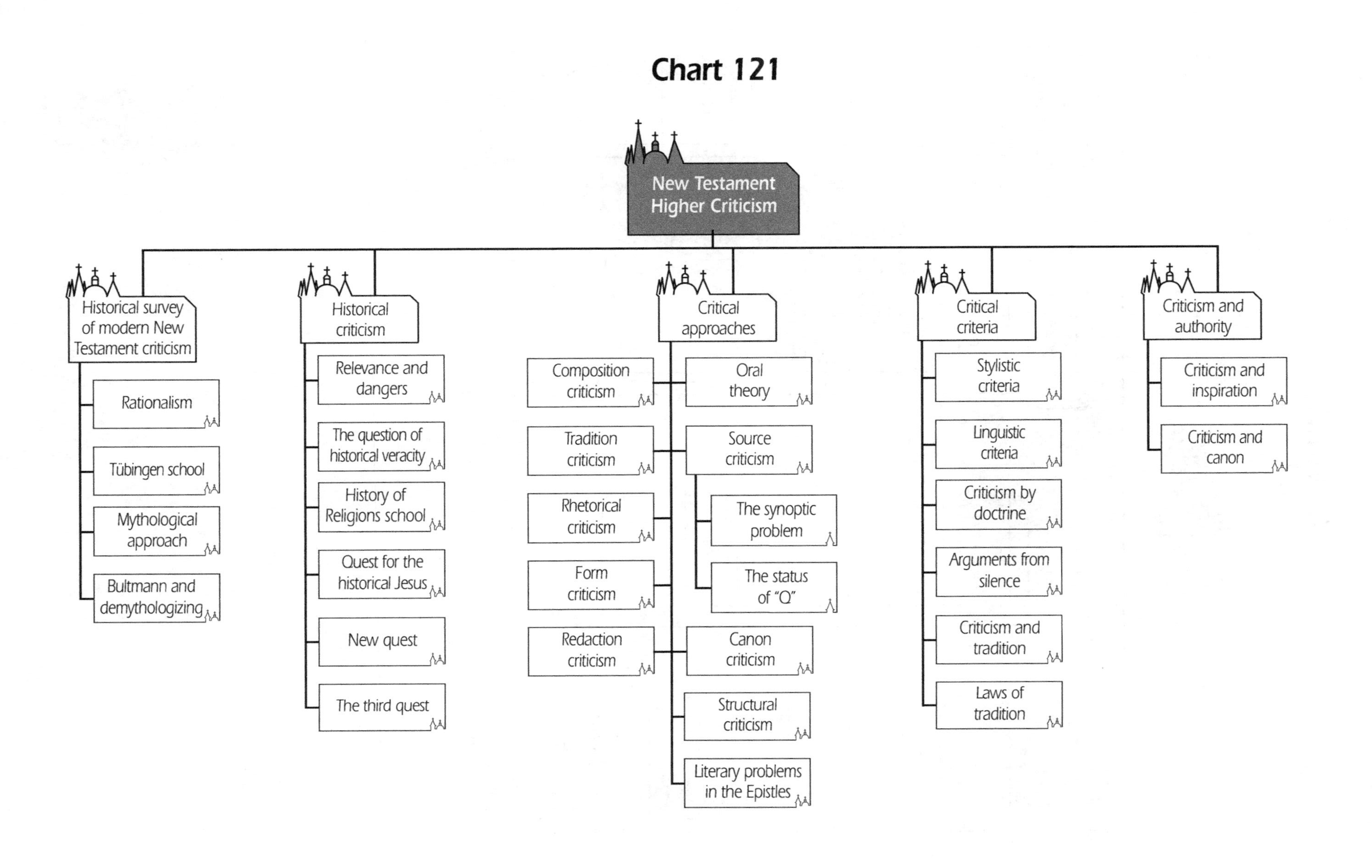
Chart 121
New Testament Higher Criticism
Historical survey of modern New Testament criticism
Rationalism
Tübingen school
Mythological approach
Bultmann and demythologizing
Historical criticism
Relevance and dangers
The question of historical veracity
History of Religions school
Quest for the historical Jesus
New quest
The third quest
Critical approaches
Composition criticism
Tradition criticism
Rhetorical criticism
Form criticism
Redaction criticism
Oral theory
Source criticism
The synoptic problem
The status of "Q"
Canon criticism
Structural criticism
Literary problems in the Epistles
Critical criteria
Stylistic criteria
Linguistic criteria
Criticism by doctrine
Arguments from silence
Criticism and tradition
Laws of tradition
Criticism and authority
Criticism and inspiration
Criticism and canon

Chart 122

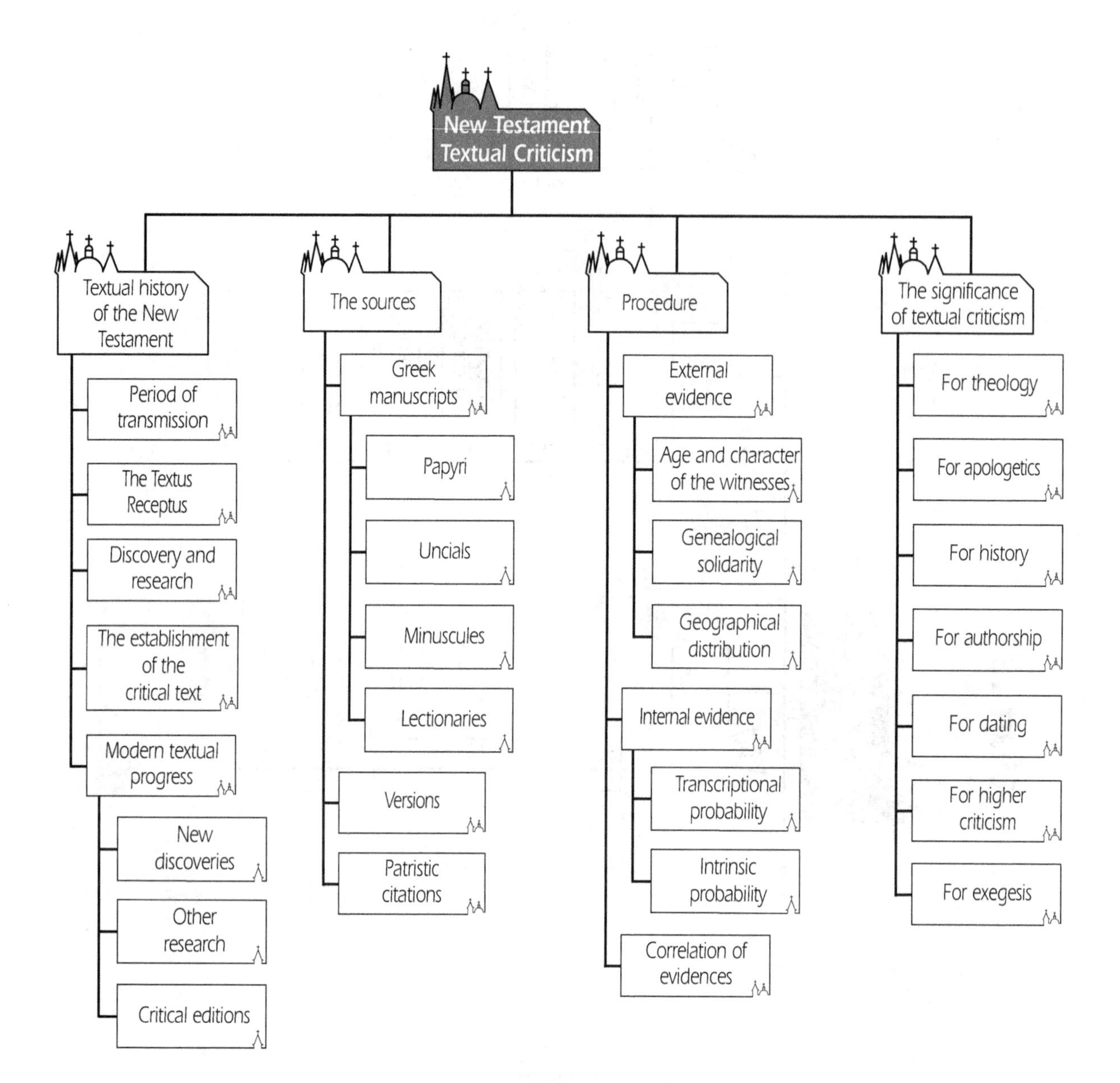

New Testament Textual Criticism
Textual history of the New Testament
Period of transmission
The Textus Receptus
Discovery and research
The establishment of the critical text
Modern textual progress
New discoveries
Other research
Critical editions
The sources
Greek manuscripts
Papyri
Uncials
Minuscules
Lectionaries
Versions
Patristic citations
Procedure
External evidence
Age and character of the witnesses
Genealogical solidarity
Geographical distribution
Internal evidence
Transcriptional probability
Intrinsic probability
Correlation of evidences
The significance of textual criticism
For theology
For apologetics
For history
For authorship
For dating
For higher criticism
For exegesis

Chart 123

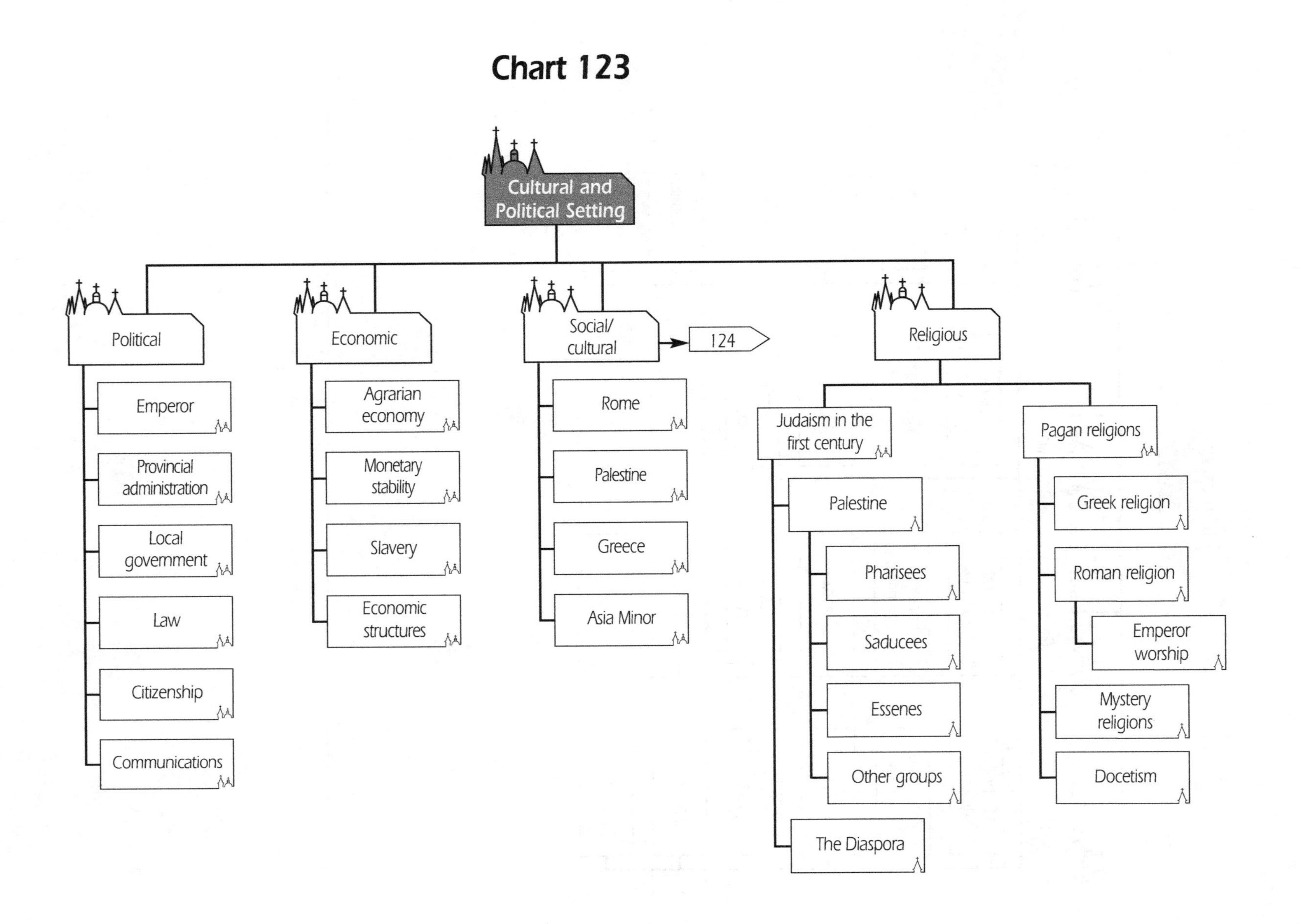
Cultural and Political Setting
Political
Emperor
Provincial administration
Local government
Law
Citizenship
Communications
Economic
Agrarian economy
Monetary stability
Slavery
Economic structures
Social/cultural
124
Rome
Palestine
Greece
Asia Minor
Religious
Judaism in the first century
Palestine
Pharisees
Saducees
Essenes
Other groups
The Diaspora
Pagan religions
Greek religion
Roman religion
Emperor worship
Mystery religions
Docetism

Chart 124

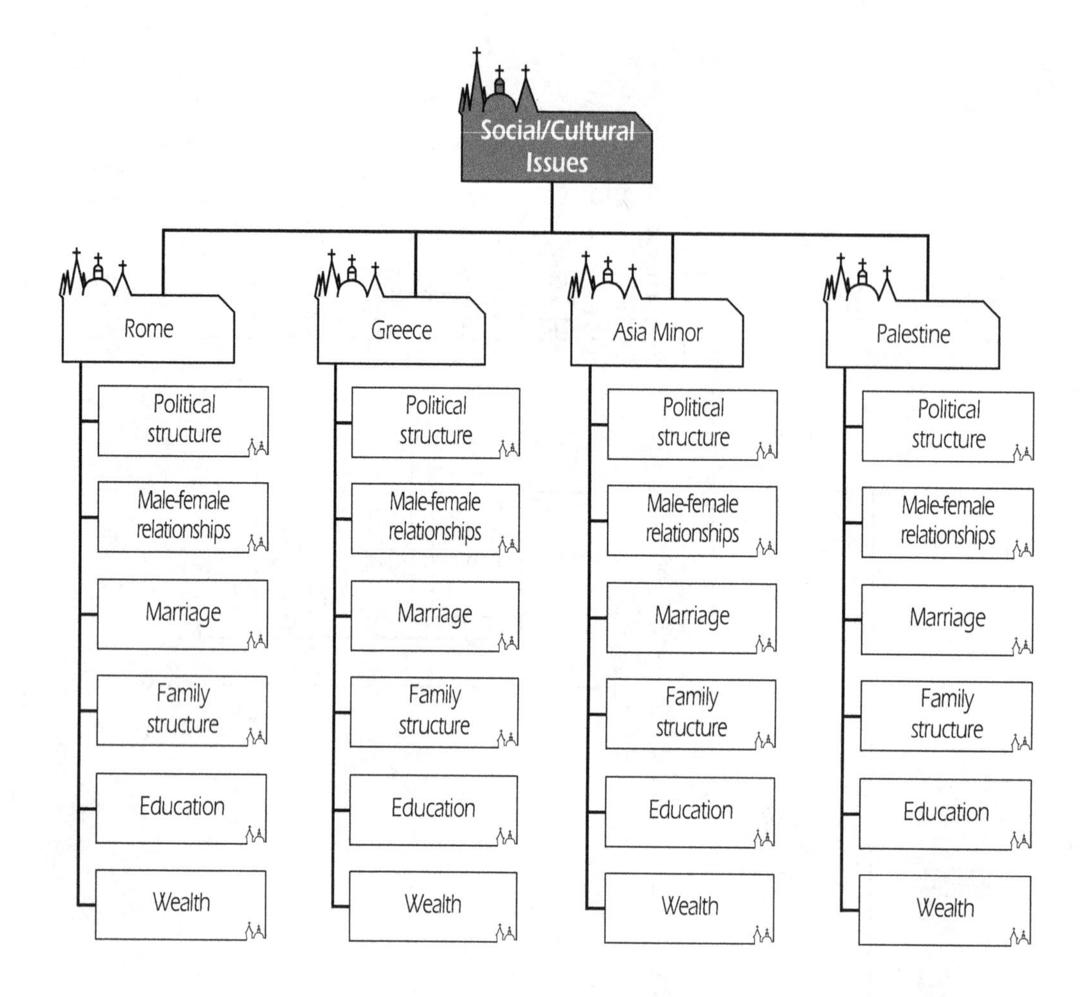

Social/Cultural Issues
Rome
Political structure
Male-female relationships
Marriage
Family structure
Education
Wealth
Greece
Political structure
Male-female relationships
Marriage
Family structure
Education
Wealth
Asia Minor
Political structure
Male-female relationships
Marriage
Family structure
Education
Wealth
Palestine
Political structure
Male-female relationships
Marriage
Family structure
Education
Wealth

Chart 125

- New Testament Theology
  - The history of NT theology
    - Origins
    - Aims
    - Development
  - Approaches
    - Descriptive
    - Topical
  - Content
    - Theology of the Synoptic Gospels
      - The Kingdom of God
      - The Messiah
      - The new age of salvation
      - The Son of Man
      - The God of the Kingdom
      - The Son of God
      - The mystery of the Kingdom
      - The messianic mission
      - The Kingdom and the church
      - The messianic problem
      - The ethics of the Kingdom
      - Eschatology
    - Pauline theology
      - The fatherhood of God
      - "In Christ"
      - Man outside Christ
      - New life in Christ
      - The person of Christ
      - The status of law
      - The Christian life
      - The church
      - The subjective work of Christ: Justification
      - The objective work of Christ: Atonement
      - The Holy Spirit
      - Ethics
      - The Pauline psychology
      - Eschatology
    - Johannine theology
      - Heaven-earth dualism
      - The fatherhood of God
      - Christology
      - Eternal life
      - The Holy Spirit
      - The Christian life
      - Eschatology
    - Other NT theologies
      - Peter
      - James
      - Jude
      - Hebrews
      - Revelation

Chart 126

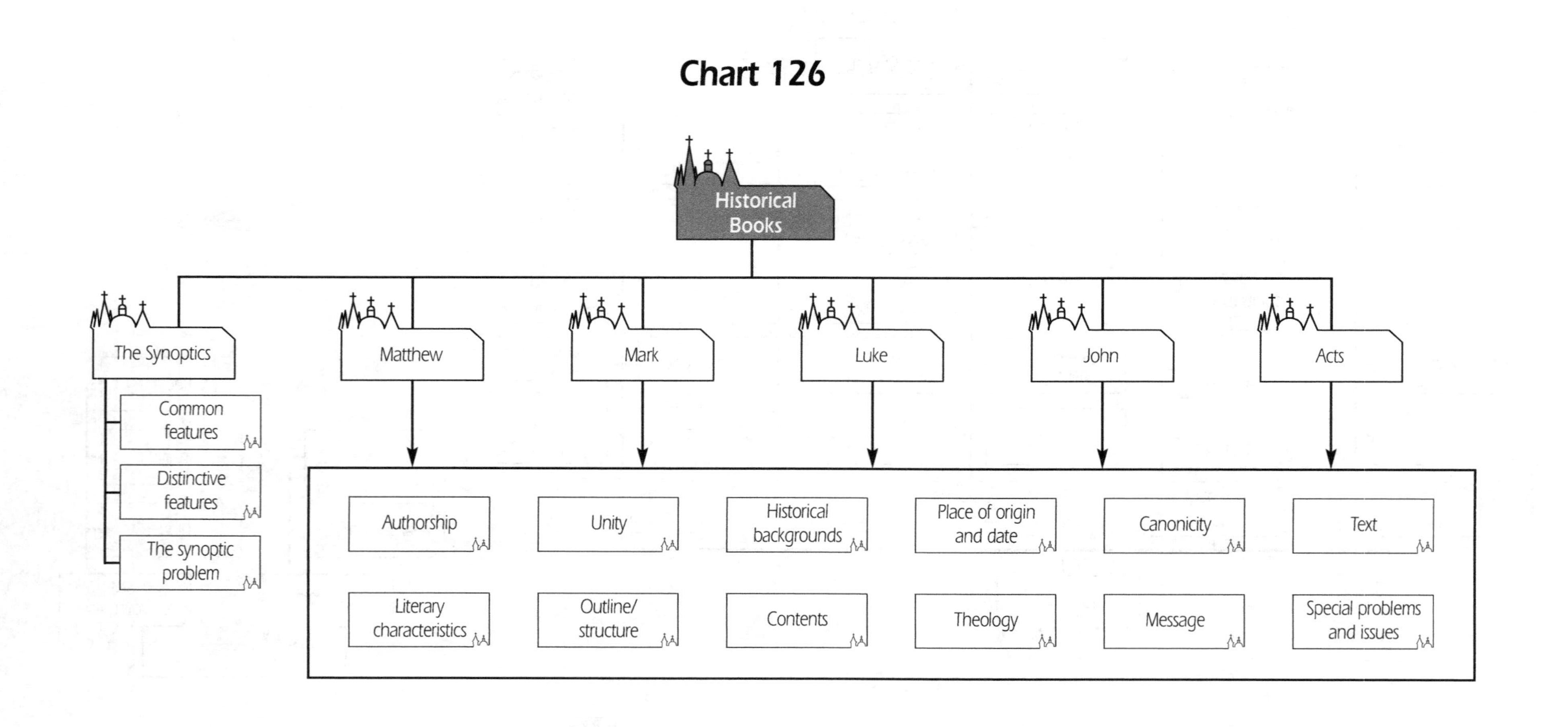
Historical Books
The Synoptics
Common features
Distinctive features
The synoptic problem
Matthew
Mark
Luke
John
Acts
Authorship
Unity
Historical backgrounds
Place of origin and date
Canonicity
Text
Literary characteristics
Outline/ structure
Contents
Theology
Message
Special problems and issues

Chart 127

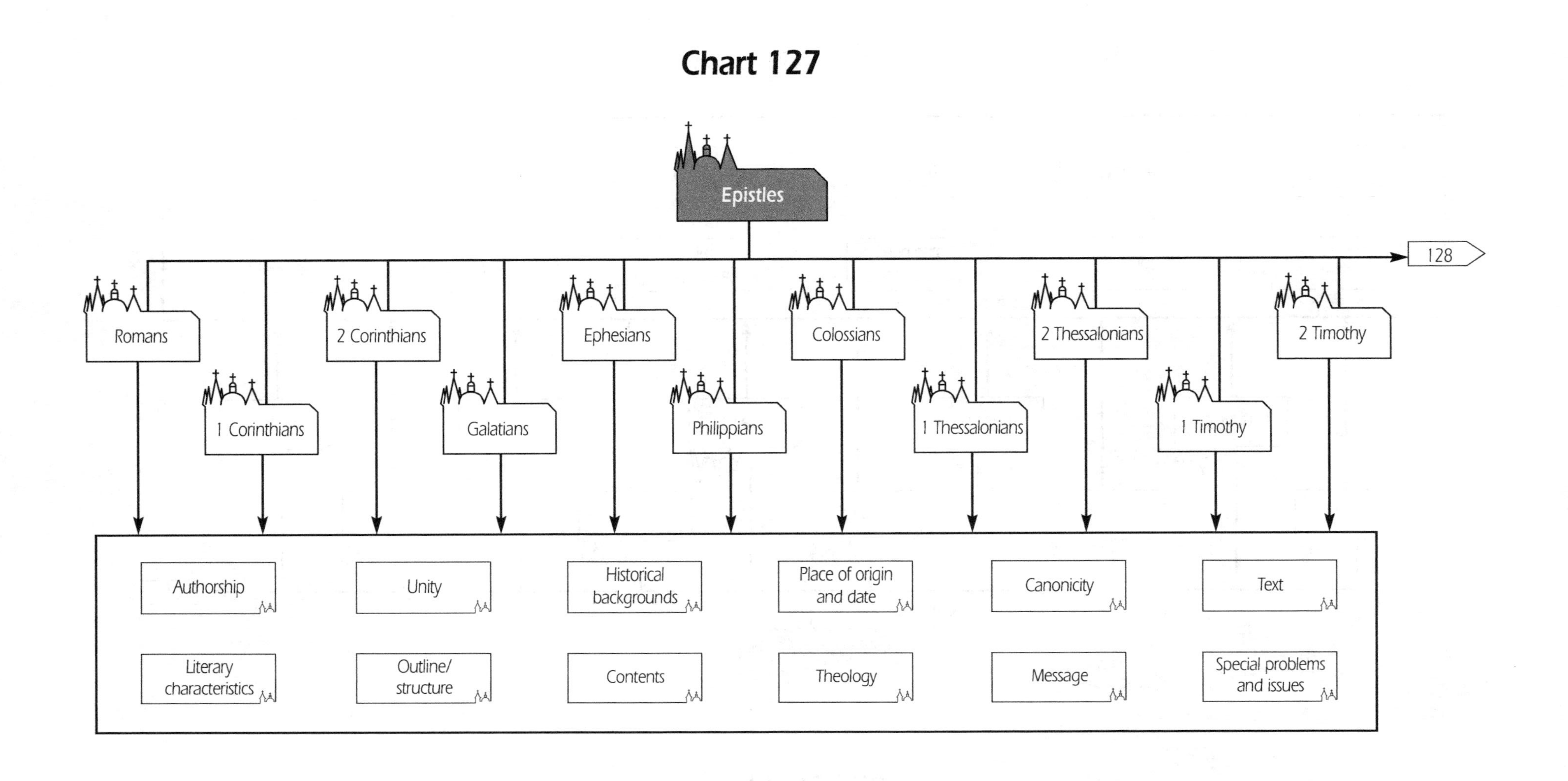

Epistles
Romans
1 Corinthians
2 Corinthians
Galatians
Ephesians
Philippians
Colossians
1 Thessalonians
2 Thessalonians
1 Timothy
2 Timothy
128
Authorship
Literary characteristics
Unity
Outline/ structure
Historical backgrounds
Contents
Place of origin and date
Theology
Canonicity
Message
Text
Special problems and issues

Chart 128

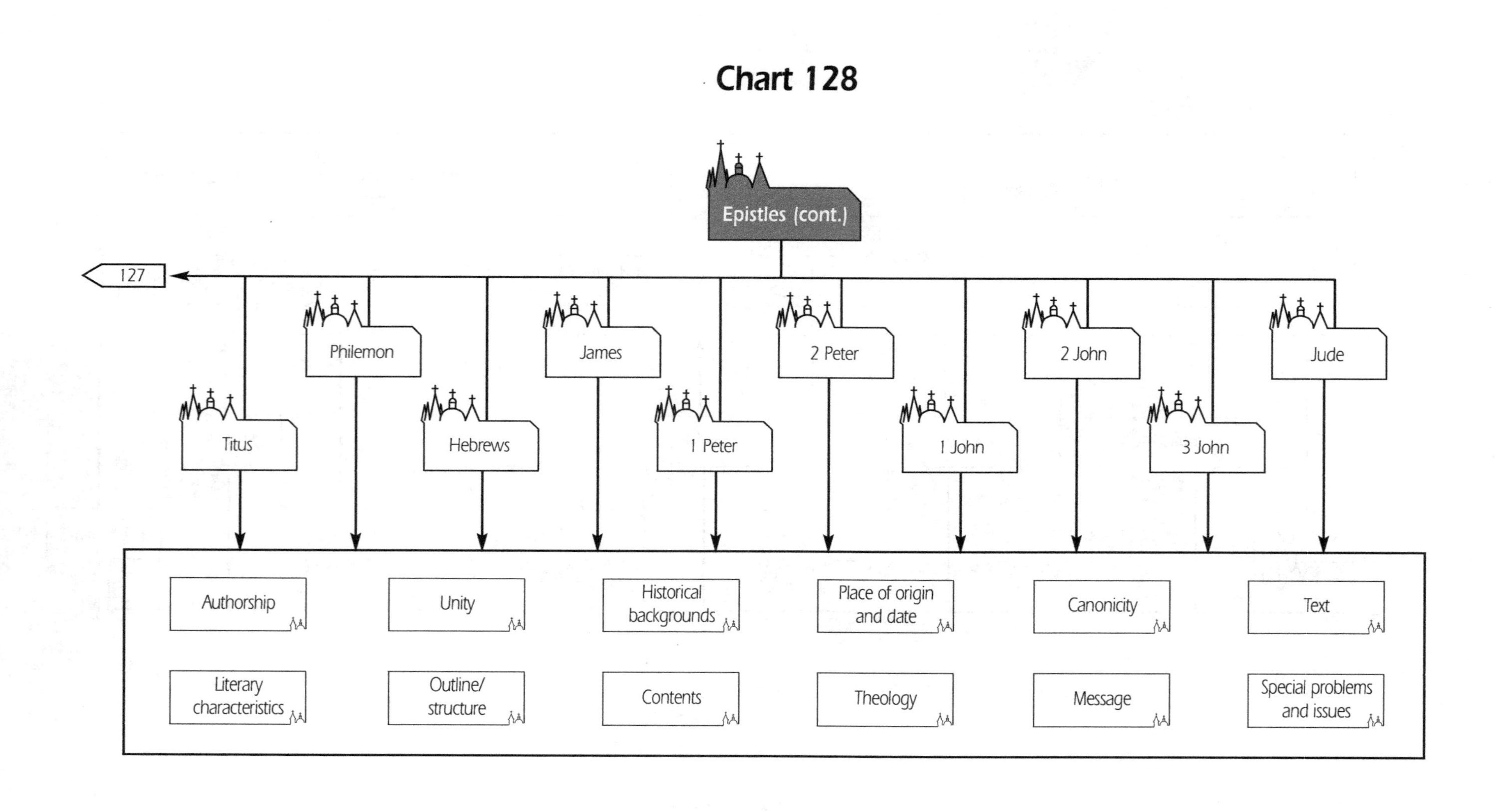

Epistles (cont.)
127
Titus
Philemon
Hebrews
James
1 Peter
2 Peter
1 John
2 John
3 John
Jude
Authorship
Unity
Historical backgrounds
Place of origin and date
Canonicity
Text
Literary characteristics
Outline/ structure
Contents
Theology
Message
Special problems and issues

Chart 129

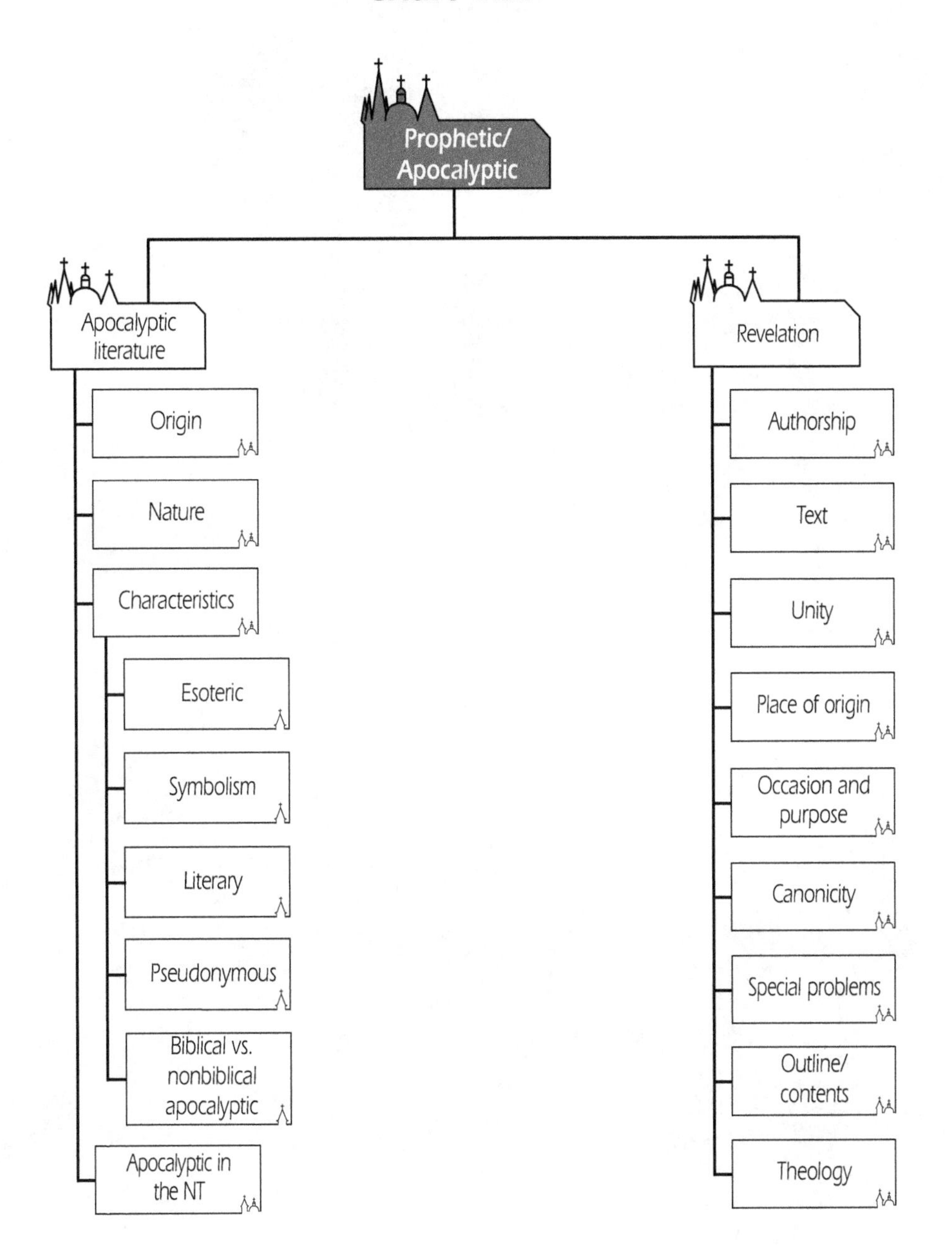

Prophetic/ Apocalyptic
Apocalyptic literature
Origin
Nature
Characteristics
Esoteric
Symbolism
Literary
Pseudonymous
Biblical vs. nonbiblical apocalyptic
Apocalyptic in the NT
Revelation
Authorship
Text
Unity
Place of origin
Occasion and purpose
Canonicity
Special problems
Outline/ contents
Theology

GLOSSARY

A

Abelard (or Abailard), Peter (1079-1142) • Controversial and colorful scholastic theologian and philosopher, remembered for his highly subjective "moral influence" interpretation of the Atonement of Christ and for *Sic et Non* (Yes and No), which demonstrated doctrinal disagreements among the church fathers.

Absolute Truth • *See* Truth.

Accommodation • The act of God whereby he condescends to human capacity in revelation. God adjusted his pattern of communication to take into account human finitude.

Adoption • The acceptance of the sinner into a familial relationship with God as Father on the basis of the completed work of Jesus Christ and through the ministry of the Holy Spirit. The term has the positive connotation of full privileges of adult sonship in family relationships (Rom. 8:15, 23; Gal. 4:5; Eph. 1:5).

Adoptionism • The Christological heresy, first proposed in the third century, that Jesus was merely a human being who was elevated (adopted) to the status of deity because of his obedience.

Albertus Magnus (1200-1280) • "The Universal Doctor." Early scholastic theologian and teacher of Thomas Aquinas. Albertus had a keen interest in the natural world and employed Aristotle's philosophy in his analysis while subjecting it to Christian revelation. His greatest work was his *Summa Theologiae.*

Allegory • An allegory is a fictional story that is intended by the author to express truths about human life and experience beyond the surface sense of the story. Examples of allegorical literature are Bunyan's *Pilgrim's Progress* and Orwell's *Animal Farm.* C. S. Lewis's *Pilgrim's Regress* is an allegory (intentionally symbolic), whereas the Chronicles of Narnia are not. In allegorism or allegorical interpretation the interpreter assigns deeper meanings to a text that was not intended by the author to be an allegory.

Already/Not Yet • *See* Eschatology.

Ambrose (c. 339-97) • Bishop of Milan. From a wealthy background, he gave his wealth away when newly converted. A great preacher and exponent of Latin theology, Ambrose was the human agent of Augustine's conversion.

Amillennialism • *See* Millennialism.

Anabaptists • ("Those who baptize again.") The fourth wing of the Reformation, which emerged in Zurich among some of Zwingli's followers who became convinced of the necessity of believer's baptism. Anabaptists were generally pacifistic and separatistic. They were persecuted by both Roman Catholics and other Protestant bodies.

Analogical • A method of reasoning whereby knowledge is acquired by seeing the similarities (analogies) between the known and the unknown. In theology it refers to inferences (analogies) that can be drawn from creation concerning the nature of God.

Analytic Judgment • *See* Justification.

ANE • Abbreviation of Ancient Near East and Ancient Near Eastern.

Angelology • The theological study of angels. Subsumed under this category are the study of demons (demonology) and of Satan (satanology).

Anointing of the Sick • One of the seven sacraments of Roman Catholicism. It involves anointing the sick and praying for healing (James 5:14-16). It became the sacrament of extreme unction in the Middle Ages and was given when death was imminent.

Anselm (1033–1109) • Scholastic theologian and archbishop of Canterbury, remembered for his *Cur Deus Homo?* ("Why did God become man?") in which he proposed the satisfaction theory of the Atonement, and as the formulator of the ontological proof of God's existence. He insisted on the priority of faith over reason, "I believe that I may understand: for this I also believe, that unless I believe I will not understand." (*See also* Atonement.)

Ante-Nicene Fathers • *See* Church Fathers.

Anthropology • The theological study of humanity, especially as it relates to the human spiritual condition and relationship to God. Because humanity is fallen, it is difficult to separate anthropology from hamartiology, the theological study of sin.

Apocalyptic Literature • Apocalypse ("Revelation") is the Greek title of the last book of the NT. Books that focus on the end of this age (world) and the coming of a new world, usually with strong imagery, are collectively called apocalyptic literature, which as a literary form was not uncommon during the NT era.

People or movements with an apocalyptic mindset view humanity as living "in the last days" and have a worldview dominated by the end of this world and the coming of the new world.

Apocrypha • Intertestamental writings that were never part of the Hebrew canon but were included in the Septuagint (LXX). These books are not part of the Protestant canon but are included in the Roman Catholic canon.

Apollinarianism • Fourth-century Christological heresy which taught that in the incarnation, Christ's body and soul were fully human but his spirit (rational faculty) was fully divine. Condemned by the Council of Constantinople (381).

Apologetics • (Gk. *apologia*, a defense) The branch of theological studies concerned with reasonably defending the faith from the attacks of skeptics and with establishing a solid intellectual basis for Christianity. Approaches include:

Evidentialism: An approach to apologetics that emphasizes the historic evidence for the veracity of the Christian faith.

Presuppositionalism: In contrast to evidentialism, denies the possibility of objective truth due to the fallenness of the human mind. Presuppositionalism assumes rather than demonstrates the veracity of the Word of God. As such it stresses proclamation of the message, trusting the power of the Word through the ministry of the Holy Spirit to bring conviction of sin and belief on the part of the hearer.

Fideism: Akin to presuppositionalism, fideism holds that Christian truth is known through faith rather than reason.

Combinationalism: Like presuppositionalism, recognizes the importance of preconceptions but insists that truth claims of worldviews and systems of thought can be tested by the three traditional tests of truth. (*See* Tests of Truth.) It is issue oriented, measuring the truth claim of Christianity on an issue-by-issue basis against the truth claims of competing worldviews, and holds that competing worldviews fail at crucial points one of the three tests of truth—e.g., modernism corresponds with reality but fails on existential viability.

Apologists • *See* Church Fathers.

Apophatic • From Greek *apophasis,* "denial." The apophatic way is the practice of inquiry into the nature of God by saying what he is not, since God cannot be conceptualized in human categories. It is formulated in apophatic theology, which is central in Eastern Orthodoxy and is closely related to negative theology or the *via negativa.*

The cataphatic (or kataphatic) approach characterizes Western theology, which makes positive statements about the person and nature of God (e.g., the attributes of God). It legitimates the approach on the basis of God's self-revelation.

Apostasy • Falling away, renouncing the Christian faith.

A Posteriori • *See* A Priori.

Apostolic Fathers • *See* Church Fathers.

Apostolic Succession • The unbroken chain of authority in the church reaching back to the apostles. Roman Catholicism bases the authority of the papacy on the succession of bishops that goes back to the apostle Peter, to whom Christ entrusted the keys to the Kingdom. Eastern Orthodoxy accepts the necessity of an unbroken succession of bishops but denies the primacy of any one bishop.

Glossary

A Priori

(a) Existing in the mind before, and independent of, experience.
(b) Not based on prior study, not analytical.
(c) Reasoning from cause to effect.

A Posteriori

(a) Not existing in the mind before, and independent of, experience.
(b) Reasoning from effect to cause.

Aquinas (1224-74) • Greatest scholastic theologian of the Middle Ages. Aquinas synthesized Christian doctrine and Aristotelian philosophy into a perspective on God, theology, and reality (Thomism) that was officially endorsed by the Catholic church at the council of Trent and remained dominant until Vatican II. Philosophically, Aquinas proposed the "five ways" or philosophical proofs of the existence of God. (*See* Theistic Proofs.)

Aramaic • A Semitic language closely related to Heb. A few sections of the OT were composed in Aramaic (Ezra 4:8-6:18; 7:12-26: Jer. 10:11; Dan. 2:4-7:28).

Arianism • The theological heresy that arose in the fourth century, led by Arius, who denied the ontological equality of the preincarnate Christ with God the Father. The position was condemned at Nicea and Constantinople but has repeatedly surfaced throughout the centuries in quasi-Christian and heretical sects such as the Jehovah's Witnesses.

Aristotelianism • *See* Platonism.

Arius • *See* Arianism.

Armenian • Non-theological term referring to the country of Armenia.

Arminianism • Theology based on the formulations of James Arminius (1560-1609) in reaction to scholastic Calvinism. Arminianism includes a heavy emphasis on the role of the free will of man in salvation and a denial of the doctrine of total depravity/inability. Included in the Arminian understanding are the conditionality of salvation (it can be lost) and divine prescience as the basis of election to salvation. (Note that *Arminian* refers to the theologian Arminius, *Armenian* to the country Armenia.)

Asceticism • A form of spiritual discipline that emphasizes abstinence from certain pleasurable things and/or activities in order to obtain salvation or further the spiritual life.

Assensus • *See* Faith.

Assurance of Salvation • Divinely given confidence that the believer is in fact saved. The means of assurance are both internal (the witness of the Holy Spirit: Rom. 8:16) and external (the promise of Scripture).

Athanasian Creed • Early-fifth-century creed, widely used among Catholics, Anglicans, and Protestants. It seeks especially to refute Arianism, Apollinarianism and Sabellianism.

Athanasius (c. 296-373) • Bishop of Alexandria and leader in the fight against the Arian heresy. He was the focal point of the controversy surrounding the definition of the Trinity that emerged from the council of Nicea and labored to subdue Arianism and establish Nicene orthodoxy.

Atonement • From Old English *at* and *one*. The work of Christ in his death on the cross, which makes possible the salvation of mankind by dealing with sin and its alienating effects. While the fact of the Atonement is central in all orthodox Christian thinking, the how of the Atonement has given rise to numerous theories.

Christus Victor: The so-called "classic" view of the Atonement that sees Christ's death as a victory over sin, death, and Satan. Subsumed under this is the ransom theory of the Atonement (*see below*).

Example theory: The theory of the Atonement propounded by Socinius. It sees Christ's death as an example of divine love for humanity rather than as embodying any objective payment for sin.

Governmental theory: Also called the relaxation theory. Proposed by Hugo Grotius (1583-1645), the theory envisions God as the moral governor of the universe who has declared "the soul that sins shall die." God, however does not want sinners to die so he "relaxed" the requirement of law and accepted the death of Christ instead of that of the sinner. In this understanding Christ is not the penal substitute but suffers as a public example of God's disapproval of sin in order to uphold the moral government of the universe. This understanding has been prevalent in Arminian circles.

Limited/Unlimited Atonement: Traditional Reformed/Calvinistic theology has held that Christ's atoning work was limited to the elect in that it was designed to objectively secure their salvation. "Four point Calvinists" (*See* TULIP), Arminians, and those of other theological traditions (Lutherans, Roman Catholic, Eastern Orthodox) contend that Christ's death paid the penalty of sin for all of mankind (not just the elect) and thus is unlimited in that it renders all savable.

Moral influence theory: The theory of Peter Abelard that Christ died in order to demonstrate God's love for mankind and that humanity would be so overcome by the magnitude of Christ's sacrifice that people would turn to God.

Penal substitution: The theory of the Atonement that emerged during the Reformation and is built on Anselm's satisfaction theory (*see below*). Since Christ's death paid perfectly and fully the penalty for human sin, the believer can say that Christ literally "died in my place." This view has had a great influence on Protestant understandings of the Atonement. It has two forms: (1) Substitution for a penalty: Christ did not pay the actual debt for sin, but his death was accepted in lieu of full and exact payment. (2)Substitute penalty: Christ paid the actual penalty for sin for all of mankind.

Ransom theory: An understanding of the Atonement that sees Christ's death as a ransom paid to Satan for humanity.

Recapitulation theory: First proposed by Irenaeus, this view teaches that Christ recapitulated in himself the life of Adam, succeeding where Adam failed and becoming the head of a new humanity.

Satisfaction theory: The theory of the Atonement, taught by Anselm of Canterbury, that sees Christ's death as appeasing. God's offended honor. The Reformers refined this view into that of penal substitution.

Attributes of God • The attributes of God are not characteristics or qualities that are attributed to God, part of God, or predicated of God. The attributes of God are descriptions of his essential being, of how God is in his simplicity. The communicable attributes are those that have a measure of correspondence in human beings, e.g., love. The incommunicable attributes have no correspondence in human beings, e.g., omniscience.

Augsburg Confession • Summary of Protestant doctrine presented to Emperor Charles V at the Diet of Augsburg (1530). It became and remains the principal confession of the Lutheran Church.

Augustine (354-430) • One of the most influential theologians in the history of the church. He was active in the Pelagian controversy (*see* Pelagianism) and the Donatist controversy concerning the nature of the church. Remembered particularly for *The City of God* and the *Confessions*, he became the foundational figure of Western Christianity and is claimed by both Catholicism and Protestantism.

Augustinian Synthesis • The synthesis of Christian theology, Platonic philosophy, and worldview that formed the basis for early medieval Catholicism.

Authentic Existence • Inauthentic Existence: A term derived from existentialism and used particularly by existential theologians with reference to the fallen human condition. It involves living life in a state of denial (either conscious on unconscious) of the realities of life, especially death and finitude. In such a state a human being does not fulfill his God given potential nor does he experience true purpose and meaning.

Authentic Existence is found by facing life's realities and by a leap of faith, accepting God's grace and justification.

Glossary

Author-Centered Meaning • *See* Interpretation, Methods of.

Authorial Intent • *See* Interpretation, Methods of.

Authority • The power or right to demand belief, action, and obedience. Protestants have historically held that the Bible is the final authority in matters of belief and practice, but most recognize some kind of subsidiary authority in the church, reason, conscience, and experience.

B

Baptism • The rite of initiation into the Christian faith that represents the washing away of sins and the beginning of a new life. Most churches consider baptism a sacrament. Baptism symbolizes identification with Christ in his death and resurrection. The main modes are:

Immersion: The person baptized is lowered into standing or running water. The practice is normative in Eastern Orthodoxy and many Protestant denominations.

Pouring: The individual has water poured over his or her head/body, symbolizing the coming of the Spirit.

Sprinkling: A small amount of water is sprinkled on the person's head, symbolizing cleansing and the coming of the Holy Spirit.

Barmen Declaration • The statement of faith by the Confessing Church in Germany in 1934, opposing any teaching (specifically Nazism) that did not place Jesus Christ at its center. Karl Barth was a major force behind the declaration.

Barth, Karl (1886-1968) • Swiss theologian and founder of Neo-Orthodoxy. In reaction to Liberalism, Barth reasserted traditional Reformed and orthodox theology at every point, except in his concept revelation and the inspiration of the Scriptures. He reasserted God's transcendence and sought to restore biblical and Reformed theology in the life of the church. Profoundly Christocentric in his thinking, Barth's influence brought an end to classic liberalism.

BHS • *Biblia Hebraica Stuttgartensia*, the standard critical edition of the Hebrew OT, published in Stuttgart, Germany.

Biblical Criticism • *See* Criticism.

Biblical Theology • *See* Theology.

Bibliology • The doctrine of the Scriptures.

Binding and Loosing • The authority given by Christ to Peter and the other apostles (Matt. 16:19; 18:1, 18). It refers to the apostles' right to discipline in the early church and to remit sin (John 20:23). In Roman Catholic understanding this authority was passed on to Peter's successors through the papacy.

Black Theology • *See* Liberation Theology.

Body of Christ • A prominent Pauline metaphor for the church that stresses its organic nature: the interdependence of believers with Jesus Christ as their spiritual head (Eph.1).

C

Calling • A divine summons either to salvation or to special service. (Ex. 3:4; Jer. 1:5; Matt. 4:21.) In Reformed theology, general calling is the call that comes to all people through external means such as preaching rather than by the internal work of the Holy Spirit. Effectual calling is God's call to the elect unto salvation, to which the elect respond in faith as the result of efficacious grace.

Calvinism • The model of theology in the tradition established by John Calvin. The term is often restricted to a conception of salvation as summarized in five points by the Synod of Dort (1618-19), commonly known by its acronym TULIP. (*See* TULIP.)

Canonical Criticism • *See* Criticism.

Canonicity • *See* Canon of Scripture.

Canonization • The process by which the various books of the Bible came to be accepted as canonical. Also refers to the process by which a person is made a saint in the Roman Catholic Church.

Canon of Scripture • The books that constitute the OT and NT and are considered authoritative by the church. The Roman Catholic Church also accepts the Apocrypha as canonical, whereas Protestant churches do not.

Cappadocians • Three fourth-century church fathers—Basil the Great, Gregory of Nyssa, and Gregory of Nazianzius—who labored to establish the Nicene faith in light of continued Arian resistance. They continue to have a profound influence on Eastern Trinitarian theology to this day.

Cataphatic • *See* Apophatic.

Catholic • (1) Universal, pertaining to the universal nature of the church. (2) Pertaining to the Roman Catholic Church. The first is generally lowercased, the latter capitalized.

Chalcedon • Council of Chalcedon (451) set forth the parameters of orthodox christological understanding and the relationship of the deity and humanity in the incarnate Christ in reaction to the errors of Nestorianism, Eutychianism, Appolonarianism, and in light of the emphases on Christ's deity and humanity as taught by the schools of Alexandria and Antioch respectively.

Charismata • (Gk. "grace gifts"; sing. *charisma*) Also called charisms. The grace (*charis*) gifts of the Holy Spirit given for the edification of the church. In contemporary usage the term is applied particularly to tongues (glossolalia), prophecy, healing, words of wisdom, words of knowledge, and the interpretation of tongues.

Chiliasm • (Gk. *chilias*, "thousand") Ancient term for millennialism, esp. premillennialism.

Chrismation • (Gk. *chrisma*) In the Eastern Orthodox Church, the practice of anointing the newly baptized person with oil and the sign of the cross. Also called chrism.

Christology • The doctrine of Christ.

Christology From Above/Below • Methods of doing Christology. Christology from above approaches the doctrine through the ancient creedal definitions (e.g.,Chalcedon), whereas Christology from below uses scientific historical research about the historical Jesus as its starting point. Some view these two perspectives as opposed to one another; others see them as complementary.

Christus Victor • *See* Atonement.

Church Fathers • The collective name given to early Christian theologians and writers. The pre-Nicene fathers (also called Antenicene fathers) wrote before, the post-Nicene fathers after the First Nicene Council (325). The pre-Nicene fathers can be further divided into the apostolic fathers, who lived in the years immediately after the NT, and the apologists, who defended the faith against pagan philosophy and prosecution. In the West, the era of the church fathers ended in the seventh century; in the East, in the eighth century. The study of the work of the early church fathers is called patristics.

Church Government

Episcopalian: Authority resides in a group of bishops.

Congregational: Authority resides in the autonomous local church. Usually churches with a congregational polity are democratic in their internal structure.

Presbyterian: Authority resides in presbyteries composed of pastors and elders from local churches.

Primitivism: Authority resides in the Holy Spirit. This approach attempts to follow only the teachings and patterns laid out in the NT (e.g., Plymouth Brethren).

Church History • *See* Historical Theology.

Church Universal • The true church, not bound by visible institutional forms and liturgies, but comprised of those who have been regenerated by the Holy Spirit throughout history and in all local (visible) churches.

Classical Theism • The doctrine of God as developed during the ancient period of the church. Often the term is used pejoratively and implies that theology became infected with Greek philosophical conceptions concerning the nature of God that are opposed to the biblical presentation.

Cognate Languages • Related languages, such as Dutch and German, that developed from common earlier forms. In OT studies it refers to Semitic languages other than Hebrew that help in understanding the nature and meaning of biblical Hebrew.

Coherence • *See* Tests of Truth.

Common Sense Realism • Also called Scottish Realism and Common Sense Philosophy. A movement that tried to counter Hume's epistemological and moral skepticism. It sees knowledge as established by intuition and common-sense experience. Common Sense Realism was the dominant epistemology in America from the late eighteenth century until the late nineteenth century. (*See* Princeton School.)

Communicable Attributes • *See* Attributes of God.

Communicatio Idiomatum • In Christology, the understanding that what is predicated of Christ's divine nature can also be predicated of his human nature and vice versa. This explanation of the relationship of the natures became a hallmark of Alexandrine Christology and was implicitly incorporated into the Christological definition of Chalcedon. The underlying truth of the explanation continues to be affirmed today.

Community • A group with common interests. As used to describe the church, the term connotes a commonality of identity, concern, and fellowship.

Comparative Religions Criticism • *See* Criticism.

Concept Inspiration • *See* Inspiration of the Bible.

Conceptualism Moderate Realism • The epistemological position espoused by Thomas Aquinas. (*See* Realism.)

Concursus • Concursus holds that every word of Scripture is at once both human and divine, and it is methodologically improper to try to separate the human and the divine in Scripture.

Condign Merit • *See* Merit.

Confirmation • A rite practiced by various Christian communities whereby the individual consciously ratifies the faith testified to at his/her baptism. In the Roman Catholic and Eastern Orthodox traditions the rite is considered a sacrament. The Eastern Orthodox form of confirmation is chrismation.

Congregational Government • *See* Church Government.

Congruous Merit • *See* Merit.

Connotation • *See* Denotation.

Conscience • The internal moral aspect of human nature that passes judgment, either positively or negatively, on the moral questions submitted.

Consistency • *See* Tests of Truth.

Constantine the Great (c. 274/80-337) • Roman emperor who legalized Christianity and was responsible for convening the first ecumenical council at Nicea (325) to deal with Arianism.

Consubstantiation • *See* Lord's Supper.

Contextualization • *See* Culture.

Contingent Being • Being that depends on conditions or powers outside itself for its existence. Thus a human being is a contingent being whose existence depends ultimately upon God.

Conversion • (Gk. *metanoia*) A "turning around" in response to the divine call in salvation. Conversion involves a radical change in mind and heart: a turning from sin (repentance) and a turning to Christ in faith/trust.

Coredemptrix • Term often applied to Mary in Catholic devotion, it reflects the special part she is thought to hold in the process of redemption.

Corporate Sin/Guilt • *See* Personal Sin/Guilt.

Corruption • The theological term for of the results of human sin, both inherited and personal.

Cosmological Argument • *See* Theistic Proofs.

Cosmos • The universe or the world. In the NT the word usually refers to the world as fallen and under the dominion of Satan.

Council of Trent • The council of the Catholic Counter-reformation that sought to reform abuses within Catholicism as well as answer Protestantism theologically. The council codified Thomism as the reigning theological perspective of the Catholic Church until Vatican II.

Covenant Theology • In Reformed theology, the perspective that divine-human relationships, especially with reference to salvation, are governed by a series of covenants. The covenants include the covenant of works and the covenant of grace. The former was made between God and Adam and Eve in the Garden of Eden; obedience to it would result in salvation, disobedience would result in death. The covenant of grace, made between God and man after the fall, makes salvation contingent upon faith/trust in God. The ultimate object of trust is God incarnate, Jesus Christ. Many covenant theologians add the covenant of redemption, made between the Father and the Son in eternity past, whereby the Father gives to the Son those elected for salvation and the Son covenants to become incarnate and die for those elect by the Father.

Crisis Experience • A specific experience that changes the direction of one's life. Conversion is seen as a crisis experience. Certain views of sanctification (Wesleyan and Keswick) see a spiritual crisis experience as necessary for holiness.

Critical Text • *See* Text of the Bible.

Criticism • A complex of methods developed for use in literary and historical studies. In this context the term is not used in the popular sense of faultfinding but in the technical sense of subjecting to critical analysis. As such it is a method of testing truth claims. Biblical criticism (the complex of historical and literary critical methods applied to the Bible) has historically been associated with anti-supernaturalistic presuppositions that deny the miraculous. Such presuppositions are not inherent to the methods themselves, and many evangelicals endorse critical methodology while eschewing the anti-supernaturalism.

Canonical criticism: The critical methodology that views each book of Scripture in its place in the canon and as contributing to the larger teaching of the Bible as a whole rather than treating each book in isolation.

Comparative-religions criticism: The comparative study of the religion of the OT and the religions of the surrounding peoples and cultures. The method looks for common features among the ancient religions and the religion of Israel.

Form criticism: Critical methodology that looks at the text of Scripture and attempts to see the "prehistory" of that text, tracing it through its oral and written stages. This is coupled with the *Sitz im Leben* (setting in life) to which the text was addressed in order to enhance understanding.

Higher criticism: The critical study of texts that looks at authorship, date, genuineness, unity, and other such factors. Higher criticism is distinguished from lower or textual criticism, which establishes the reliability of the received text of a document. As originally practiced higher criticism was accompanied by an anti-supernaturalistic mentality that denied the possibility of divine revelation and miracles.

Historical criticism: The use of critical historical methodology to ascertain the validity of the historical information in the text.

Literary-source criticism: Studies documents in their final, finished form, focusing on what the text as it stands says. It assumes that the text creates a world that can be investigated in its various dimensions by studying the linguistics, genre, style, and forms of the text.

Lower criticism or textual criticism: The study that attempts to reconstruct the original form of the text based on the existing copies.

Narrative criticism: The exegetical method that approaches the text from the literary perspective of the story and finds meaning in the literary structure and plot.

Reader-response criticism: The view that meaning is created by the reader of the text rather than being communicated by the author.

Redaction criticism: The critical methodology that attempts to identify the editorial methods and predisposition of an author and how the authors shaped the material taken from other sources. Particularly used in the study of the Synoptic Gospels.

Rhetorical criticism: The analysis of the text based on its rhetorical structure.

Source criticism: The critical method that seeks to identify the source documents underlying the written documents of Scripture. (*See also* Documentary Hypothesis.)

Structural criticism: The critical exegetical method that looks beyond surface structure and finds meaning in the underlying deep structure of the text.

Textual criticism: Lower criticism.

Culture • Culture is the integrated pattern of language, beliefs, and behavior that gives a society and the individuals in it a coherent understanding of reality. Culture exists wherever humanity exists and extends its influence invisibly over all members of a society.

Contextualization: The process of adapting the expression of the timeless truths of theology to the culture and condition of the audience.

Enculturation: Embedded in culture. In biblical studies the term is used with reference to the fact that divine revelation was given in preexisting cultural frameworks and must be analyzed to determine what portion of the revelation is universal and what portion is merely cultural.

Supracultural: That which is above culture or transcends the limitations of a particular culture and has universal validity.

Transcultural: Across culture. Meaning in Scripture that is valid "across cultures" for all people at all times and in all places. While some aspects of Scripture may be culture-bound, its message was designed for all humanity.

Cultus • The form and practice of worship in a religion, particularly the rites and rituals associated with worship.

Cyprian (200-258) • Bishop of Carthage and martyr during the Decian persecution. His contribution lay in his stress on the episcopal as opposed to theological unity of the church.

Cyril of Jerusalem (c. 310-87) • Opponent of Arianism who played a major role at the Council of Constantinople (381).

D

Damnation • Condemnation, used especially of eternal condemnation to hell.

Darkness • Biblical metaphor for chaos, ignorance, evil, destruction.

Day of the Lord • Term associated with the special presence of God either in judgment or blessing. Most prominently the term has negative connotations in that it involves God visiting his people in judgment for their unfaithfulness. In the NT it is associated with the Tribulation and the Second Coming of Christ.

Death • The biblical concept of death has at its root the idea of separation. Thus, spiritual death is separation from God, physical death the separation of the soul from the body.

Deconstructionism • Late-twentieth-century literary critical method that assumes that language refers to itself rather than to external reality. Deconstructionism denies the legitimacy of the author's intended meaning as the goal of interpretation and instead asserts multiple conflicting meanings that must be analyzed according to political, philosophical, and social implications.

Deductive • *See* Inductive.

Definitive Sanctification • *See* Sanctification.

Degrees of Guilt • The recognition that knowledge or ignorance of the divine will makes the offender liable for greater or lesser punishment (Luke 12:47-48).

Deification • *See* Theosis.

Deism • Enlightenment view that true knowledge of God is available via reason and that revelation is unnecessary and impossible. God created the universe, which runs by natural laws, much like a clock. Miracles are impossible since God would not break his own laws. Morality is built into the structure of the universe and final judgment will be based upon good works.

Deity of Christ • The equality of Jesus Christ with God the Father by virtue of his participating fully in the essence of godhood. Jesus is understood to be fully God rather than merely reflecting the influence or character of God. He is God rather than merely divine.

Demonology • *See* Angelology.

Demon Possession • Demon possession is the total domination of a person by evil spirits, rendering the individual incapable of voluntary actions. Demon oppression is the effect of the demonic on human individuals whereby the individual experiences the evil influence of demons or the demonic yet without falling into the complete enslavement of demonic possession.

Demythologizing • *See* Myth.

Denial • A psychological defense mechanism involving a conscious or unconscious unwillingness to confront emotionally painful realities and consequences that are the result of either personal decision (sin) or of abuse (being sinned against).

Denotation • The denotation of a word is the meaning of a word that is shared by all speakers of the language; its connotations are what the word evokes in an individual or group of individuals. The denotation is "objective," the connotation subjective—e.g., abortion objectively refers to a medical procedure, but it has widely differing connotations to opponents and proponents of abortion rights.

Deontology • Also called ethics of moral obligation or duty. A system of ethics based upon principles of rightness without regard to outcome.

Depravity • (Lat. *depravare*, "to make corrupt") Theological term used to describe the theological and moral condition of mankind as sinful and wicked apart from God since the fall (Gen. 3).

Total Depravity: The condition of humanity, since every aspect of human existence is tinged by sin. The term does not mean that an individual or humankind generally is as bad as could be but that every aspect of existence is affected by sin.

Determinism • The philosophical position that all actions are determined by rigid cause and effect. Determinism denies the reality of human freedom. In its extreme form it becomes fatalism.

Freedom: The idea that the individual is free to create his or her own destiny based on choice, apart from fate or divine predestination. Proponents of radical freedom argue that any form of divine foreordination or foreknowledge negates the concept of freedom and thus must be denied.

Christianity acknowledges the legitimacy of human freedom, within certain boundaries, as inherent in the concept of personhood and being created in the image of God. These boundaries include human fallenness, human finiteness, and the sovereignty of God.

Diachronic • In language study, diachronic refers to the study of a language as it has evolved over time, synchronic to the study of a language as it appears at a particular point in time. Thus, a diachronic study of a Greek NT word includes tracing the history of the word from its earliest known form and occurrence through classical antiquity up to NT times. A synchronic study of the word limits itself to its usage in NT times.

Dialectic • A method of reasoning where truth is seen to emerge from the tension between two opposing views.

Diaspora • The dispersion of the Jews among the nations, beginning at the Babylonian exile (586 B.C.).

Dichotomism • *See* Holism.

Disciplines • Religious practices intended to enhance the spiritual life and promote spiritual growth, such as prayer, solitude, simplicity.

Dispensationalism • A theological movement within evangelicalism that stresses an apocalyptic understanding of history. Its peculiarities arise from an interpretation of the history of redemption that sees the OT and NT united eschatologically in a way that is consistent with a historical-grammatical (sometimes referred to as "literal") interpretation of OT and NT, and consistent with the fulfillment of the OT promises to national Israel of an earthly kingdom ruled personally by the Messiah, Jesus Christ. It is a philosophy of history with adherents in the Calvinistic, Arminian, and Pentecostal and Charismatic traditions.

Divine Enthronement • *See* Enthronement Psalms.

Divine Image • *See* Image of God.

Divinity of Christ • *See* Deity of Christ.

Docetism • Proto-gnostic heresy already evident in the first century. It argued that Jesus only seemed or appeared to be human but was not truly manifest in flesh.

Documentary Hypothesis • Also called the JEDP theory. The early biblical critical theory that the Pentateuch was compiled from four earlier documents/traditions, identified by the name of God used in each: the J(Y)ahwistic, the Elohistic, the Deuteronomic, and the Priestly. This reconstruction dated the Pentateuch late in Israel's history and denied Mosaic authorship.

Dogmatic Theology • *See* Theology.

DSS • Dead Sea Scrolls.

Duns Scotus (c. 1264-1308) • Late-medieval scholastic philosopher-theologian and opponent of Aquinas's teaching. He separated philosophy from theology and reason from faith, arguing that faith was a matter of the will rather than the result of logical proofs.

Dynamic Monarchianism • *See* Monarchianism.

Dynamic Theory • View of inspiration held by A. H. Strong similar to but less specific than plenary inspiration and emphasizing the dynamic work of the Spirit in the inspiration process.

E

Eastern Orthodox Church • *See* Orthodoxy.

Ebionitism (Ebionism) • Early Jewish-Christian sect in Palestine in the second and third centuries that believed in the continuing relevance of the Mosaic law for believers and saw Jesus as the son of Joseph and Mary upon whom the Holy Spirit descended so that he became "Son of God."

Ecclesia • *See* Ekklesia.

Ecclesiology • The doctrine of the church.

Economic Trinity • *See* Trinity.

Effectual Calling • *See* Calling.

Efficacious Grace • *See* Calling.

Eisegesis • *See* Exegesis.

Ekklesia • Greek word for church. The term is derived from the Greek political context and has reference to those who are "called out."

Election • *See* Predestination.

Empiricism • *See* Epistemology.

En Christo • *See* In Christ.

Enculturation • *See* Culture.

Enthronement Psalms • OT psalms that celebrate the enthronement of Yahweh as the true king of Israel.

Episcopalian Government • *See* Church Government.

Epistemology • The study of how human knowledge is obtained. Major theories include:
Rationalism: Human reason is the arbiter of truth. Rationalism denies the necessity and possibility of supernatural revelation, although it may allow for the existence of God. It sees religion as a cognitive phenomenon.
Phenomenalism: All knowledge arises from an interplay of incoming sensory experience and innate categories of the mind that process that experience. Phenomenalism denies the ability to know the "thing in itself." One can only know a thing as it is experienced.
Existentialism: The only way to know truth is through human subjectivity and participation in reality ("being").
Empiricism: Knowledge comes through experience or sense perception.

Erastianism • Named for Thomas Erastus (1524-83), the position that the state has the right to exercise authority over the church in all areas.

Eschatology • The study of last things. Personal eschatology or individual eschatology deals with the fate of the individual at death, general eschatology with the return of Jesus Christ, the final judgment of earth, and the establishment of the millennial and eternal kingdoms.
Realized eschatology: The view that the eschatological passages of the NT do not look toward a future fulfillment but were fulfilled in the life and ministry of Christ.
Already/Not Yet: The view that the kingdom of God has already been inaugurated but is not yet fully manifested. The full manifestation awaits the second coming of Christ. (*See also* Millennialism.)

Estrangement • The condition of withdrawal from relationship. Often seen as a result of sin which distances the individual from right relationship with God, others, and self.

Eternal Security • The doctrine espoused by the Reformed/Calvinistic tradition that a person who has once truly believed in Jesus Christ as Savior and has become regenerate by the Holy Spirit will never lose his or her salvation. (*See also* TULIP: Perseverance of the Saints.)

Eternal State • The ultimate state of the individual, either heaven or hell. Also, the eternal kingdom after final judgment.

Eternity • *See* Time and Eternity.

Eucharist • *See* Lord's Supper.

Eutychianism • The fifth-century Christological heresy that held that Jesus had only the divine nature, by which his human nature was absorbed.

Evangelists • The title given to the writers of the four Gospels.

Evidentialism • *See* Apologetics.

Evil • That which is morally bad or harmful or opposes the will or character of God. It has been described as "the absence of good" (Augustine) and may be personal or structural (functioning in social structures and institutions).

Example Theory • *See* Atonement.

Excluded Middle • *See* Laws of Thought.

Exegesis • The "bringing out" of the author's intended meaning of the text of Scripture by means of proper use of the rules of hermeneutics. This is the opposite of eisegesis, the reading into the text of the interpreter's ideas.

Existential • That which is important to the experience of one's existence.

Existentialism • Philosophy originating with Søren Kierkegaard. It stresses that the only way to know truth is through human subjectivity and participation in reality ("being"). Christian existentialism uses existential categories and insights within a Christian framework and stresses the personal element of decision and commitment that affects one's entire existence. Atheistic existentialism asserts the absurdity of life and the universe and the need to create meaning for oneself by personal decision.

Ex Opere Operato/Operantis • *See* Sacraments.

Expiation • Atonement or covering of sin by sacrifice, specifically the death of Christ. Propitiation is understood as a turning away of divine wrath, whereas expiation does not imply divine wrath.

Extent of the Atonement • *See* Atonement.
Extreme Unction • *See* Anointing of the Sick.

F

Faith • In historic orthodoxy, faith has three aspects:

Understanding: (Lat. *Notitia*): The intellectual, factual component.

Assent: (Lat. *Assensus*): Acknowledgement of the intellectual component as truth.

Trust: (Lat. *Fiducia*): The personal element of trust.

Saving faith: Trust in Jesus and his death to save one from sin and to gain eternal life. Saving faith in Christ goes beyond understanding and assent.

Fallenness • The spiritual condition of humanity as sinners after the fall of Adam into sin (Gen. 3).

Falsifiability • *See* Verifiability.

Fathers of the Church • *See* Church Fathers.

Fear of God • Fear of God may be either servile fear, which is based on the threat of punishment, or filial fear, which stands in awe and reverence and seeks not to offend God.

Fellowship • (Gk. *koinonia*) Participation, sharing, fellowship in a common life. In an objective sense, fellowship exists among Christians by virtue of participation in the life of Christ. The term is used even in the sense of the financial giving by which lives are shared. It also refers to the experience of unity, community, and belonging that emerges from common participation (see 1 John 1).

Feminist Theology • *See* Liberation Theology.

Fideism • The view that faith as opposed to reason is the means to knowledge of God. Often used in a pejorative sense of a theology that focuses on subjective experience to the exclusion of reason. (*See also* Apologetics.)

Fiducia • *See* Faith.

Figures of Speech • Word pictures that can communicate more powerfully than simple, literal language. Figures are not opposed to literal meaning but presuppose that a literal truth is being communicated. All languages use figures of speech for communication. The most common figures include:

Simile: The comparison of two things by use of *like* or *as*.

Metaphor: The comparison of two things without the use of the terms *like* or *as*. More generally, the term metaphor is used broadly to speak of figurative language.

Filioque • (Lat. "and the Son") The filioque clause was added to the Nicene creed in the West during the early Middle Ages to teach a double procession of the Spirit from the Father and from the Son. The doctrine became the theological reason for the separation of the Eastern and Western Churches in 1054.

Final Judgment • The last judgment of God on all humanity. It will determine whether an individual will spend eternity in the presence of God or in Hell.

Finitude • The condition of being finite and therefore limited and unable to transcend the physical and mental boundaries of existence. All created beings are finite and limited.

Flesh • Used in Scripture literally of the physical body and figuratively of humanity in its weakness as it exists in a sinful condition apart from God (Rom. 8:4-8; Gal. 5:16ff.).

Forensic Act • A legal act or pronouncement. The term is usually used with the doctrine of justification, which is understood as a legal pronouncement of the sinner's righteousness. God declares (not makes) the sinner righteous/justified through faith in Jesus Christ and his Atonement.

Forgiveness • Pardon, remitting an offense. Forgiveness restores an open and honest relationship with God, others, or self, after that relationship has suffered alienation through an offense.

Formal/Material • A distinction made by many between words and the ideas expressed by words. The term also has wider application in areas such as the recognition of the canon of Scripture: the books of Scripture had material authority as inspired from the time they were written; formal authority arose gradually as the books of the canon as a group were recognized as divine.

Form Criticism • *See* Criticism.

Formgeschichte • German for form criticism. (*See* Criticism.)

Frame of Reference • A set of assumptions, ideas, or conditions that determine how something will be approached, perceived, or understood.

Freedom • *See* Determinism.

Futurism • *See* Eschatology.

G

General Calling • *See* Calling.

General Eschatology • *See* Eschatology.

General Revelation • *See* Revelation.

Genre • A literary form that can be distinguished from other literary forms in aim, form, and technique. Major genres found in the Bible are poetry, narrative, and wisdom literature. The recognition of the genre of a text (e.g., Is this text history or poetry?) is essential to its proper interpretation.

Glorification • The "future tense" of salvation (justification = past tense, sanctification = present tense). It includes eternal life, the final purification from all that remains of sin, and the renewal of the body without the weakness experienced in this life.

Glory • Brightness, splendor, greatness. Glory is an attribute of God.

Gnosticism/Gnostic • A second- and third-century constellation of religious movements that stressed salvation by means of some esoteric knowledge. For a time Christian versions of gnosticism became serious rivals of orthodox Christianity. Gnosticism was in many ways parallel to the New Age movement of the late-twentieth century.

Governmental Theory • *See* Atonement.

Grace • Unmerited favor. The grace of God is given to sinful humanity in the form of salvation and forgiveness through Jesus Christ, not because of any merit but out of divine love and compassion. Dealing with humanity on the basis of merit would bring a deserved condemnation.

Great Schism • The split between the the Eastern and Western (Orthodox and Roman Catholic) churches in 1054.

Great Tribulation • *See* Tribulation.

Gregory the Great (540-604) • Pope from 590 until his death, he was the transitional figure between the ancient and medieval church. His reforms set the direction for the development of the church seen in the medieval period. He standardized worship, introduced the Gregorian chant, encouraged missionary activity, and became the official interpreter of Augustine for the medieval church.

H

Hagiographa • *See* Canon: OT.

Hamartiology • *See* Anthropology.

Hard Sciences • Physical sciences.

Heart • Biblically, the center of human mental and spiritual activity from which emotions and values arise. The heart can be evil (Jer. 17:9) or pure (Matt. 5:8).

Heaven • The dwelling place of God and the future eternal abode of those who inherit salvation through Jesus Christ. Heaven is pictured as a place and condition of bliss and joy apart from sin and evil and characterized by the presence of God.

Hell • The place of future eternal punishment for the wicked, characterized by suffering, torment, and a lack of the presence of God. (Rev. 20:13-15).

Helplessness • The condition of the sinner before God, unable to act to extricate himself from his bondage to sin. Inability.

Heresy • A belief consciously chosen in contradistinction to the official teaching of a church body and understood to be dangerous to the spiritual health of the church. The most serious heresies surround the doctrine of the Trinity and the person and work of Christ.

Heterodox • *See* Orthodox.

Higher Criticism • *See* Criticism.

Hilary of Poitiers (c. 315-67) • Bishop of Poitiers and opponent of Arianism in the West. Wrote *De Trinitate*, a significant work on the Trinity.

Historical Critical Method • A methodology that approaches the biblical text with a view to establishing what the texts meant in their earliest forms and contexts.

Historical Criticism • *See* Criticism.

Historical-Grammatical • *See* Literal Interpretation.

Historical Theology • The study of the teachings of the church and its theologians in their historical context. Closely related to, but distinct from, church history.

Church History: The study of the people and events which comprise the legacy of the church from the first century to the present.

History of Doctrine: The tracing of the development of individual doctrines diachronically through the ages of the church.

History of Christian Thought: The study of the development of Christian thought and doctrine synchronically within its various eras of development.

Historical Truth • Truth that is derived from the historical process and as such is contingent rather than absolute and timeless. Part of the uniqueness of Christianity is that it is grounded in the contingency of history rather than the timeless and "necessary truth of reason."

History • The record of people and events that have had enduring significance for subsequent generations of mankind. Historical events are those whose significance goes beyond the mere fact that they actually happened in space and time.

History of Christian Thought • *See* Historical Theology.

History of Doctrine • *See* Historical Theology.

History of Religions School • Late-nineteenth-century approach to the study of religion that assumes an evolutionary continuity between ancient religions. It seeks to trace the historical development of polytheistic thought, its evolution into monotheism in Israel, and the phases of religious development in Judaism and Christianity. Also known by its German name, *Religionsgeschichte*.

Holiness • The condition of being separated unto someone or something. In both OT and NT, holiness is a pre-ethical concept, looking at the fact or condition of separation rather than at moral purity. In Christian theology the term has taken on a moral sense of living in conformity with divine standards.

Holiness Movement • The mid- to late-nineteenth-century theological revival of Wesley's doctrine of entire sanctification. Placing it in a new context and stressing absolute perfection in a way foreign to Wesley, the holiness movement became the catalyst for numerous new denominations as well as exerting significant influence on the development of Keswick theology.

Holism • The three main views of the relationship between body, soul, and spirit are as follows:
Holism: The person is a unified being that cannot be subdivided.
Dichotomism: The person consists of two parts, the material (body) and immaterial (soul/spirit).
Trichotomism: The person is composed of three parts: body, soul, and spirit. Ancient trichotomous understanding saw the soul as the life principle and the spirit as the rational principle. Contemporary understandings see the soul as including the rational and the spirit as the aspect of human nature that relates to God.

Holy Orders • In the Roman Catholic Church, ministries of the Church requiring ordination.

Holy Spirit • The third person of the Trinity who with the Father and Son is to be worshiped, praised, and adored.

Homoousia • (Gk. "of the same substance or essence") Term adopted in the Nicene Creed (325) to explain the eternal divinity of the Word/Son and his relationship to God the Father.

Hope • The expectation of the future fulfillment of God's covenant promises despite present circumstances. The Christian hope is based on the completed work of Jesus Christ and the present ministry of the Holy Spirit (Rom. 8:18-25; 1 Peter 1:3ff).

Human Freedom • *See* Determinism.

I

Icon • A picture, image, or representation. In the Eastern Orthodox Church, icons are two-dimensional images of saints and other venerated persons, traditional in form and content, that are intended as aids to devotion.

Idealism • *See* Realism.

Identity • *See* Laws of Thought.

Image and Likeness • *See* Image of God.

Image of Christ • The goal of redeemed humanity is conformity to the incarnate Son of God as the visible example of perfect humanity (Rom. 8:29; 1 John 3:2, etc.), who is himself the exact representation of the invisible God.

Image of God • The nature and status of man, based on Gen. 1:26. The image of God (Lat. *Imago Dei*) has been seen as moral capacity, as rationality, as spirituality, as relationship, as sonship, and even as form. By whatever definition, the possession of the divine image marks man off as unique among God's creatures and as having a status that is qualitatively different and higher than that of the rest of the created order. The Fall has distorted the divine image but not erased it; numerous times after the Fall are humans said to be in God's image, which implies a continuing dignity despite the present fallen condition. In the Hebrew text of Genesis 1-2, the terms *image* and *likeness* are interchangeable synonyms and intensify the concept of mankind's likeness to God. In theology, *image* and *likeness* have been used to refer to different aspects of man's being.

Imago Dei • Lat. "Image of God." (*See* Image of God.)

Immanence • *See* Transcendence.

Immanent Trinity • *See* Trinity.

Immediate Imputation • *See* Imputation.

Immersion • *See* Baptism.

Imminence • The view that the return of Christ and God's final judgment upon humanity may occur at any time. This was the faith of the church during the earliest ages but not reasserted again in the nineteenth century. Imminence must be distinguished from immediacy. Christ's return is imminent, but it may not be immediate. (Spelling not to be confused with *immanence*.)

Immortality • The condition of not being mortal and thus not subject to death. God alone possesses immortality within himself, but those who receive salvation as a gift from God also receive immortality as a part of that gift.

Impassability • The theological understanding that God does not change and is thus not affected by contingent developments in the created order. The concept emphasizes God's changeless consistency. Recently the concept has been attacked by process thinkers who charge that this view finds its origin in Greek philosophy rather than in the Bible.

Imprecatory Psalms • Psalms in which the psalmist calls down the curse of God upon his (and God's) enemies.

Imputation • To attribute or reckon to one's account. With reference to sin, guilt, and righteousness, Paul indicates that sin and guilt are imputed to Adam's descendants while Christ's righteousness is imputed to those who believe (Rom. 5:12-21).

Immediate imputation: The sin of Adam is placed on the account of each of his descendants in such a way as to make each personally guilty of Adam's sin (federal headship).

Realistic imputation: The theory that all humanity was actually present in Adam and thus actual though unconscious participants in Adam's sin (seminal headship).

Mediate imputation: While not actually guilty of Adam's sin, humanity is born physically and morally depraved and thus falls under divine condemnation. (*See also* Infused Grace.)

Inauthentic Existence • *See* Authentic Existence.

In Christ • Pauline reference to the radical identification of the believer with the person and work of Jesus Christ.

Incommunicable Attributes • *See* Attributes of God.

Individual Eschatology • *See* Eschatology.

Inductive • Method of reasoning that infers conclusions from observed patterns in data under study. Induction is the basis of the scientific method. Deductive reasoning deduces conclusions that are logical and necessary consequences of the premises.

Indulgences • In Roman Catholic theology, a releasing from the temporal effects of sin that remain after repentance and the forgiveness of guilt. The concept is built on the concept of the merit of Christ and works of supererogation of the saints which the church stores up in a treasury of merit to be dispensed at its discretion. It was abuse of this system that gave impetus to the Protestant Reformation.

Indwelling of the Holy Spirit • The personal presence of the Holy Spirit in the life of the believer. The believer is said to be a temple of the Holy Spirit by virtue of his presence (1 Cor. 6:19).

Inerrancy • *See* Inspiration of the Bible.

Infallibility • *See* Inspiration of the Bible.

Infralapsarianism • *See Ordo Salutis.*

Infused Grace • The Roman Catholic understanding of justification as grace poured into the individual by the Holy Spirit whereby he/she is made righteous. Protestants, by contrast, understand justification as a declaration of the individual's standing as right before God based on the imputed (not infused) righteousness of Christ, while the making righteous is the process of sanctification that is based on justification.

Injustice • A moral/ethical wrong that involves failure to render to another person what is due.

Inner Man • The aspect of human existence that is transformed by the redeeming power of Jesus Christ and indwelt by the Holy Spirit.

Inspiration of the Bible • The process whereby God guided the authors of Scripture in the recording of his revelation (2 Tim. 3:16; 2 Peter 1:21).

Concept inspiration: God inspired the ideas of Scripture but left to the human authors the task of choosing the actual words to employ in expressing the inspired ideas.

Verbal inspiration: God inspired both the ideas of Scripture and the words employed by the human authors to express those ideas.

Plenary inspiration: Scripture is fully (extensively) the Word of God.

Verbal-plenary inspiration: An intensification of the idea of plenary inspiration make explicit that both extensively (all of Scripture) and intensively (the very words) the Scriptures are divine in origin and therefore totally trustworthy. The corollary doctrine is inerrancy.

Inerrancy holds that the Bible is without error in all that it affirms, including historical and scientific facts. Inerrantists recognize that this is a faith position and that there are difficulties that preclude the demonstration of the doctrine beyond challenge.

Infallibility refers to the understanding that the Bible does not fail in its purpose. Until recent decades the term was a virtual synonym of inerrancy. Today, many assert the infallibility of the Bible while denying that it is necessarily without error in scientific, historic, and geographic details.

Instantaneous Resurrection • *See* Resurrection.

Intermediate State • *See* Resurrection.

Interpretation, Methods of

Author-centered meaning: meaning is centered in the mind of the author, hence psychoanalysis of the author or a climbing inside the author's mind becomes necessary to grasp the meaning of a text.

Textually centered meaning: the text exists independent of the author and meaning may be unrelated to any authorial intent.

Reader-centered meaning: meaning is found/created in the interaction between the reader and the text.

Authorial intent: In hermeneutics and biblical interpretation, the message and intention that the original author of Scripture was trying to communicate. Traditional evangelical hermeneutics sees a dialectic between author-centered meaning and textually-centered meaning in that the text as it exists may lend itself to several competing interpretations, only one of which is within the perview of the message intended by the author. The goal of the hermeneutical process is the rediscovery of this intended message.

Introspection • The practice of looking inward at one's own thoughts and feelings. Often this practice becomes a morbid exploration trying to unearth past sins in order to gain forgiveness.

Invisible Church • *See* Church Universal.

Irenaeus (c. 130-200) • Bishop of Lyons. Apologist who wrote *Against Heresies* (c. 180) to refute the positions of the Gnostics. Also contended with the Montanists and wrote *The Demonstration of the Apostolic Preaching,* one of the earliest theological treatises.

J

Jesus Seminar • The contemporary ongoing study of the Gospels from the radically skeptical perspective that sees little historical reliability in the gospel records of the sayings and acts of Jesus. Led by Robert Funk, the Jesus Seminar has self-consciously sought to bring the results of radical skeptical scholarship to the awareness of the general public.

John Chrysostom (c. 347-407) • Patriarch of Constantinople and representative of the school of Antioch. The greatest preacher of the ancient church, he was later called "Chrysostom" (golden mouth). He was devout, ascetic, and reforming in character. His fearless zeal and devotion led to two exiles from his post on trumped-up charges. He died during his second exile under the harsh treatment of his captors, but was vindicated after his death.

John of Damascus (c. 675-749) • Eastern monk, scholar, and Christian representative at the caliph's court, he represents the apex and final form of Eastern Orthodox theology and is the last recognized Greek father.

Judgment • The evaluation of one's guilt or innocence. Usually used in a negative sense of condemnation.

Justification • The judicial declaration by God that the sinner is not guilty but righteous (in the right relationship with God) based on the righteousness of Christ (Rom. 3:24-26; 4:25; 5:16-21). The result of justification is peace with God (Rom. 5:1) and the indwelling of the Holy Spirit (Rom. 8:9).

Justification by Faith

As synthetic judgment: The Protestant perspective on justification by faith that sees justification as a divine judgment based on a righteousness synthesized from the alien righteousness of Christ and imputed to the sinner's account.

As analytic judgment: The Roman Catholic perspective on justification that sees justification as a divine judgment based on actual divine righteousness imparted to and inherent in the individual's life by God's grace.

Justin Martyr (c. 100-165) • Christian apologist who used philosophy as a tool to explain the faith. He emphasized the fact that Christianity inherits the promises of Israel. Martyred for his testimony.

K

Kataphatic • *See* Apophatic.

Kenotic Christology • Nineteenth-century approach to Christology that finds its basis in Philippians 2:5-11 and focuses on the idea of Christ's self-emptying. The emphasis is upon an emptying of the incarnate Christ of deity in some measure and emphasized the full humanity of Christ. The radical versions represented a break with historic orthodox Christology while the mild to moderate versions fell with the parameters of Chalcedonian orthodoxy.

Kerygma • *See* Proclamation.

Keswick • A modified holiness understanding of sanctification with roots in the higher-life theology of Robert Boardman, Hannah Whitehall Smith and Robert Pearsall Smith. It stresses the overpowering reality of sin, the necessity of confession of all known sin to enjoy the presence of God, and the necessity of the Spirit-filled life. It is characterized by a practical perfectionism. Although it has declined as a distinct movement, Keswick theology has affected most of American evangelicalism with reference to its understanding of sanctification and the spiritual life.

Keys to the Kingdom • A phrase from Jesus' saying about spiritual authority in Matthew 16:19. Roman Catholicism sees this reference as giving primacy to Peter and his successors, thus legitimizing the papacy. Protestantism sees it as dealing with spiritual authority in the church. (*See also* Binding and Loosing.)

Kierkegaard, Søren (1813-1855) • Danish philosopher and Lutheran critic of the established Danish church. He argued that ministers were more ministers of the state than of Christ. He was also the father of existential philosophy, linking truth to the subject rather than to an object. He stressed the "leap of faith" as a personal commitment.

Knowledge • The organization of ideas or the ways in which reality is perceived. (*See* Epistemology.)

Knowledge of God • Human awareness of God and who he is on either a cognitive or an experiential level (see Hosea 4:1; 6:6; Col. 1:10; 2 Peter 1:2).

Koine Greek • The common Greek that was used throughout the Roman Empire. The NT was written in Koine Greek.

Kyriakos • Greek term for the church; it means "belonging to the Lord."

L

Language Games • Phrase coined by Ludwig Wittgenstein (1889-1951) to describe the fact that all words are used within a larger system that provides rules for the way words may be used and interpreted within a given context. These games effect the way reality is perceived and must be understood in order to correctly comprehend what is being communicated.

Laws of Thought • In classical logic, the laws of identity, non-contradiction, and the excluded middle.

Identity: The principle that "A is A." As a law of thought it is considered basic to both theological and philosophical reasoning.

Non-Contradiction: "That which is A cannot be non-A." A thing cannot be both itself and something else.

Excluded middle: "A thing is either A or non-A." There is no middle ground.

Lectionary • A book comprising daily Scripture readings for the liturgical year, designed either for private use or public worship.

Legal Fiction • A condition accepted legally as true that does not conform with existential reality. Critics of justification by faith have charged that the doctrine is a legal fiction because the justified person is not in fact righteous. (*See* Forensic Act.)

Legalism • An ethical system or a relationship that is governed by obedience to law or rules. In Christianity the term is generally used in the negative sense of a strict adherence to the letter of the law that ignores the spirit and intent of the law and may lead to the adoption and enforcement of nonbiblical norms as necessary for spirituality (pharisaism).

Leo I (the Great) (d. 461) • Bishop of Rome from 440. Leo's great theological contribution to the Christological debates, *The Tome of Leo*, became the basis for the Calcedonian definition of the nature of Christ.

Liberalism • Properly, the theological tradition that originated with nineteenth-century theologian Friederich Schleiermacher. It attempted to reformulate theology in light of the Enlightenment critique of revealed religion. It focused on religious experience at the expense of objective truth, elevated reason, taught essential human goodness and the continuity of the human with the divine. Theologically, liberalism denied every key doctrine of historic orthodoxy. As a movement it suffered defeat at the hands of WWI and Karl Barth's critique.

Liberation • Release from anything that would enslave to a state of freedom. Biblically, liberation is a metaphor of salvation, which is seen as liberation from the bondage and slavery of sin.

Liberation Theology • A variety of theologies, ultimately related to Moltmann's theology of hope, that see the gospel primarily in terms of liberation from social injustice and oppression in its various forms (economic, gender, race, political, spiritual) rather than in terms of personal sin and redemption. Stress in these movements is on praxis as opposed to doctrine, and priority is given to social activity rather than individual spirituality. Black theology, feminist theology, and Latin American liberation theology are manifestations of liberation theology.

Limited Atonement • *See* Atonement.

Literal Interpretation • Also called historical-grammatical interpretation. A method of interpretation that understands the words, phrases, and sentences of a text in their normal everyday sense, as opposed to some spiritualized or allegorical sense. Literal/normal interpretation does not imply "woodenly literal" understanding. Instead, it recognizes figures of speech and various literary genres as part of the normal communication process. However, it insists that the goal of interpretation is the author's intended meaning.

Literary Source Criticism • *See* Criticism.

Liturgical • (From Gk. *leitourgia*, "work of the people") Having to do with worship." As the term is generally used it refers to formal worship style, often accompanied by symbolic ritual and prescribed order and content of service. Roman Catholic, Eastern Orthodox, and a number of Protestant churches have a liturgical worship style.

Local Church • The visible assembly of Christians at a particular location as opposed to the universal/invisible church, composed of all believers at all places and times.

Logos • (Gk. "word") A dominant first-century concept both in Greek philosophy and Jewish thought, encompassing reason on the one hand and wisdom on the other. The term is used by John to describe the pre-incarnate Christ (John 1:1ff.).

Logos Doctrine • The doctrine developed concerning the pre-incarnate person of Christ, especially in his relationship to the Father and the created order, and used by second- and third-century theologians and apologists to communicate the nature and person of Christ to the Hellenistic philosophical mindset.

Lordship Salvation • The theological position within Calvinistic evangelicalism that denies the common evangelical distinction between "Jesus as Savior" and "Jesus as Lord." Lordship advocates decry "easy believe-ism" and assert that without visible evidence of salvation in the form of good works there is no salvation.

Lord's Supper • Also called Eucharist (Gk. *Eucharistia*, "thankfulness," "gratitude") and Communion. A sacrament in most churches, it is understood in a variety of ways.

Consubstantiation: The term popularly used to describe the Lutheran understanding of the nature of the Lord's Supper. Lutheranism holds that the elements are not physically transformed into the body and blood of Christ but that the body and blood of the risen Christ are in, with, and under the bread and wine in a special way.

Memorial Presence: The understanding of the Lord's Supper propounded by Zwingli and characteristic of most of American evangelicalism. In contrast to Catholicism, Lutheranism, and Calvin, the Lord's Supper is simply to be understood as a memorial. There is no grace conveyed by the sacrament nor is there a special spiritual presence of the risen Christ.

Mystery Presence: The Eastern Orthodox understanding of the Eucharist, which sees a real presence of Christ in the rite but refuses to speculate as to the nature of that presence, simply asserting it as beyond human explanation and hence "mystery."

Spiritual Presence: The view of the Lord's Supper taught by Calvin that sees an actual spiritual feeding upon Christ at the Eucharist.

Transubstantiation: The Roman Catholic understanding of the Eucharist, which holds that the bread and wine are changed in their substance (not appearance) into the literal body and blood of Christ. The Mass is thus a re-sacrifice of Christ.

Lower Criticism • *See* Criticism.

Lutheranism • The theological and denominational tradition tracing its roots back to the Protestant Reformation and Martin Luther. Confessionally committed to the Book of Confessions (1580) and the Augsburg Confession (1530). At the center of Lutheran theology stands the doctrine of justification by faith alone.

LXX • Septuagint. (*See* Text of the Bible.)

M

Majority Text • *See* Text of the Bible.

Manuscripts of the NT

Papyri: The earliest surviving fragments of the NT, written on papyrus, a paper-like substance derived from reeds growing along the Nile in Egypt.

Uncial: A Greek script that used only capital letters. The oldest surviving manuscripts of the NT are written in this script and are therefore called uncials.

Minuscule: The later, cursive Greek script that was used from the ninth century on. The majority of the surviving Greek NT manuscripts are minuscules.

Marcionism • Second- and third-century radically anti-Jewish Christian heresy with gnostic tendencies. Marcion and his followers rejected the OT and accepted only Paul (minus the pastorals) and an edited version of Luke. The heresy forced the church to deal with the extent of canon.

Masoretic Text • *See* Text of the Bible.

Material • *See* Formal/Material.

Means of Grace • The ways in which the blessings of God are received by humans. Protestants have traditionally seen the means of grace as the Scriptures, the sacraments, and prayer.

Mediate Imputation • *See* Imputation.

Memorial Presence • *See* Lord's Supper.

Merit • The worth or the value of an act. Protestantism denies that there is any merit toward salvation in human good works. The only act of merit for salvation is the atoning death of Christ.

Condign merit: The medieval scholastic teaching that supernatural grace could enable an individual to merit eternal life.

Congruous merit: The late-medieval view that denied that salvation could not be earned by works in a strict sense but saw it as appropriate for God to reward good works and faithfulness to God with eternal life.

Treasury of merit: In Roman Catholic teaching, the idea that the good works of the saints and of Jesus Christ (works of supererogation) can be stored up and used for the benefit of others. The concept of the treasury of merit lay behind the practice of indulgences in the medieval church.

Metaphor • *See* Figures of Speech.

Metaphysics • (Lit. "beyond the physical") Philosophical terms for those issues having to do with ultimate reality. This branch of philosophy is closely related to theology and has had an impact on theological thinking.

Meter • *See* Poetry.

Midrash • Comments on and explanations of the Hebrew Scriptures (OT) produced from the time of the Babylonian exile until the twelfth century.

Millennialism • The doctrine of the millennial kingdom (also called chiliasm in the early church). There have been several interpretations of the kingdom throughout the history of the church including:

Premillennialism: Jesus Christ will personally return to establish an earthly kingdom over which he will reign for 1,000 years.

Postmillennialism: Jesus Christ will physically return to Earth in final judgment after an extended period of peace and prosperity during which the church will mediate Christ's presence on the earth to such an extent that it will be identified as a kingdom age.

Amillennialism: There will be no earthly reign of Christ during which the kingdom promises to Israel will be fulfilled.

Minuscule • *See* Manuscripts of the NT.

Miracles • An extraordinary event that cannot be accounted for by the laws of nature. Theologically, miracles are a revelation of God's purposes and person.

Modalism • *See* Monarchianism.

Monarchianism • Movement that flourished during the second and third centuries as the doctrine of the Trinity was being formally developed. It emphasized the rulership of one God, as opposed to polytheism and even Trinitarianism. It took two forms.

Modalistic Monarchianism: Sabellianism, Modalism, patrapassionism. There are not three eternal personal subsistences in the Trinity, but the three Trinitarian persons are three successive historical revelations of the same God. God revealed himself under the image of Father in the OT, Son in the Gospels, and Spirit in the present age.

Dynamic Monarchianism: The man Jesus was endued with the power (dynamis) of God that came upon him either at his birth or at his baptism and left him prior to the crucifixion.

Monophysitism • The heretical teaching that Christ had only one nature. It arose after the council of Calcedon.

Monothelitism • The heretical teaching that Christ had only one will, the divine. It arose after the condemnation of monophysitism.

Montanism • Second-century heretical Christian ascetic sect that stressed the advent of the age of the Spirit and the renewal of prophecy through the agency of Montanus. The sect continued into the sixth century.

Moral Argument • *See* Theistic Proofs.

Moral Influence Theory • *See* Atonement.

Moralism • The belief that one can obtain salvation acting according to moral principles. The concept of salvation in classical liberalism is moralistic.

Morphology • In grammar, the patterns of word formation. In written language, the way the letters are formed.

Motif • Dominant idea or a central theme.

MT • Masoretic Text. (*See* Text of the Bible.)

Mystery Presence • *See* Lord's Supper.

Mysticism • The experience of a direct, intuitive apprehension of God and of things divine, apart from rational reflection. Christianity is mystical insofar as it asserts the reality of a direct personal relationship with and knowledge of God. The term is also used of the experience of spiritual ecstasy.

Myth • In biblical studies the term is not used in the sense of a purely fictitious fable or fairy tale. Rather, it is a literary genre in which truth is presented in a symbolic-imaginative way in a story or account that is not historically verifiable. Myth thus describes spiritual realities and truths.

Demythologizing: The process of biblical interpretation proposed by Rudolph Bultmann. It involves stripping away the "mythological" in Scripture (in the sense of prescientific understandings that are meaningless to the modern hearer) and re-presenting the point of these myths (the *kerygma*) in the form of existential philosophy.

Mythological approach: The approach taken by rationalistic NT scholars to the miraculous in the Bible. This perspective was pioneered by David Strauss in his *Leben Jesu* in the mid-nineteenth century

N

Narrative Criticism • *See* Criticism.

Natural Revelation • *See* Revelation.

Natural Theology • The knowledge of God attained solely through the created order and apart from special revelation. Natural theology has been emphasized in Roman Catholic thought since Aquinas. Protestant thought has been divided on the possibility of constructing a natural theology.

Neo-evangelicalism • The term applied to American evangelicalism in the 1950s indicating a move away from fundamentalism, the development of social conscience, and the embracing of higher education while remaining theologically conservative.

Neoliberalism • Used in two senses: (1) negatively of neo-orthodoxy by those who saw it as a new form of the old liberalism; (2) of the re-emergent liberal theology after WWII that was heavily influenced by process thought.

Neologians • Nineteenth-century British label for German rationalistic theologians.

Neo-orthodoxy • The theological tradition originating with Karl Barth that reacted to both nineteenth-century liberalism and seveneenth-century Protestant confessionalism. Neo-orthodoxy stressed divine transcendence, human sinfulness, and the centrality of Christ as God's revelation to mankind.

Neoplatonism • The dominant philosophical position/worldview in the third through fifth centuries. Neoplatonism involved a melding of Plato, Aristotle, and Stoicism.

Nestorianism • The Christological heresy that saw the union of the human and the divine in Christ as moral rather than organic. Condemned by the Council of Ephesus in 431.

New Age • A constellation of spiritual movements that gained prominence in the 1970s. They share common themes, including reincarnation, astrology, holism, self-fulfillment.

New Creation • The spiritual state of one who has been regenerated by the Holy Spirit. Also, the future remaking and restoration of the created order after the final judgment.

New Israel • Theological name for the church.

New Life • Salvation.

New Quest • *See* Quest of the Historical Jesus.

New Testament Theology • *See* Theology.

Nicea, Council of • The first ecumenical council of the church (325), called to deal with the Arian heresy. It gave the first formal statement of Trinitarian doctrine.

Nicene Creed • The first ecumenical creed of the church, composed at the council of Nicea in answer to Arianism. Expanded by the Council of Constantinople in 381 to include a more specific statement about the person of the Holy Spirit.

Nominalism • The epistemological position, espoused by William of Occam and dominant in late-medieval theology, that universals do not exist. They are labels created by the mind without objective reality.

Nomism • (Gk. *nomos*, "law") Perspective based upon law.

Noncontradiction • *See* Laws of Thought.

Non Posse Peccare/Posse Non Peccare • (Lat. "not able to sin/able not to sin") Used in the debate of concerning the possibility of the incarnate Christ to sin. Some argue that by virtue of the incarnation and the *communicatio idiomatum* it was not possible for Christ to sin. Others argue that in order for Christ to be genuinely tempted there must have been the possibility of sin.

Notitia • *See* Faith.

Novatian • Third-century theologian and author of *On the Trinity*, martyr, and rival Roman bishop/pope who precipitated a schism in the Roman church over the treatment of those who had lapsed during persecution.

O

Occult • The belief in and practice of contacting the invisible spiritual powers for guidance and power. All occult practices are condemned both in the Bible and by the church.

Ontic Trinity • *See* Trinity.

Ontological Argument • *See* Theistic Proofs.

Ontological Trinity • *See* Trinity.

Oppression • The condition of being treated unjustly. The term is used with reference to economic, racial, and gender-based injustice. It is also used with reference to demonic harassment at a level less severe than possession.

Order • Especially in Roman Catholicism, institutions or communities of monks or nuns, e.g., the Jesuits.

Ordination • The act of setting apart unto professional ministry. Sacramental traditions see ordination as conferring spiritual powers, while non-sacramental communities see the rite as a recognition of God's call in the life of an individual.

Ordo Salutis • In Reformed theology, the logical order of the decrees of salvation.

Supralapsarianism: The decree to predestine particular individuals to salvation falls logically before the decree to permit the fall of mankind into sin. In this scheme, election is understood to be a sovereign act of God who works all things after the council of his own will. It is often objected that this position makes God harsh, unjust, and arbitrary.

Sublapsarianism: (also called Infralapsarianism): The decree to predestine particular individuals to salvation falls logically after the decree to permit the fall of mankind into sin. Thus, election is understood to be an act of grace and mercy by God who contemplates individuals in their helpless and sinful condition. The charge that God is unfair and arbitrary is avoided because those chosen are seen as being already under a sentence of just condemnation.

Origen (185-253) • Brilliant Alexandrine exegete, textual scholar, philosopher, and theologian who sought to explain Christianity as the true gnosis and who popularized the allegorical interpretation of Scripture in the ancient church.

Original Sin • The effects of the sin of our first parents on all succeeding generations of humanity. The effects include the loss of original righteousness and a defacing of the image of God in humanity. Original sin speaks of a condition of corruption permeating the individual prior to any independent moral action and may include liability for punishment.

Orthodox, Orthodoxy • (Gk. *orthodoxos*, "right belief") Antonym: heterodox.

1. Beliefs that are common to all Christian traditions. Also referred to as historic orthodoxy or historic Christianity.

2. That which is accepted as correct or proper belief and teaching by a church or group of churches.

The theological tradition that was defined formally in the Great Schism of 1054 when the church in the East broke with the Roman Catholic Church in the West. Also known as the Eastern Orthodox Church, its main branches are the Greek Orthodox and the Russian Orthodox churches. Eastern Orthodoxy accepts only the first seven ecumenical councils as authoritative. The Orthodox tradition is sacramental, personalist, and mystical in its perspective on the faith.

Oxford Movement • Mid-nineteenth-century renewal movement that decried the spiritual state of the Anglican church and sought to move toward Roman Catholicism in doctrine and worship.

P

Papyri • *See* Manuscripts of the NT.

Paradigm • A model, example, or pattern. Often used as a synonym for worldview.

Paradigms provide the structure that organizes a mass of data into some kind of comprehensible form. In theology it is used of the different organizing patterns from which doctrines arise, e.g., Lutheran, Reformed, and Arminian ways of interpretation.

A paradigm shift is the replacement of one operative model of reality for a new one which better or more simply explains the totality of the data contemplated. When a paradigm shift occurs there is a revolution in understanding, e.g., from Newtonian physics to quantum mechanics.

Parallelism • *See* Poetry.

Participation in the Divine Nature • *See* Theosis.

Particularism • The view that salvation is related to the response of the individual to the gospel as opposed to universalism, which sees all humanity as being saved.

Particular Redemption • *See* Redemption.

Patristics • *See* Church Fathers.

Peace • (Heb. *shalom*; Gk. *eirene*) Theologically, the concept involves more than tranquillity. Following the OT *shalom*, it refers to completeness, wholeness, and well-being, together with righteousness. Peace exists as a gift from God.

Pelagianism • Late fourth-/early fifth-century heresy that denied human depravity and the absolute necessity of the work of Christ for salvation. Pelagianism denied original sin, made freedom of the will absolute, and taught the plenary ability of man to please God apart from any divine intervention. Opposed by Augustine, who argued for original sin, total depravity, total inability, and predestination.

Semi-Pelagianism is the position that the human condition has been injured by sin and that man is spiritually sick and needs rescuing but retains some measure of freedom to turn to God apart from the prior work of the Holy Spirit.

Penal Substitution • *See* Atonement.

Penance • In Roman Catholicism and Eastern Orthodoxy, a discipline placed upon the believer as a means of showing contrition and sorrow for sins confessed.

Pentecostalism • Protestant theological tradition that originated with the Azusa Street revival in 1900. It emphasizes the sign gifts of the Holy Spirit, particularly the gift of tongues.

Perfectionism • The theological teaching that one can in this life be totally free from sin. Perfectionism may be seen as moment by moment (more usual) or absolute (radical).

Perseverance of the Saints • *See* TULIP.

Personal/Personalist • A perspective in philosophy and theology that emphasizes the value, perspective, and experience of the individual. It sees the personal experience of self-consciousness as basic to one's reality.

Personal Eschatology • *See* Eschatology.

Personal Sin/Guilt • Sin committed by one person, for which the individual alone bears responsibility. Personal guilt is the condition of the individual human being having violated divine law.

Corporate Sin/Guilt: sin committed by a group, society, or the human race. All members of a group are involved in corporate sin, although an individual member of the group may not consciously participate in the act. The result is corporate guilt: the liability of the group for punishment as a result of corporate sin.

Personhood • That sense of self-conscious individual identity that marks off the individual as distinct from other selves and as morally responsible.

Phenomenalism • *See* Epistemology.

Philosophical Proofs • *See* Theistic Proofs.

Philosophy • ("Love of wisdom") The study of the overarching issues of life and of ultimate reality by the use of human reason as distinct from divine revelation.

Physical Salvation • Salvation as rescue from dire or difficult circumstances. This is the predominant understanding of salvation in the OT.

Pietism • A seventeenth- and eighteenth-century renewal movement within confessional Lutheranism emphasizing vital spiritual experience as the heart of Christianity. Used in a pejorative sense for an overemphasis on the devotional life and an emphasis on the leading of the Holy Spirit that devalues the intellectual aspects of the faith.

Platonism • The idealistic philosophy associated with Plato that has had a continuing influence on Christian theology. Platonism encouraged the use of the mind and exalted spiritual reality over empirical reality.

Aristotelianism: The philosophical perspective based on Aristotle that stresses facts, logic, and causation. Aristotelianism provided the framework for the theology of Thomas Aquinas and medieval scholasticism and post-Reformation Protestant scholasticism.

Pluralism • The diversity of religions and cultures in which each is to co-exist without enforcing hegemony over competing understandings.

Plymouth Brethren • A Protestant body founded in the early 1800s in reaction to the perceived apostasy of the Anglican Church. The Plymouth Brethren practice ecclesiastical primitivism, denying the validity of an ordained clergy and stressing lay leadership. Dispensationalism was born in the Plymouth Brethren context.

Pneumatology • The doctrine of the Holy Spirit.

Poetry (OT) • A highly figurative and structured genre of literature represented in the OT by the books of Job, Psalms, Song of Solomon and many of the prophets. Whereas English poetry is largely characterized by rhyme, a major literary feature of Hebrew poetry is the juxtaposition of parallel ideas or structure, coupled with meter (rhythmic patterns).

Posse Non Peccare • *See Non Posse Peccare.*

Postmillennialism • *See* Millennialism.

Postmodernism • The contemporary intellectual and theological climate that has rejected Enlightenment claims of the universality of truth and knowledge. Instead, it insists that all knowledge is relative and arises out of the perspective of the community in which one is a participant.

Pouring • *See* Baptism.

Pre-understandings • An interrelated complex of experiences, conceptions, thoughts which form a coherent pattern for comprehending new information. (*See also* Paradigm, Worldview, Frame of Reference.

Predestination • The activity of God in foreordaining that certain events come to pass. Predestination may have reference to actions and activity or to the eternal destiny of human beings (election: the two terms are often used as synonyms). Within the Reformed tradition, faith unto salvation is seen as the result of predestination (election), while in the Arminian tradition predestination (election) is understood to be based upon the faith God foresees the individual exercising.

Pre-existence • With reference to Christ, the fact that as the second person of the Trinity Christ existed before the Incarnation.

Premillennialism • *See* Millennialism.

Presbyterian Government • *See* Church Government.

Presuppositionalism • *See* Apologetics.

Pride • Usually negative, the exaggerated value of self, or overarching self-love at the expense of care for others. The term may be used positively in a sense of realistic self-esteem and satisfaction in one's accomplishments.

Priest • One who mediates between God and man. The OT appointed a perpetual, hereditary priesthood. The NT replaces this with the priesthood of all believers with Jesus Christ as the High Priest.

Primitivism • *See* Church Government.

Princeton School • The distinctive American form of Reformed theology wedded to Scottish Common Sense Realism associated with old Princeton Seminary (through 1929) generally and Charles and A. A. Hodge and B. B. Warfield particularly. The representatives of the Princeton School are referred to as Princetonians.

Process Theology • A school of thought arising from the philosophical perspective of Alfred North Whitehead and given theological shape by Charles Harthshorne. It focuses on dynamic change over static "being" and emphasizes divine participation in the evolving creation and divine development and change as a result of that involvement.

Proclamation • (Gk. *kerygma*) The public preaching of the gospel of the good news of Jesus Christ, often as distinct from teaching. Proclamation is directed to the heart and not just the head.

Progressive Revelation • *See* Revelation.

Progressive Sanctification • *See* Sanctification.

Projection • Attributing one's own thoughts, feelings, ideas, or motivations to another. Externalizing personal guilt, blame, or anxiety as a psychological defense mechanism.

Proofs of God's Existence • *See* Theistic Proofs.

Prophet • One who speaks the message of God, on behalf of God, usually addressing God's people. The prophets' predicting (foretelling) the future is incidental to their proclaiming (forth-telling) of God's message.

Propitiation • *See* Expiation.

Provenance • Origin or source.

Providence • God's gracious continual personal superintendence and preservation of his creation for his purposes and for the benefit of humanity.

Purgatory • In Roman Catholicism, the place of punishment/purification where the faithful after death are purified from all that remains of sin in their lives and made worthy and fit for eternity in God's presence. Purgatory is understood to be a place of disciplinary suffering.

Q

Q. • *See* Synoptic Problem.

Quest of the Historical Jesus • The Enlightenment and liberal critical investigation into the religious personality of Jesus and the environment that shaped him. The aim was to get to the simple human being behind the religious figure as it had been developed over the centuries. Numerous scholars participated in the quest, but the results were a projection of nineteenth-century human ideals onto the person of Jesus rather than historical discovery. Albert Schweitzer proclaimed the enterprise a failure in the early twentieth century.

Second Quest or New Quest: The efforts by Rudolph Bultmann to demythologize the NT records in order to recover the real Jesus without any mythical overlays.

Third Quest: Begun in 1953 by Ernst Käsemann in reaction to Bultmann, this quest has a firmer methodological foundation than the first quest and is not radically rationalistic as was the first quest. Recognizing that history is vital to Christianity, scholars from across the theological spectrum are participants.

(*See also* Jesus Seminar.)

R

Ransom Theory • *See* Atonement.

Rapture • In premillennialism, the catching of the church up in the air to meet Christ at his return (1 Thess. 4:17). Also, an intense religious experience.

Rationalism • *See* Epistemology.

Reader-Centered Meaning • *See* Interpretation, Methods of.

Reader-Response Criticism • *See* Criticism.

Realism • Realism is the epistemological view that asserts the objective reality of objects apart from human knowledge of them.

Idealism, by contrast, sees ideas present in the human mind as basic to understanding reality. Idealism has its roots in Platonic thought and has had significant influence on theological history.

Realistic Imputation • *See* Imputation.

Realized Eschatology • *See* Eschatology.

Recapitulation Theory • *See* Atonement.

Reconciliation • The bringing together of two parties that are estranged. Theologically, the estrangement of sin is overcome in an objective sense by the death of Christ so as to effect reconciliation between God and man in salvation (2 Cor. 5:16-21). Because of the fact of divine reconciliation, Christians are to reflect in their lives reconciliation to others (Matt. 5:23-24).

Reconstructionism • Recent theological movement arising from within Reformed theology that seeks to restructure society along the lines of OT Law, which is held to be permanently binding.

Redaction Criticism • *See* Criticism.

Redemption • (Lit. a "buying back") Redemption involves the "buying back" of humanity from slavery to sin. Theologically it involves Atonement, reconciliation, and liberation from sin, death, and the powers of evil through the death of Christ. (*See* Atonement.)

Particular redemption: Limited atonement.

Universal redemption: Unlimited atonement.

Reformed Theology • The theology following in the tradition of John Calvin. "Reformed" refers to the broad scope of theology as well as a comprehensive world-and-life view, whereas "Calvinism" is often used more narrowly of the soteriological position defined by TULIP. (*See* TULIP.)

Regeneration • (Lit. "being born again") The work of the Holy Spirit in giving new and spiritual life to the repentant sinner who believes in Christ.

Reincarnation • The nonbiblical belief that after death one is born again into a new physical body. Also called transmigration of the soul.

Relaxation Theory • *See* Atonement.

Religionsgeschichte • *See* History of Religions School.

Remonstrants • The followers of Arminius in Holland, who put forth the Remonstrance in opposition to the then-dominant scholastic Reformed theology with its emphasis on divine sovereignty. The protest occasioned the convening of the Synod of Dort (1618-19) which formulated the TULIP of Calvinism as a refutation of Arminianism.

Repentance • (Gk. *metanoia,* "a changing of one's mind") It encompasses the act of turning to God from sin. The beginning of repentance is expression of faith in Christ.

Resurrection • A raising from the dead. Specifically the resurrection of Christ and the future raising of all the dead unto final judgment and reward or punishment.

Instantaneous resurrection: After death the individual experiences immediate resurrection rather than an intermediate state or "soul sleep." At death the soul steps out of linear time and into eternity.

Intermediate state: The condition and abode of the soul between death and resurrection. For unbelievers this is understood to be a place of conscious torment (hades, Luke 16), for believers a state of spiritual peace and comfort.

Soul sleep: The view that at death the soul sleeps (or is in an unconscious state) until awakened at the resurrection.

Return of Christ • *See* Second Coming.

Revelation/Natural revelation • Truth about God seen by all humanity through nature, conscience, and history.

General revelation: God's self-disclosure in nature, history, and conscience to all people at all times, revealing his power, wisdom, eternity, and moral nature.

Special revelation: God's particular, personal, and redemptive self-disclosure at specific times and places to humans in their fallen, sinful state through, e.g., dreams, visions, audible voice, theophanies, the Incarnation. Scripture is understood to be special revelation in durable form.

Progressive revelation: God's revelation in Scripture reflects a continuing process by which later revelation builds on that which preceded it. Progressive revelation implies that new revelation can occur but cannot contradict that which has preceded.

Reward • The view in Roman Catholic moral theology that final salvation comes as a result of a believer's cooperation with God's grace, doing good works that accrue as merit before God.

Rhetorical Criticism • *See* Criticism.

Righteousness • The Hebrew and Greek biblical terms stress the establishing and maintaining of a right personal relationship between God and man. The relationship is established by God apart from human merit. Linguistically the term is pre-ethical, but as commonly used it refers to moral purity.

Rites and Rituals • Set forms of religious expression that represent in symbolic form religious experience or theological truth.

S

Sabellianism • *See* Monarchianism.

Sacraments • Signs or rituals instituted by God as symbols of an inward spiritual reality/grace. Sacraments are the liturgical rituals of the church. Roman Catholicism recognizes seven sacraments, Protestants recognize two.

Ex opere operato: (Lat. "from the work done") The Roman Catholic view of the Sacrament that emphasizes its objective nature and sees its spiritual validity in its nature as sacrament rather than the worthiness of the priest or the recipient.

Ex opere operantis: (Lat. "out of the work of the worker") The view that sees the efficacy of the sacrament as dependent upon (1) the spiritual condition of the one who administers the sacrament and (2) the spiritual condition of the recipient.

Sacred and Taboo • Sacred is that which is holy or able to instill a sense of the presence of the divine. Taboo is that which is proscribed for fear of harm from the deity.

Saint • Biblically, all those who have been saved by Jesus Christ are saints. Popularly, one who is especially devoted to God. In Roman Catholicism, one who has been canonized.

Salvation • Comprehensive term for the activity of God in delivering human beings from their sinful condition and giving them righteousness and fellowship with him as a gift, based upon the Atonement of Christ. Biblical images for salvation vary widely, and each image contributes uniquely to understanding the magnitude of the divine project.

Sanctification • The "present tense" of salvation. (justification = "past tense"; glorification = "future tense"). The process involves the progressive spiritual growth of the individual following justification (progressive sanctification) whereby he or she is more and more conformed to the image of Christ and is able to progressively deny sin in his or her life and produce good works (Eph. 2:10).

Definitive sanctification: The recognition in Reformed theology that the regenerate individual, by virtue of incorporation into and identification with Christ, is by definition "a saint" or "sanctified," despite any personal sin and weakness which may still plague him/her.

Satisfaction Theory • *See* Atonement.

Saving Faith • *See* Faith.

Schism • *See* Great Schism.

Schleiermacher, Friederich (1768-1834) • German theologian and philosopher and father of liberal theology. He saw true religion as the feeling of absolute dependence upon God.

Scholasticism • Method of philosophy and theology developed at the newly emergent European universities during the High Middle Ages. Scholasticism combined the philosophy of Aristotle with the teachings of the Fathers, particularly Augustine. During the post-Reformation period both the Lutheran and the Reformed traditions adopted the methodology of scholasticism as they constructed their systems of theology. This period is referred to as the era of Protestant scholasticism.

Scientific Materialism • The worldview that asserts that the material universe is the entirety of reality and that it can be understood through science alone without reference to any deity or transcendent spiritual reality.

Scofield Reference Bible • The study Bible edited by C. I. Scofield (1909) that popularized dispensationalism in America in the early-twentieth century.

Sealing • The work of the Holy Spirit in setting an identifying mark of ownership on the believer that assures final redemption (Eph. 4:30).

Second Coming • The literal bodily return of Jesus Christ from heaven (Acts 1; Rev. 20) to establish his kingdom.

Second Helvetic Confession • Written by Bullinger in 1562, this became the most prominent of the Swiss Reformed creeds and was accepted by Reformed churches throughout Europe.

Self • *See* Personhood.

Semantics • The aspect of language study that has to do with meaning.

Semi-Pelagianism • *See* Pelagianism.

Septuagint • *See* Text of the Bible.

Session (Christology) • The present work of Christ in heaven.

Seventieth Week of Daniel • In premillennialism, the seventieth week in Daniel is generally understood to be the period of the Great Tribulation.

Shame • The feeling arising from the realization that one has failed to live up to standards and expectations or that one has acted dishonorably and disgracefully.

Shame involves the desire to hide the true self from condemnation and often involves denial of responsibility and shifting of blame for failure (Gen. 3).

Simile • *See* Figures of Speech.

Simple Truth • *See* Truth.

Simul iustus et peccator • (Lat. "at once both righteous and a sinner") Luther's description of the sinner justified by grace through faith.

Sin • The comprehensive term used to describe the human condition of failing to reflect divine righteousness. Scripture uses a variety of terms to describe this condition. Sin may be willful and deliberate, or it may be inadvertent. It always needs forgiveness.

Sitz im Leben • (Ger. "setting in life") The cultural and intellectual context in which a particular passage of Scripture originated. A form-critical term.

Social Gospel • The late nineteenth- and early twentieth-century movement within liberal American Protestantism that sought to apply the social implications of the gospel to the conditions of industrialized society, focusing on the poverty and economic oppression suffered by urban factory workers. The stress of the movement was the establishment of the moral ethical kingdom of God, often at the expense of the personal redemptive aspects of the gospel.

Socinianism • The rationalist theology espoused by Faustus Socinus (1539-1604), who disavowed the Trinity and the deity of Christ and the Atonement, as well as other cardinal Christian doctrines. American Unitarianism reflects the Socinian theological perspective.

Sociology of Knowledge • The contemporary discipline that denies the Enlightenment perspective that truth/knowledge is objective. Rather, the context of the knower determines what will be perceived and accepted as truth/knowledge. Radical understandings deny the reality of objective truth, moderate perspectives see an objective reality but insist that it is inevitably colored its subjective apprehension.

Soft Sciences • Social sciences.
Sonship • The relationship with God as Father. The sonship of Jesus Christ is unique in that it is eternal and by nature, whereas the sonship of the Christian is by virtue of adoption.
Soteriology • The doctrine of salvation.
Soul • In the OT, refers primarily to the life principle (Gen. 2:7). In the NT the term is used regularly for one's life (Matt. 2:20) or of existence after death (Luke 21:19). (*See* also Holism.)
Soul Sleep • *See* Resurrection.
Source Criticism • *See* Criticism.
Spirituality • The spiritual aspect of human existence. Christian spirituality is grounded in the presence of the Holy Spirit in the life and experience of the believer. Protestantism stresses the Bible and prayer as means to maintain spirituality. (*See* Disciplines.)
Spiritual Healing • (1) The curing of diseases both physical and spiritual by nonphysical means, e.g., prayer and faith. (2) The healing of the inner self from the damage done by sin, particularly victimization and abuse.
Spiritual Presence • *See* Lord's Supper.
Spiritual Warfare • A NT image of the struggle of the Christian with the cosmic forces of evil that are the enemies of the believer. In recent decades the term has come to be popularly applied to direct confrontation with demonic forces in which the believer binds Satan, verbally rebuking him by authority of the risen Christ.
Sprinkling • *See* Baptism.
Structural Criticism • *See* Criticism.
Sublapsarianism • *See Ordo Salutis.*
Substitution • *See* Atonement.
Succession of Bishops • *See* Apostolic Succession.
Succession of Doctrine • The handing down of Christian truth/doctrine from one generation to the next (2 Tim. 2:2).
Suffering • To experience deep physical, emotional or spiritual pain distress or injury. While not good in itself, within the framework of God's sovereignty suffering is a vehicle to bring believers to maturity.
Supracultural • *See* Culture.
Supralapsarianism • *See Ordo Salutis.*
Synagogue • Place of worship in Judaism. The synagogue originated during the Babylonian exile. After the destruction of the temple in A.D. 70 it became the center of Jewish religious life.
Synchronic • *See* Diachronic.
Syncretism • A blending of two or more ideas to form a third. The term is used of the blending of Christian and non-Christian elements into a view that compromises the Christian faith at crucial points.
Synergism • (Lit. "working together") In theology, the concept of synergism as advocated by Arminians and Semi-Pelagians holds that initial salvation is a cooperative effort between the divine will and the human will.
Synod of Orange (529) • Synod that accepted a semi-Augustinian position (rejecting Augustine's doctrine of double predestination) as the official position of the church with reference to the doctrines of sin and grace.
Synoptic Problem • The problem of the literary interrelationship of the first three (synoptic) Gospels. The most common view is that Matthew and Luke depended on Mark (Marcan priority) and that all three used common source material. A hypothetical source, Q, is often assumed to be the basis for material that is common to Matthew and Luke but not found in Mark.
Synoptics • The Gospels of Matthew, Mark, and Luke.
Syntax • The grammatical structure of a language.
Synthetic Judgment • *See* Justification.
Systematic Theology • *See* Theology.

T

Taboo • *See* Sacred and Taboo.

Taxonomy • An orderly classification or ranking according to natural relationships. A theological taxonomy assumes that certain doctrines are foundational while others are of secondary and tertiary importance.

Teleological Argument • *See* Theistic Proofs.

Temple of the Holy Spirit • As used by Paul, the corporate church as well as the individual believer is the temple of the Holy Spirit.

Tests of Truth • The three classic tests of truth are:

Coherence: For a particular belief or to be considered as true it must be capable of being put into a logical, systematic, and coherent form.

Consistency: A truth claim must be self-consistent and without internal contradictions.

Utility: In order for a proposition to be accepted as true, it must work. (If it is true it will work; not to be confused with pragmatism, which says that if it works it is true.)

Tertullian (c. 160-c. 220) • Brilliant Latin-speaking lawyer, apologist, and theologian who gave to Western Christianity much of its legal cast. Influential in the developing doctrine of the Trinity and also in the coining of theological terminology, he was a moral rigorist who ultimately joined the Montanists because of their ascetic practices and the laxity he perceived in the orthodox church.

Text of the Bible

Septuagint: (LXX): Greek translation of the OT, completed about a century before Christ. The designation LXX, the Roman numeral for seventy, is based on the apocryphal Letter of Aristes, which states that the Septuagint was translated by seventy scholars in seventy days.

Textus Receptus: (TR) The received edition of the Greek NT based on the work of Erasmus. The TR is based on a few late Greek manuscripts. It was the basis for translations of the NT up until the late nineteenth century when Westcott and Hort introduced the critical text based on collations of manuscripts nearly a millennium older.

Majority Text: The text of the NT as represented by the majority of the surviving manuscripts. By virtue of numbers the majority text is Byzantine in type although not identical with the Textus Recptus.

Masoretic Text: (MT) The text of the Hebrew OT, copied and preserved by the Masoretes.

Dead Sea Scrolls: (DSS) A collection of scrolls found in a cave at Qumran on the Dead Sea in 1948. They represent the oldest known Hebrew manuscripts, some dating from before the time of Christ.

Critical text: The printed Hebrew OT text or Greek NT text, of the OT or NT respectively based on the comparison of available manuscripts. The critical text is determined by means of textual criticism and uses proven methods to eliminate errors that have crept into the hand-copied manuscripts over centuries of transmission.

(*See also* Criticism: Textual Criticism.)

(*See also* Manuscripts of the NT.)

Textual Criticism • *See* Criticism.

Textually Centered Meaning • *See* Interpretation, Methods of.

Textus Receptus • *See* Text of the Bible.

Theistic Proofs • The so-called "proofs for the existence of God," popularized by Thomas Aquinas. These proofs play a major part in the attempts of natural theology to demonstrate to the unbeliever that God exists, apart from the revelation of Scripture.

Cosmological argument: Since every effect must have a cause, the universe itself must have a first cause, God.

Moral argument: The universal nature of morality and the necessity for a transcendent moral reality upon which to base this universal phenomenon lead to the conclusion that the source of this transcendent morality must be God.

Motion argument: Similar to the cosmological argument. The world and created order is not static but in motion, everything that moves is moved by something else. There must be at some point an "unmoved mover" who is himself unmoved. That unmoved mover would be God.

Ontological argument: God is "that than which nothing greater can be conceived." This must include existence. Originally formulated by Anselm.

Teleological argument: The design and evident purpose seen in the created order proves the existence of God.

Theocracy • Ruled by God. In the OT, Israel was originally a theocratic state with Yahweh as king. The term has also been used to refer to human attempts to set up a kingdom ruled by the religious establishment, e.g., the Puritan theocracy.

Theology

Natural theology: Theology based on God's self-disclosure in nature, history, and conscience to all people at all times, revealing his power, wisdom, eternity, and moral nature (general revelation). Natural theology is by definition nonredemptive.

Systematic theology: Christian theology comprehensively presented in a coherent, orderly fashion around a central organizing principle. Especially characteristic of the Reformed tradition. Systematic theologies must have an underlying philosophical perspective and method in order to be a true system.

Dogmatic theology: Systematic theological reflection based primarily but not exclusively on received church dogma such as a creed or confession. A virtual synonym of Systematic Theology.

Biblical theology: The historical and descriptive discipline that sets forth and synthesizes the teachings of the biblical authors in their own thought forms and categories without imposing upon the biblical material later theological understanding. Major areas are OT theology, NT theology, Johannine theology, and Pauline theology.

(*See also* Historical Theology.)

(*See also* Liberation Theology.)

Theology of Hope • *See* Liberation Theology.

Theopneustos • (Gk. "God-breathed") Used by Paul to describe the divine origin of the OT Scriptures (2 Tim. 3:16).

Theosis • Theosis (or deification) is the predominant Eastern Orthodox conception of salvation. It is understood as a process by which the Christian becomes a participant in the life of God or united with Christ's divine nature in its energies, not its essence (2 Peter 1:4: "participate in the divine nature").

Eastern theology holds that deification is the goal of every Christian, not just the "saints." There are significant parallels with the Protestant concept of progressive sanctification.

Therapeutic • Having to do with healing. Biblically, salvation is to be a therapeutic process of restoring to spiritual and emotional health those who have been caught in the sickness of sin.

Third Quest • *See* Quest of the Historical Jesus.

Third Use of the Law • In Reformed theology, the concept that the law is a normative guide to the believer, revealing the will of God for life.

Third Wave • The Vineyard movement, frequently thought of as the Third Wave of the outpouring of the Holy Spirit in the twentieth century. (First Wave: Pentecostalism; Second Wave: charismatic movement.)

Emphasis has been placed on healing and prophecy more than on tongues, which characterized earlier movements.

Time and Eternity • Time is understood to be the period between creation and the final consummation. Eternity is distinct from time and has no beginning and no end. Properly it belongs only to God as an attribute. More popularly, the time after the final consummation is referred to as eternity future. Theologians debate as to whether this period is an infinite extension of time in one direction or if it is qualitatively different from time.

Torah • First of the three parts of the OT canon, consisting of the five books of Moses (Pentateuch). The other two parts are the Nebiim (Prophets) and the Ketubim (Writings or Hagiographa).

TR • Textus Receptus (*See* Text of the Bible).

Tradition History • A critical approach to OT studies.

Traducianism • The view on the origin of the human soul that sees it as traduced from human parents rather than directly created by God (creationism). Tertullian was the first advocate of this view.

Transcendence • God's being above and apart from the created order.

Immanence: God's presence and actions within the created order.

Transcendentalism • Nineteenth-century idealistic movement associated with Ralph Waldo Emerson, emphasizing the spiritual realities beyond space and time.

Transcultural • *See* Culture.

Transmission of Sin • The passing of sin from generation to generation (Rom. 5). Pelagians have held that sin is individual and that no necessary link exists between Adam and his posterity other than a bad example. Orthodox theology has held that the corruption resulting from Adam's fall is passed from generation to generation, affecting the entirety of the race. While the means of the transmission have been debated, the fact of the transmission is virtually universally accepted.

Transubstantiation • *See* Lord's Supper.

Treasury of Merit • *See* Merit.

Trent • The Council of Trent (1545-63), convened by the Roman Catholic Church to reform abuses and answer the Protestant Reformation. Trent elevated to dogma many of the perspectives of Thomas Aquinas.

Tribulation • Generally, the suffering and anguish of God's people. Tribulation is a characteristic experience of the Christian in the world.

In premillennialism, "the Tribulation" or "the Great Tribulation" refers to the period of unparalleled human suffering under divine judgment prior to the return of Christ.

Trichotomism • *See* Holism.

Tridentine • Pertaining to the Council of Trent.

Trinity • The uniquely Christian understanding that the one God is three eternal persons, Father, Son, and Holy Spirit, while remaining one in essence. This tri-unity has reference to eternal intrapersonal distinctions within the single essence of the Godhead (ontological Trinity or immanent Trinity) and not just to God's relationship to the world (economic Trinity).

Triumphalism • A perspective on the Christian life and the life of the church that sees victory and blessing as normative and tribulation and opposition as an indication of divine disfavor.

Trust • *See* Faith.

Truth • That which is in correspondence with reality or is genuine. Theologians debate whether truth is propositional or personal. Such a dichotomy is false, since Scripture speaks of both perspectives. God is true, trustworthy, and reliable, Jesus is the truth, and the Scripture is God's true revelation given in durable form.

Absolute Truth: That which is universal and unchanging. Ultimately God alone is absolute truth.

Simple Truth: Correspondence with reality.

TULIP • Acronym for a Calvinistic conception of soteriological doctrines formulated by the Synod of Dort (1618-19) in answer to the Arminian Remonstrance.

T: Total Depravity: *See* Depravity.

U: Unconditional Election: The basis of election unto salvation is only the good pleasure of God's will, not foreseen faith or merit in human beings.

L: Limited Atonement: *See* Atonement.

I: Irresistible Grace: The work of the Holy Spirit whereby he draws the individual to salvation, breaking down obstacles in the process.

P: Perseverance of the Saints: Those who are genuinely regenerated by the Holy Spirit will continue in their faith until the end. Differs from the doctrine of eternal security in that the latter bases confidence of one's salvation on one's initial profession of faith. Perseverance looks at life from the end rather than the beginning and sees the fact that one has remained steadfast as proof of the genuineness of conversion.

U

Uncial • *See* Manuscripts of the NT.

Unconditional Election • *See* TULIP.

Unction • Anointing as a symbol of consecration. (*See also* Anointing of the Sick.)

Undistributed Middle • The logical fallacy in which neither premise of a syllogism makes a universal statement that does not occur in the conclusion.

Union with Christ • The believer's radical identification with Christ in his atoning death and resurrection. (*See also* In Christ.)

Unitarianism • *See* Socinianism.

Universal Church • *See* Church Universal.

Universal Redemption • *See* Redemption.

Unlimited Atonement • *See* Atonement.

Utility • *See* Tests of Truth.

V

Vatican I (1869-70) • Roman Catholic council that declared as dogma the doctrine of papal infallibility.

Vatican II (1962-65) • Roman Catholic council that dethroned the traditional Thomistic perspective in theology, casting the doctrines of revelation, Scripture, salvation, and the church in new frameworks, as well as enacting far-reaching reforms.

Verbal Dictation • *See* Inspiration of the Bible.

Verbal-Plenary Inspiration • *See* Inspiration of the Bible.

Verifiability • In logical positivism, any statement that is neither verifiable (that cannot in principle be shown to be true) nor falsifiable (that cannot in principle be shown to be wrong) is nonsense or irrelevant. E.g., the statement "Christ is risen" can in principle be falsified by the discovery of his body. Verifiability and falsifiability determine whether or not a statement is nonsense, not whether it is true.

Victimization • Theologically, an interpersonal effect of sin. While ultimately sin is a divine-human issue, it is also an interpersonal and community issue. The effects of sin often leave trauma and lifelong scars upon those who are sinned against.

Visible Church • *See* Local Church.

W

Wesleyan-Arminian Theology • The theological tradition that originated with James Arminius and John Wesley. This tradition stresses human freedom, the possibility of loss of salvation by means of apostasy, and the goal of entire sanctification/holiness in this life.

Westminster Confession • The Presbyterian (Calvinistic/Reformed) confession of faith composed by the Westminster Assembly and published in 1648. It has become the standard Reformed confession in the English-speaking Presbyterian and Reformed tradition.

Wholeness • The condition of being whole or complete. In theology, salvation is seen as a therapeutic process of being progressively restored to spiritual health/wholeness from the sickness of sin.

Wisdom Literature • OT Literature that contains practical perspectives on living in accordance with God's will. Included are Job, Proverbs, Ecclesiastes.

Wish-Fulfillment • God has no objective reality but is the projection of our desires. We create God in our own image. Position of nineteenth-century anti-theologian Ludwig Feuerbach.

Witness of the Spirit • The ministry of the Holy Spirit whereby he testifies to the divine origin and veracity of the Scriptures and to the status of the Christian as child of God.

Women's Liberation • *See* Liberation Theology.

Worldview • A complex of pre-understandings that gives a conceptual framework by which an individual understands reality. The term is sometimes used in reference to a philosophy of life or outlook on life.

Worship • Giving praise and glory to God in action and attitude. In Christianity, worship is to be Trinitarian, praising the Father through the Son in the power of the Spirit.

Writings • The third section of the Hebrew canon of the OT, along with the Torah (Law) and the Prophets.

Yahweh • The personal name of the covenant-keeping God of Israel. It is derived from the four Hebrew radicals (consonants) YHWH. Older English translations render God's personal name variously as Lord or Jehovah.

We want to hear from you. Please send your comments about this book to us in care of the address below. Thank you.

GRAND RAPIDS, MICHIGAN 49530 USA

WWW.ZONDERVAN.COM

CPSIA information can be obtained
at www.ICGtesting.com
Printed in the USA
LVHW062238120822
725812LV00005B/8